Slavery and Racism
in American Politics,
1776–1876

D1231486

Slavery and Racism in American Politics, 1776–1876

MICHAEL C. THOMSETT

Foreword by Ken West

McFarland & Company, Inc., Publishers

Jefferson, North Carolina

ISBN (print) 978-1-4766-7099-7
ISBN (ebook) 978-1-4766-3634-4

LIBRARY OF CONGRESS AND BRITISH LIBRARY
CATALOGUING DATA ARE AVAILABLE

On the cover: Currier & Ives lithograph, 1862 (Library of Congress)

Printed in the United States of America

McFarland & Company, Inc., Publishers
Box 611, Jefferson, North Carolina 28640
www.mcfarlandpub.com

Table of Contents

Foreword by Ken West

Who controls the past controls the future. Who controls the present controls the past.—George Orwell

Today's understanding of slavery in America's past, especially as it relates to the Democrat and Republican parties, has been flipped in a false narrative. Democrats are portrayed as the party that fought against slavery, and for civil rights. This is not the truth. How this happened is only part of the story told by Michael Thomsett in this unique and extensively researched book. The historical record is clear yet unknown to most Americans. Thomsett's book sets the record straight.

I've known Michael Thomsett for only a short time, but have been impressed with his broad knowledge of American history. In this book, he tells the story of why slavery lasted so long in America, with compromise upon compromise that never struck at the root of slavery's evil.

Two competing visions of slaves spanned across the years: Was a slave "property" or was he or she a person? Was this an issue of "states' rights" or a Federal concern? And what political party was in power, not only in the White House, but in Congress and in the Supreme Court? For me, the most shocking truth is that the Federal government guaranteed and enforced slavery until Lincoln's election and the Civil War.

So, what's in this book for you? You'll be armed with facts to answer the falsehoods that flood the media and public discussion. *Slavery and Racism in American Politics, 1776–1876,* will give you a solid grounding and understanding of what really happened in our history and why. Here are just a few of the questions that Thomsett's book answers:

Why did slavery last as so long?
Why didn't the Supreme Court step in and end slavery?

1

Did the Emancipation Proclamation free the slaves?
How did the Ku Klux Klan gain power ... and lose it?

This book is a valuable piece of scholarship, and a reaffirmation of truth.
This is an important book, and a fascinating, enlightening read.

Ken West is past president of the New England chapter of the National Speakers Association and the Association of Objectivist Businessmen. He is the author of Achieve Your Purpose.

Preface

This book examines a long-standing core issue in American history: How slavery was created, evolved, and finally ended with the conclusion of the Civil War.

The process includes examination in Part I of legislative, political, and judicial decisions concerning the nature of slavery versus human rights.

Part II examines the politics leading up to the Civil War and the politics during that struggle, including politicians and their statements about slavery, the evolution of the Copperhead movement, and resistance to Lincoln's government in the Northern states.

Part III concludes with the period of Reconstruction. This includes Andrew Johnson's administration as well as those of presidents Grant and Hayes, and the activities of the Ku Klux Klan.

This evolution was by no means easy or sudden. Although the Founding Fathers set forth a gradual reduction and elimination of the slave trade, it became such an integral attribute in the economy of the South that conclusion of the institution by way of armed conflict became inevitable.

The research for this book included study of numerous published books, published papers and articles, and newspaper editorials and archives from the period. This research was augmented by examination of published papers at JSTOR, Google Scholar, and published sources for numerous societies and universities. All of these sources are cited fully with endnotes for each chapter, and also in the bibliography.

PART I

Slavery, Political Parties and the Supreme Court

1

A Pill Too Bitter to Swallow[1]

his book focuses not on the purely political aspects of U.S. history, but specifically on the racial element that has dominated the political scene from the beginning. In the 19th Century, the focus of this debate was on slavery. The issue divided the political, economic, and moral points of view for both political parties, and was largely responsible for the emergence of the two parties dominating political life today: Democrats and Republicans.

The obvious split of philosophy between Democrats and Republicans originally was centered on the single issue of slavery as expressed as a matter of states' rights versus a strong federal government.

Pro-slavery and anti-slavery forces cannot be simplified in this analysis. The underlying political motivations had roots in the Declaration of Independence and the Constitution, where slavery was accepted by some states as a means for gaining approval by all states. The Three-Fifths Compromise was one of the devices placed into law in order to gain Southern approval for the Constitution. Under this rule, slaves were counted as three-fifths of their numbers for the purpose of determining how many representatives each state would have in Congress. As a result, the South had significant influence beyond the number of voters, which were white males in each of the states. This condition, lasting up to the Civil War, has been called the "slave power" because voters in states where slavery was practiced were able to control Congress and, up to 1861, the presidency as well. Of the first 15 presidents, nine (60 percent) were members of the Democratic Party.[2] The "Caricature of Slavery" illustration predates the Declaration of Independence by 38 years and is a commentary on the condition of slaves.

As a consequence of the Democratic domination over Congress and the presidency, a majority of Supreme Court nominees between 1800 and 1861 were appointed by Democratic Party presidents. Between 1836 and 1861, the most critical period for slavery-related cases, all but one of the justices were appointed by Democratic Party presidents. This resulted in one-sided rulings favoring slave states and slaveowners, culminating in a decision that slaves could never be citizens of the United States.

"Caricature of Slavery" (1738). Many of the Founding Fathers and early presidents were slaveowners, presenting a dilemma for the drafters of the Declaration of Independence.

The great division between the parties as pro-slavery (Democrats) and anti-slavery (Republicans) had its roots in racial challenges and policies going back to the beginning of the 19th Century, not only in political parties, but also in legislation and court decisions. The evils of slavery defined much of life from 1776 through to the Civil War. But the focus in this book is on the primary issue involving race and racism: The formation of both political parties was based largely on the debate over slavery, the very policies that led to the Civil War. Slavery was the primary issue—with related struggles over political power and questions of morality—that led to the most devastating war in U.S. history, in which an estimated 620,000 people died in battle, from disease, and as prisoners.[3]

The Presentation of a Complex History

The organization of this book begins with the struggle faced by the Founding Fathers in developing a new nation. In a sense, the leadership of the new nation inherited the vast problem of slavery. As an institution, slavery was heavily invested in the agricultural economy of the South, making it impossible to easily or quickly relinquish slavery. As a moral issue, the Founding Fathers struggled with the conflict between ideals of the Declaration of Independence and the Constitution, versus the glaring contradictions of slavery. This led to the passage by Congress of many laws intended to settle the question or arrive at a compromise. However, at each step, the problem was made worse by legislation, not better. From the Three-Fifths Compromise and the birth of the slave power, Congress tried to resolve the problem of slavery with dozens of new laws. These included the Northwest Ordinance of 1787, the Fugitive Slave Act of 1793, the Slave Trade Act of 1794, the Act Prohibiting Importation of Slaves of 1807, the Missouri Compromise, the Compromise of 1850, and the Kansas–Nebraska Act of 1854, among others. In each and every case, the new laws failed to settle the conflict between pro-slavery and anti-slavery interests and introduced new problems at every turn.

A similar problem was encountered by the Supreme Court, which was dominated by Democratic president appointees through the decades up to 1861. Between 1836 and 1861, the makeup of the Court consisted of Democratic appointees with only one exception; moreover, the Court itself was highly political, with a clear bias favoring slave states and slave-owners. They used the Constitution's Commerce Clause, the nullification debate, and the Supremacy Clause in many of their pro-slavery decisions. These direct and precedent decisions included *The* Antelope, *McCullough v. Maryland, Gibbons v. Ogden, New York v. Miln, The* Amistad, *Prigg v. Pennsylvania, Strader v. Graham, Jones v. Van Zandt, Dred Scott v. Sandford, Winny v. Whitesides, Rachel v. Walker,* and *Ableman v. Booth.* The most crucial of these was the Dred Scott case, in which the Court decided that an ex-slave could never be a citizen and, as a result, did not have the ability to sue in court. This decision was so extreme that the only Whig on the Court resigned, the only time a justice left the Court on a disagreement of principle.

As a consequence of these repeated attempts by Congress and the Supreme Court to solve the disagreement between states, the issue became polarized geographically as well, developing into the anti-slavery North and the pro-slavery South. The debate over states' rights and slavery was centered less on areas where slavery existed and more on how new territories would be classified as they became states. The stalemate was continued with admission of states in equal numbers on each side to maintain the balance of power in Congress. Political parties were developed along the same lines. The first system was divided between Federalists (the party of Washington and Adams) and Democratic Republicans (later renamed the Democratic Party), which was dominated by the thinking of Jefferson, and later by the political philosophy of Andrew Jackson.

As the Federalist Party went into decline, most of the anti-slavery forces moved to a new party, the Whigs. During the three decades leading up to the Civil War, the Democrats dominated the presidency, Congress, and the Supreme Court. In the 1850s, a new party was formed specifically in opposition to federal law concerning slavery. This new Republican Party nominated its second candidate, Abraham Lincoln, in 1860. This was a great turning point, in which the prevailing slave power was ended through the Civil War and the abolishment of slavery; but this was a difficult, expensive, and tragic process. At the core of the struggle and the Civil War were the two parties, Lincoln's anti-slavery Republican Party and the South's pro-slavery Democrats.

As further sections of this book reveal, the Civil War did not end the debate. Instead, it led to further polarization between the industrial, Republican North and the rural, Democratic South.

Although United States history has been labeled as "racist," a modern understanding of racism also has to be explained in the context of the times from 1776 to 1876. This idea has not always been understood or agreed upon universally. Today, the label of racism is used, often casually, to attack opposition in many ways.

Racism in Context

The modern-day definition of racism is simple. A racist is any person who does not like a member of another race, and who wants to deny members of that race any form of equality. Racism is

> prejudice, discrimination, or antagonism directed against someone of a different race based on the belief that one's own race is superior.... The belief that all members of each race possess characteristics, abilities, or qualities specific to that race, especially so as to distinguish it as inferior or superior to another race or races.[4]

The Oxford English Dictionary traces the earliest use of the term "racism" to 1936 in *The Coming American Fascism* by Lawrence Dennis. A second usage was found in a 1938 translation of a book entitled *Racism* by Magnus Hirschfield, originally published in 1933 in German.

Because the terms "racism" and "racist" are relatively new, it is not entirely accurate to describe individuals or political parties as "racist" before the Civil War. However, by modern definitions of these terms, there clearly was a racial element involved in the support of slavery. As obvious as this is, there is a distinction and a consequence in modern times.

The distinction is found in a past acceptance of the idea that people of a different color, often from parts of the world with less developed civilizations, were inferior to the European race. This assumption was used to justify enslavement. The purpose in creating the institution of slavery was based on the need for labor, which was very difficult to find in colonial America. Indentured servants from Europe often returned home after fulfilling their term of service and had to be replaced. With this severe labor shortage in a rapidly expanding society (especially in the agricultural South), slavery solved one problem while creating another. Apart from this, the moral aspects of slavery were conveniently overlooked among Southern farmers and plantation owners out of what they perceived not only as necessity but also as their right to enslave fellow humans based on economic need as well as a belief in racial superiority.

The nationalism of the South before and during the Civil War—over issues of slavery as part of a broader states' rights debate—defined the Democratic Party with its regional distinctions (agricultural versus industrial, beyond pro-slavery and anti-slavery). This party became the part of slavery by its own internal conflicts and sense of nationalism:

> Whenever and wherever nationalism has developed in notably vigorous form, it has been in circumstances of conflict between the nationalizing group and some other group. In such a situation, the rejection of the out-group not only strengthens the cohesion of the in-group, but imparts to the members of the in-group a greater awareness of what they share.... The problem of the South in 1860 was not a simple one of southern nationalism versus American nationalism, but rather one of two loyalties coexisting at the same time—loyalty to the South and loyalty to the Union.[5]

This explains the fierce division between South and North, but at the same time the irrational differences in opinions about slavery have created a great contradiction. The Democratic Party dominated the South as a pro-slavery force in political life up to the beginning of the Civil War and beyond.

This first part of this book describes the three major segments of the government from its founding up to 1861: legislation (Chapter 2), evolution of the political parties (Chapter 3), and slavery-related decisions by the Supreme Court (Chapter 4). All of the events up to 1861 reveal the truth about the racially-based positions of the Democratic Party in each and every branch of government.

This caused an understandable loyalty among ex-slaves to the opposition party. Black voters were nearly entirely Republican following the Civil War and emancipation:

> The first year Southern blacks were able to participate in federal elections was 1868.... In most of the South, majority turnout for Republicans ... is a fair indicator

of black enfranchisement, since Republicans could not win elections in most of the South without overwhelming black support. [There was a] high Republican vote in the same areas in the South where blacks were concentrated.[6]

This party division carried over into voting trends. The blame for a long history of repression of the black vote belongs to the Democratic Party:

> It was nearly a century before the next civil rights bill was passed, because in 1876 Democrats regained partial control of Congress and successfully blocked further progress. As Democrats regained control of the legislatures in southern States, they began to repeal State civil rights protections and to abrogate existing federal civil rights laws. As African-American US Rep. John Roy Lynch (MS) noted, "The opposition to civil rights in the South is confined almost exclusively to States under democratic control...."[7]

This lengthy era of unequal relations between the races was typified by numerous black codes, found primarily in the Democrat-controlled South and later called Jim Crow laws.

Jim Crow

The end of slavery was not the end of discrimination, a well-documented history. As shameful as the actions of the Democratic Party were during the years before the Civil War, their actions afterwards were designed to suppress the black vote and were equally noteworthy. A large part of the rewritten history—in which the Democratic Party has recast itself as the champion of the minority citizen—has had to ignore the truth about Jim Crow.

The phrase "Jim Crow" was first used in reference to a series of laws in 1892. An article in the *New York Times* discussed a series of voting laws in Southern states designed specifically to ban or curtail voting among black citizens. The phrase goes back more than a half century earlier, however. A caricature of blacks in a song and dance routine called "Jump Jim Crow" is traced back to 1832. A white actor in blackface named Thomas Rice performed the routine and, ever since, the expression "Jim Crow" has come to mean "Negro." Among the many variations, the most often referenced refrain is:

> Come, listen all you gals and boys, Ise just from Tuckyhoe;
> I'm goin, to sing a little song, My name's Jim Crow.[8]

As laws were passed toward the end of the 19th Century in Democrat-controlled Southern legislatures, they were given the catch-all name, Jim Crow laws.[9]

The illustration on the next page dates from 1879, revealing how literacy tests as part of the Jim Crow era prevented emancipated black citizens from voting.

"The color line still exists in this case" (1879). Steps like literacy tests were used in the Jim Crow era to prevent black voters from being able to vote.

These laws included enactment of many provisions, including literacy tests, poll taxes, segregation enforcement, primaries limited to white voters only, extreme voting eligibility tests, and intimidation leading to violence. Although the origin of these laws was during the period of Reconstruction after the Civil War, many Jim Crow laws remained on the books until 1965.

At the origin of these anti-black laws was the formation by the Democratic Party of paramilitary organizations to intimidate black voters and to force Republican candidates out of office. The White League began in 1874 in Grant Parish, Louisiana. Chapters were rapidly added in New Orleans and other parts of the state. Another group, the Red Shirts, was formed in Mississippi, North Carolina, and South Carolina in the same era. Members of both groups were later rolled into state militia and National Guard units. The Red Shirts were described during the formative years as "the military arm of the Democratic Party."[10]

This effort by the Democratic Party to use intimidation to regain power was successful. By 1877, Democrats had regained control of every Southern state, and that control would last for nearly 100 years, as would the Jim Crow laws. With domination in all of the previous Confederate states, from 1890 to 1910 the Democratic Party was able to achieve passage of new laws and amendments to state constitutions that nearly completely forbade black citizens from voting.

The most infamous of groups formed during Reconstruction, the Ku Klux Klan, originated within the postwar Democratic Party and was populated nearly exclusively with Democratic Party members:

Founded in 1866, the Ku Klux Klan (KKK) extended into almost every southern state by 1870 and became a vehicle for white southern resistance to the Republican Party's Reconstruction-era policies aimed at establishing political and economic equality for blacks. Its members waged an underground campaign of intimidation and violence directed at white and black Republican leaders.[11]

The Democrats were the party supporting slavery as a states' right issue, who wanted to see the institution expanded into territories and newly admitted states. The same party supported the Confederacy during the Civil War and in 1864 ran candidate George McClennan, a man committed to surrender to the South, continuation of slavery, rejection of emancipation, and capitulation to end the Civil War. A broadside during the election year compared the choice between the two parties:

Elect Lincoln and the Republican ticket, you will bring on Negro equality, more debt, harder times, another draft, universal anarchy, and ultimate ruin.

Elect McClennan and the whole Democratic ticket, you will defeat Negro equality, restore prosperity, re-establish the Union in an honorable, permanent and happy peace.[12]

The next three chapters examine the history of legislation, political parties, and court cases all related to the issue of slavery and states' rights versus the federal government. This study demonstrates the truth about the parties, in which beliefs among many citizens are based not on history itself, but on the revised history that led to it.

2

The Most Oppressive Dominion[1]

We hold these Truths to be self-evident, that all Men are created equal, that they are endowed by their Creator with certain unalienable Rights, that among these are Life, Liberty, and the Pursuit of Happiness...[2]

T he inspiring simplicity of the Declaration's statement also points to a glaring contradiction that has defined the political history of the United States. If "all men are created equal," why did the "peculiar institution"[3] persist for nearly a century after these words were written?

It was not a simple matter of right and wrong. In fact, the status of slaves in the newly formed Republic was complex, both politically and economically, not to mention morally. Over the first 100 years of United States history, a great struggle took place to reconcile conflicting interests and to resolve the question of slavery in moral, cultural, political, and economic terms. The story is worth telling as one of the foundations of the United States, as the country's leaders (legislative, executive, and judicial) attempted to resolve the debate over slavery, but each attempt only made matters worse. The country did not begin with harmonious agreement between the ideal stated in the Declaration and the stark reality of the struggle over slavery. In fact, the compromises made by the Founding Fathers were part of a larger effort to arrive not only at a consensus, but at a unanimous consensus. To achieve this, the anti-slavery founders compromised with pro-slavery founders. This chapter chronicles the legislative effort within the country to resolve the issues surrounding slavery and ultimately to eliminate it entirely.

As events unfolded, it became clear that each subsequent attempt to restrict or abolish the practice introduced new problems and aggravated the divide between North and South. The impossible dilemma finally was resolved between 1861 and 1865, but no legislative, political, or legal remedies worked over the decades from 1776 to 1861. The tragedy of slavery led to the tragedy of the Civil War. The fate of four million slaves was de-

15

cided in that conflict, with most of this slave population located in seven states: Alabama, Georgia, Louisiana, Mississippi, North Carolina, South Carolina, and Virginia.[4] The war led to the highest number of casualties of any U.S. war before or since, at an estimated 618,000 deaths in battle and from disease.[5]

The argument concerning slavery during the years prior to the Civil War was not limited to a debate focused solely on the right or wrong of the institution, but on a larger scope of issues including much more, with a focus on political power and influence in Congress and based on how slavery was to be treated in newly admitted states. The debate, broadly speaking, was between states' rights and associated property rights on one hand, and Federalism and centralized control on the other. Although slavery was the central theme in the years from 1776 to 1861, North and South were at conflict over much more. By the 1850s, the sectional conflict was more precisely defined by the differences between the industrial North and the agricultural South, and was focused more on slavery policies and laws in territories to be admitted as states in the future than on the status of the free and slave states already part of the Union.

The cultural difference contained subtle attributes, including priorities about centralized versus decentralized government, competitive attitudes, and progressive or conservative thought. The North tended, as a generalization, to be more competitive and technologically advanced; the South tended, also as a generalization, to be more static and in favor of the status quo, which included economic reliance on slavery to support the needs of an agrarian society based largely on the farming of cotton and tobacco.

While the states' rights concept refers to many issues today, in the period before the Civil War it was a question of whether the federal or state governments had jurisdiction over slavery. Many attempts have been made over the history of the United States to rationalize or even to contradict the concept of "all men are created equal" in some manner. Some, including Nathaniel Macon (D–NC), a pro-slavery member of Congress and sixth Speaker of the House of Representatives, argued that the phrase "all men are created equal" was not relevant because the Declaration of Independence was not a part of the Constitution.[6]

The debate at the time of drafting the founding documents certainly carries over to the modern day, and the issue of slavery has evolved into discussions about the issue of civil rights. The argument, however, is very similar: It's a question of equality or lack of equal opportunity between the races. However, this debate did not begin with the Declaration of Independence. The issue goes back hundreds of years, when the slave trade was introduced in the New World. Once the Declaration of Independence was written and published and the founders took their position concerning equality, the glaring contradiction had to be addressed and ultimately resolved. How that would occur was a constant challenge to all sides.

Slavery in the New World

The contradiction was not a new one—it had been developing for over 150 years. The origins of chattel slavery in the U.S. are traced back well before the Revolutionary War to the days when Jamestown was still a remote outpost. This institution of slavery refers to "chattel" because under the system, slaves are treated as an owner's personal property: "Such chattel slaves are used for their labor, sex, and breeding, and they are exchanged for camels, trucks, guns and money. Children of chattel slaves remain the property of their master."[7]

The practice of slavery in Colonial America developed gradually over time. In the early formation of the Chesapeake Bay settlements (areas today parts of Maryland and Virginia) it was difficult to find and hire laborers to work farmlands. Labor was most likely to be found among British indentured servants willing to work for a specified period (usually between four and seven years) in exchange for later being accepted as permanent residents. For local farmers who invested in the transport, training, and maintenance of indentured service, the biggest problem was that many servants chose to leave after their contract expired. With improvements in the British economy, indentured servants were more likely to return home than to seek permanent residence in the American colonies.

In the early 17th Century, colonial settlers imported the first slaves from Africa. These arrived in 1619 in Jamestown, Virginia, after being seized from a Spanish slave ship originally bound for Europe. However, under English law, anyone baptized as a Christian could not be enslaved, so these captured slaves were given the same status as indentured servants and eventually were freed from servitude. Matters changed two decades later; the first legal decision favoring slavery occurred in 1640 in Virginia, when an indentured African named John Punch tried to escape. He was recaptured, and the Court sentenced him to slavery.[8]

Massachusetts was the first colony to legalize slavery with enactment of the Body of Liberties in 1641. Under this law, slavery was forbidden with three exceptions: when the individuals were captured during war, when they sold themselves into slavery or were purchased from another owner, and when they were sentenced to slavery by a court.[9]

By 1654, a civil case redefined an indentured servant to a slave. The servant, John Casor, claimed that his owner had held him in service beyond the agreed term. A neighbor, Robert Parker, offered to testify in Casor's behalf in exchange for agreeing to a seven-year term of indenture for him. Casor agreed. Even though the original owner, Johnson, then freed Casor, Johnson later sued and won on a claim that he had a legal right to hold Casor "for the duration of his life."[10]

Under English and colonial law, Africans were not recognized as English subjects, so they were exempt from provisions of common law. So crucial was this distinction that it was possible for a slave to gain freedom by establishing a relationship to an Englishman. In Virginia in 1656, a mixed-race woman named Elizabeth Key Grinstead gained freedom for herself and her son by establishing her relationship with Thomas Key, an Englishman.[11]

A turning point was a new law passed in the royal colony in 1662, in which the principle of *partus sequitur ventrum* ("the offspring follow the condition of the mother") was codified. Under this new law, children of slave mothers were also considered slaves, no matter whether the father was a slave or free. So if an Englishman or other Christian fathered a child with a slave, that child would still be classified as a slave. Further solidifying the status of slaves as property was the 1705 slave codes passed in Virginia. This set of codes declared that

> all servants imported and brought into the Country ... who were not Christians in their native Country ... shall be accounted and be slaves. All Negro, mulatto and Indian slaves within this dominion ... shall be held to be real estate.[12]

With passage of similar laws in other colonies, the general understanding in colonial times was that a slaveowner had a legal right to claim and recapture escaped slaves even if they managed to make their way to a free colony (or later, to a free state), without first requiring permission from the local jurisdiction.

By the time of the Revolutionary War, slavery had spread throughout the 13 colonies, but some Northern states abolished the practice during this period. In 1777, Vermont's Constitution freed all male slaves over the age of 21 and females over 18. In 1780 Pennsylvania passed a new law entitled "An Act for the Gradual Abolition of Slavery." Under this law, all children born after passage were declared free. However, at the same time, slavery had become so institutionalized in the South that a new crisis arose. How should citizens be counted in the newly founded country for purposes of determining representation in Congress? With some states containing large populations of slaves, distortion would occur in apportionment of representatives if a compromise was not reached to maintain a balance of power between the newly emerged yet distinct free and slave states.

This matter dominated legislative thinking during the defining phases of the Constitution, resulting in a growing conflict between free and slave states and, eventually, to a political system in which newly admitted states had to maintain the artificial balance between free states and slave states. Thus, the major difference between "north" and "south" developed in the same manner.

The Three-Fifths Compromise

The first attempt at reconciling the difficulties between states regarding slavery occurred once freedom had been won from Great Britain. The idea of a three-fifths compromise—counting slaves at 60 percent of their numbers—originated in the 1783 Constitutional Convention; however, at that time the concept was applied only to taxation and not to levels of representation in Congress, as it was later. In assessing taxes among the states, the debate centered around the counting of 60 percent of slaves versus 100 percent of free citizens. This proposed compromise originally would have lowered taxes for the slave states. Later, when this became an issue of representation, the proposal became more controversial.

The Founding Fathers attempted to address the moral and economic realities of slavery as the 1787 Constitutional Convention convened. The convention took place from May 25 through September 17, 1787, in Philadelphia and slavery was one of the first issues tackled directly. The debate centered on the method by which states were to be apportioned in the lower house of Congress (later named the House of Representatives). Some favored equal weight for all states, and others argued for representation based on combined property holdings and population. During the debate, Thomas Jefferson wrote in his notes that Southern states were to be taxed "according to their numbers and their wealth, while the northern would be taxed on numbers only."[13]

The property segment of this argument was dropped because of the difficulty in assigning value to assets. Because population was the dominant factor in determining representation, delegates from the slave states wanted slaves to be included in the population statistics, meaning those states' representation would be increased in Congress. This led to the final version of what became known as the Three-Fifths Compromise, in which slaves would be counted at only 60 percent while non-slaves would be counted at 100 percent. The idea was first proposed by Pennsylvania delegate James Wilson.[14]

As one of the signers of the Declaration of Independence, Wilson proposed the Three-Fifths Compromise as a way to create consensus between delegates from Southern slave states and Northern free states. The uncomfortable inclusion of this compromise was the price paid by anti-slavery participants at the 1783 Constitutional Convention to achieve acceptance of the Constitution by all sides.[15]

Wilson's introduction of the idea was seconded by Charles Pinckney of South Carolina. However, while introduced in the hope for consensus, this idea led to further debate. Gouveneur Morris of New York argued against the plan as it would give Southerners an incentive to import more slaves, increasing their share of power in Congress. Morris explained

> that the inhabitant of Georgia and S.C. who goes to the Coast of Africa, and in defiance of the most sacred laws of humanity tears away his fellow creatures from their dearest connections and damns them to the most cruel bondages, shall have more votes in a Govt. instituted for the protection of the rights of mankind, than the Citizen of Pa or N. Jersey who views with a laudable horror, so nefarious a practice.[16]

Beyond the struggle over slave versus free states, another criticism of the Three-Fifths Compromise persists to this day: the idea that the Founding Fathers considered a slave as only three-fifths of a person. However, this was, and still is, political rhetoric and technically untrue:

> The three-fifths compromise was not proposed because the delegates believed that African slaves were only 60 percent human. Rather, the fraction "three-fifths" was intended as a rough approximation of the measure of wealth that an individual slave contributed to the economy of his or her state.... One individual, the bristly Elbridge Gerry, cut through the linguistic fog in blunt language when he opposed giving a three-fifths weight to slaves. Gerry noted that "blacks are property...."[17]

Thomas Jefferson argued that levels of wealth would determine how Southern states would be taxed under his idea of how slaves should be counted.

Elbridge Gerry, the outspoken delegate, became the fifth vice president of the U.S. under President James Madison. However, he is best remembered for the use of his name in the process of drawing electoral districts, or "gerrymandering."[18]

The controversy has never subsided despite its clear meaning in the original Three-Fifths Compromise. This continues to be misrepresented and has been cited by politicians as recently as 1999 as evidence of the racism practiced by the Founding Fathers: "When the Constitution was written, there was a shameful compromise.... African Americans were counted as three-fifths of a person."[19]

This was a mischaracterization of the Constitution's Three-Fifths Compromise, which was based not on all African Americans, but on the number of slaves in each state. The Three-Fifths Compromise never alluded to slaves as three-fifths of a person, but was solely applied to decide how many representatives would be assigned to each of the states, and how the population was to be counted. The language that ended up in the Constitution refers to "all other Persons," meaning specifically slaves owned at the time:

> Representatives and direct taxes shall be apportioned among the several States which may be included within this Union, according to their respective Numbers, which shall be determined by adding to the whole Number of free Persons, including those bound to Service for a Term of Years, and excluding Indians not taxed, three fifths of all other Persons.[20]

This clause was abolished in 1865 with the passage of the Thirteenth Amendment. In 1868, the Fourteenth Amendment replaced the clause with new language, stating that "representatives shall be apportioned ... counting the whole number of persons in each State, excluding Indians not taxed."[21]

American statesman Elbridge Gerry (portrait made in 1860) argued that black persons were property and should not be granted the rights of citizens.

The most immediate consequence of the Three-Fifths Compromise was greater representation among slave states in the House of Representatives than would have been the case if only free populations had been counted. This disparity, affecting legislative voting outcomes, appointment of Speaker of the House, and approval of nominees to the Supreme Court, endured until the Civil War. In 1793, the Southern states had 47 representatives, but would have had only 33 without the Three-Fifths Compromise; in 1812, the difference was 76 representatives versus only 59; and in 1833, the difference was 98 versus 73.[22]

The debate surrounding this issue went to the heart of slavery as an institution. The compromise did not address the underlying issue of whether slaves should be treated as persons or as property; it was devised to break the deadlock at the Constitutional Convention rather than to add definition to the issue of slavery. Complicating the debate was the fact that two separate matters were involved: the method for apportioning representatives and the amount of taxes levied on the states by the federal government. Central to this debate was the unaddressed concern about the immorality of slavery. Representatives focused on coming to agreement and did not address this larger issue:

> Much has been said of the impropriety of representing men who have no will of their own.... They are men, though degraded to the condition of slavery. They are persons known to the municipal laws of the states which they inhabit, as well as to the laws of nature. But representation and taxation go together.... Would it be just to impose a singular burden, without conferring some adequate advantage?[23]

The Slave Power

Due to the Three-Fifths Compromise, many in Congress were deeply concerned about the South having more representation in Congress than the North, meaning that the slave-owning South had greater power. This concept, referred to as a "slave power" or "slaveocrary," was a recurring theme for many decades and aggravated the growing conflict—economically and politically—between the two sides.

In the days leading up to the Civil War, party lines were drawn between Democrats as supporters of states' rights (including slavery) and Republicans and members of the Free Soil Party as opponents of slavery and its expansion. Of these two parties on the anti-slavery side, they

> both vehemently opposed the expansion of slavery. But ... motivations varied. Some men and women clamored for free soil because they opposed slavery, or because they opposed its expansion. But others joined the free-soil ranks largely because they hated and feared blacks. "Free soil" in their minds meant "whites

only." Still others supported free soil because they despised Southern planters. To them the fight over free soil in the West was just part of the larger battle against the "slave oligarchs."[24]

The issue of slavery—and by association, degrees of political power—was by no means clear between the two sides. However, as legislative and legal actions leading up to the Civil War progressed, the two sides became more polarized. The Free Soil Party, for example, did not survive because its members lacked a focused platform. Many Free Soil members, notably the anti-slavery group, ended up later joining the Republican Party with a clear and unwavering opposition to the expansion of slavery as well as to its continuation even in slave states. Other Free Soil Party members, preferring expansion in the West to belong only to white persons, did not find a home in the Republican Party and much later, during the Civil War, became "Peace Democrats" or "Copperheads."[25]

These so-called Peace Democrats were from the group of Free Soil members whose anti-black bias led them to oppose the expansion of slavery. They wanted Western expansion to be a "whites only" movement. Later, during the Civil War, these same Peace Democrats, even those residing in Union states, favored secession and formation of a separate Confederate States of America, complete with legalized—but isolated—slavery as part of its national charter. As the war progressed, these same Peace Democrats opposed Lincoln and his efforts to end the war and the practice of slavery. Even after the war, the divide between Republicans and Democrats was as pronounced as ever. In 1868, the Democratic Party candidate, Horatio Seymour, ran under the slogan of Democrats as "the white man's party."

The free soil movement was controversial due to the racial undertones involved. "The Hurly-Burly Pot" is a political cartoon portraying the struggle between free soil advocates and abolitionists. The artist attacks abolitionist, Free Soil, and other sectionalist interests of 1850 as dangers to the Union. Shown are abolitionist William Lloyd Garrison, Pennsylvania Free Soil advocate David Wilmot, New York journalist Horace Greeley, and Southern states' rights spokesman Senator John C. Calhoun. The three wear fool's caps and gather, like the witches in Shakespeare's "Macbeth," around a large, boiling cauldron, adding to it sacks marked "Free Soil," "Abolition," and "Fourierism" (added by Greeley, a vocal exponent of the doctrines of utopian socialist Charles Fourier). Sacks of "Treason," "Anti-Rent," and "Blue Laws" already simmer in the pot.

> WILMOT: "Bubble, bubble, toil and trouble! / Boil, Free Soil, / Ther Union spoil; / Come grief and moan, / Peace be none. / Til we divided be!"
>
> GARRISON: "Bubble, bubble, toil and trouble / Abolition / Our condition / Shall be altered by / Niggars strong as goats / Cut your master's throats / Abolition boil! / We divide the spoil."

Greeley: "Bubble, buble [*sic*], toil and trouble! / Fourierism / War and schism / Till disunion come!"

In the background stands the aging John Calhoun. He announces, "For success to the whole mixture, we invoke our great patron Saint Benedict Arnold." Benedict Arnold rises from the fire under the pot, commending them, "Well done, good and faithful servants!"

The slave power debate was as complex as the motives of Free Soil Party members. Some Northern opponents of slavery recognized that membership of the slave power (Southern slaveowners, their Congressional representatives, and other supporters) would defend slavery fiercely, whether for economic, political, or moral reasons. There was some truth in this as evidenced by attempts on the part of slave state congresmen to add new states with slavery allowed within their boundaries, and to extend slavery as a property rights issue even in free states.

This argument between the two sides added to the antagonism affecting the many issues over which the Civil War was fought. It also evolved into a modern-day conflict between Republicans and Democrats over a broad range of issues growing out of the civil rights movement.

Legislation intended to resolve the slave power conflicts made the debate more complex. From 1787 to 1861, a series of new laws were passed

THE HURLY-BURLY POT.

"The Hurly-Burly Pot" (1850). The debate concerning slavery between Free Soilers and abolitionists led to accusations of treason by each side against the other.

or amended to fix the conflicts over slavery; the Supreme Court also ruled on numerous cases in the interest of settling questions of slavery's legality in various territories and states. These attempts, both legislative and legal, only made the problem worse. The issue did not go away or find resolution; it had only been given different names.

A distinction has to be made between the political concerns among Northern state politicians and abolitionists. The political interests saw increasing power among Southern states as a threat to the balance of representation in Congress; in comparison, abolitionists were opposed to slavery not for political reasons, but as a moral point. The political threat was not characterized primarily by the treatment of slaves, but as a threat to the core philosophy of republicanism, which eventually led to formation of the Republican Party. The concept of republicanism that arose as part of this debate was not just a political stance; in the minds of Northern politicians, it "represented more than a particular form of government. It was a way of life, a core ideology, an uncompromising commitment to liberty, and a total rejection of aristocracy."[26]

Another argument put forth by anti-slavery political interests was that slavery was economically inefficient and that a free labor market worked far better. The political interests that later formed the Republican Party also viewed slavery as an inhibiting factor to the long-term development and modernization of the United States. However, more than any other factor, the imbalance of representation favoring Southern slave states was viewed as a movement gradually taking over Congress as well as executive and judicial branches of the federal government. In other words, slaves were counted in the way that representatives were sent to Congress, but had no vote, making white slaveowners far more influential than Northern citizens. This argument was strongly supported by Salmon P. Chase and Charles Sumner.

Chase had a long-standing political career. He was governor of Ohio, a senator, and later, the sixth chief justice of the Supreme Court. In Lincoln's administration, Chase served as Secretary of the Treasury. He referred to the "slave power conspiracy" and led a Northern state movement against slavery. He wrote a manifesto based on these ideas entitled "The Appeal of the Independent Democrats in Congress to the People of the United States," which became an early version of the creed of the Republican Party.[27]

The problems of political balance of power persisted, however, despite efforts in Congress and in the courts to remedy the growing divide. Among the proposed solutions to the issue of imbalance between north and south was the Northwest Ordinance of 1787, which attempted to set up a system for creating new territories while also curtailing the spread of slavery. However, intended solutions turned ineffective as its provisions eventually were modified by the Supreme Court and did not apply to future territorial areas set to be added to the Union. As a result, the Northwest Ordinance did nothing to resolve the political conflict.

The Northwest Ordinance of 1787

Beyond the Constitution and its compromise in how representatives were to be apportioned, the delegates further passed legislation to limit future growth of slavery in the country. One of the first actions of the Congress of the Confederation was passage of the Northwest Ordinance (also known as the Freedom Ordinance or Ordinance of 1787) on July 13, 1787.

This ordinance created the Northwest Territory, consisting of land west of the Appalachian Mountains between British Canada and the Great Lakes, bounded to the South by the Ohio River and to the west by the northern section of the Mississippi River. It was a first step in attempting to limit the spread of slavery and, eventually, to its abolition. Under this ordinance, all states to be newly admitted to the Union would prohibit slavery. The ordinance specified that its conditions "shall be considered as Articles of compact between the original States and the people and states in the said territory, and forever remain unalterable, unless by common consent."[28]

The U.S. Supreme Court confirmed the authority of the Northwest Ordinance in 1851, but altered the original provisions, banning application of its provisions to states admitted to the Union in the future. This led to future controversy on the question of slavery, especially in the years prior to the Civil War when westward expansion again raised the question of slavery.[29]

By prohibiting slavery in the territories, the effective boundary between free states and slave states became the Ohio River. This boundary set the stage for controversy in coming years, whether this was intentional on the part of the Continental Congress or not. It is more likely that their initial purpose was to limit and eventually abolish slavery over time within the expanding geographic reach of the country. In addition to a prohibition of slavery in the new territory, the ordinance also established a fugitive state clause, specifying that an escaped slave "may be lawfully reclaimed and conveyed to the person claiming his or her labor or service...."[30]

Central to the debate over slavery was a balance of power between free and slave states. Because the number of senators was fixed at two per state, neither side favored upsetting the balance between the two sides. Ultimately, as it turned out, new states admitted to the Union had to be created in equal numbers, half free and half slave. However, because slave and free states often bordered on one another, a related problem arose regarding what to do about slaves escaping from slave states into free states. The question also raised a related issue of jurisdiction. Did the federal government have the authority to dictate laws about escaped slaves at the state level?

The Fugitive Slave Law of 1793

The federal government attempted to resolve the ongoing crisis between slave and free states with passage of the Fugitive Slave Law of 1793, "an act respecting fugitives from justice, and persons escaping from the service of their masters." In this new law, the U.S. Constitution was cited as authority for the federal position:

> No Person held to Service or Labor in one State, under the Laws thereof, escaping into another, shall, in Consequence of any Law or Regulation therein, be discharged from such Service or Labor, but shall be delivered up on Claim of the Party to whom such Service or Labor may be due.[31]

This clause created debate concerning states' rights versus the power of the federal government. The Kentucky and Virginia Resolutions of 1797 and 1798 disputed federal authority to make laws such as the Fugitive Slave Law, claiming that this law was contrary to states' rights as defined in the Constitution. One of the features of the Kentucky and Virginia Resolutions was called the Principles of '98, with opposition to the federal government's stated policy concerning escaped slaves.[32]

The Fugitive Slave Law required the federal government to pursue escaped slaves in any state or territory to protect the property rights of slaveowners.[33] In the opinion of the anti–Federalist camp, the Fugitive Slave clause in the Constitution, along with the Fugitive Slave Law of 1793, violated states' rights by citing slaveowners' property rights.[34]

Jefferson (author of the Virginia Resolution) and Madison (author of the two Kentucky Resolutions), in opposing Federalist support for slaveowners and their property rights, created long-lasting controversy. The Kentucky and Virginia Resolutions have been described as "a recipe for disunion."[35] The arguments set forth by the anti–Federalists were based on the belief that states held the right to decide if and when the federal government's actions were constitutional. This was at least in part an effort by Jefferson, Madison, and their supporters to strengthen the states' position under the Constitution.

The Slave Trade Act of 1794

The Constitutional Convention established the structure of the U.S. government and defined the balance of power, methods of election of Congress, and more, including a measure to end the slave trade beginning in 1808. The Slave Trade Act of 1794 banned "carrying on any trade or traffic in slaves, to any foreign country; or for the purpose of procuring, from any foreign kingdom, place or country, the inhabitants of such kingdom, place or country, to be transported to any foreign country, port, or place whatever, to be sold or disposed of, as slaves...."[36]

The attempt to abolish slavery was a long process, but it began with the prohibition against slave trade in the 1794 act. Even so, the legacy of slavery had been set for over 200 years by the end of the 18th Century, and the path toward civil war was set in motion. The debate over this issue also defined the creation of both major political parties, divided over the issue of slavery and, in a larger sense, over the inherent racism that grew from it: "Slavery was not born of racism; racism was the consequence of slavery."[37]

Ending the institution was not a simple matter, as the ownership of slaves was widespread in the states and not limited to the South. Many states had adopted the policy of "gradual emancipation," in which slaves would eventually be granted freedom.[38] Among the 55 delegates to the 1787 Convention, 25 (over 45 percent) were slaveowners.[39] Slaves represented an estimated 20 percent of the total states' population at the time, with 90 percent living in the South.[40]

The economic and moral issues surrounding slavery were in direct conflict at the time the Constitution was drafted. Several Southern states took the position that they would not agree to join the Union unless slavery was left intact as a legal institution. Under a compromise designed to achieve ratification, Congress was granted the power to ban the slave trade, but only with the 20-year delay leading to the 1808 deadline.[41]

The method of division between slave and free states was a complex problem. The counting of only three-fifths of slaves created great controversy about its meaning, rather than only establishing agreement among the delegates. Many in Congress adopted the argument about greater Southern influence under the Three-Fifths Compromise. This concern was aggravated in 1803 by the Louisiana Purchase. This acquisition doubled the size of the United States, consisting of 828,000 square miles.[42] Critics predicted that this massive addition of land would forever destroy the balance of power between slave and free states, assuming that the states forged out of the new territory would allow slavery. This fear was confirmed with the defeat of a series of bills designed to limit or curtail the expansion of slavery into the newly acquired lands.

Act Prohibiting Importation of Slaves of 1807

In 1808, the Act Prohibiting Importation of Slaves of 1807 became U.S. law. The act specified that no new slaves could be imported into the United States. This act was passed in response to the Slave Trade Act of 1794, in which the date of 1808, the year named in the Constitution, was selected to begin the prohibition:

> The Migration or Importation of such Persons as any of the States now existing shall think proper to admit, shall not be prohibited by the Congress prior to the Year one thousand eight hundred and eight, but a tax or duty may be imposed on such Importation, not exceeding ten dollars for each Person.[43]

The move toward abolishing slavery was growing, even among leaders who themselves owned slaves. Thomas Jefferson, in his annual message to Congress in 1806, anticipated the 1808 deadline to abolish further importation:

> I congratulate you, fellow-citizens, on the approach of the period at which you may interpose your authority constitutionally, to withdraw the citizens of the United States from all further participation in those violations of human rights which have been so long continued on the unoffending inhabitants of Africa, and which the morality, the reputation, and the best interests of our country, have long been eager to proscribe. Although no law you may pass can take prohibitory effect till the first day of the year one thousand eight hundred and eight, yet the intervening period is not too long to prevent, by timely notice, expeditions which cannot be completed before that day.[44]

Although the new law outlawed importation from 1808 onward, it was not enforced. The practice of importing slaves continued up until at least 1859. In fact, the volume of ships in American ports with a cargo of slaves apparently was not affected by the 1808 law:

> The act outlawing the slave trade in 1808 furnished another source of demand for fast vessels, and for another half century ships continued to be fitted out and financed in this trade by many a respectable citizen in the majority of American ports. Newspapers of the fifties contain occasional references to the number of ships sailing from the various cities in this traffic. One account stated that as late as 1859 there were seven slavers regularly fitted out in New York, and many more in all the larger ports.[45]

The Missouri Compromise

By 1819, slavery was routinely debated as an issue involving newly admitted states, as a states' rights issue, and also regarding the balance of power in the House of Representatives. The question was whether newly admitted states would be slave states or free states. Congressmen opposed to slavery argued that the Declaration of Independence clearly was written against the institution of slavery and that, as a result, newly admitted states should not be allowed to practice slavery within their borders. By 1819, Missouri had petitioned for admission as a slave state, creating renewed debate and disagreement in Congress.[46]

Prominent pro-slavery congressmen included John Randolph of Virginia, a strong supporter of states' rights, and John C. Calhoun of South Carolina, a prominent defender of slavery. Their position was that the ideal of "all men are created equal" did not apply to black people.[47] Both of these men were members of the Democratic Party.[48]

A proposed solution to this debate was the Missouri Compromise, which banned slavery in the Great Plains (the "unorganized territory" of the time) but permitted slavery in the new states of Missouri and Arkansas. The idea was proposed by Henry Clay, Sr., Democratic Party member and U.S. senator from Kentucky; he also served in the House of Representatives, as Speaker of the House, and as Secretary of State. Clay ran for president three times, in 1824, 1832 and 1844.

Clay's suggestion led to the compromise, in which the slave state of Missouri was accompanied by a division of Northern Massachusetts to create the state of Maine as a free state. This kept intact the equal balance between free and slave states. On February 13, 1819, New York Representative James Tallmadge (also a member of the Democratic Party) offered what was called the Tallmadge Amendment.

This amendment suggested admitting Missouri as a free state. Tallmadge hoped that conditions in his bill would eliminate slavery altogether within a generation. It included terms

John C. Calhoun of South Carolina (photographed by Mathew Brady in 1849) was one of the prominent members of Congress who favored slavery under the banner of "states' rights."

affecting all slave states, that further expansion of slavery was to be prohibited, and that all children born to slaves would become free at the age of 25. Although the House approved the amendment three days after it was introduced, the Senate rejected it. Debate on the merits of the amendment continued, but the Missouri Compromise survived and slavery was allowed to spread to newly admitted states.[49]

A Second Missouri Compromise followed in 1820. It combined admission of Maine with an enabling act for Missouri (which did not restrict slavery but left the Missouri question of whether to be a slave or free state up to the state). Admission of Missouri was debated in 1820 and 1821 in Congress, and the final admission of Missouri was finalized. This Second Missouri Compromise resulted in statehood and was a symptom of the power struggle between North and South (free and slave states). Thomas Jefferson wrote in a letter to John Holmes on April 22, 1820, that the issue would lead to the end of the Union:

> This momentous question, like a fire bell in the night, awakened and filled me with terror. I considered it at once as the knell of the Union. It is hushed indeed for the moment, but this is a reprieve only, not a final sentence. A geographical line, coinciding with a marked principle, moral and political, once conceived and held up to the angry passions of men, will never be obliterated; and every new irritation will mark it deeper and deeper.[50]

The ongoing debate concerning slavery and how widely it would be allowed to spread set the stage for the Civil War four decades later. Tocqueville wrote of this and offered insight into the character of the nation and of the debate:

> Thus it is in the United States that the prejudice which repels the Negroes seems to increase in proportion as they are emancipated, and inequality is sanctioned by the manners while it is effaced from the laws of the country. But if the relative position of the two races that inhabit the United States is such as I have described, why have the Americans abolished slavery in the North of the Union, why do they maintain it in the South, and why do they aggravate its hardships? The answer is easily given. It is not for the good of the Negroes, but for that of the whites, that measures are taken to abolish slavery in the United States.[51]

The Wilmot Proviso

The Missouri Compromise appeared to have settled a portion of the question of slavery, at least for the moment. However, an unending series of anti-slavery petitions made their way to the floor of the House of Representatives in the years following.

Among these, the most significant was the Wilmot Proviso, so named for Congressman David Wilmot of Pennsylvania. He introduced the clause as a rider to another bill; it would prohibit slavery in territories acquired from Mexico after the Mexican-American War. The specific language within the Wilmot Proviso stated that as part of acquiring territory from Mexico, "neither slavery nor involuntary servitude shall ever exist in any part of said territory...."

The proviso stirred up debate and controversy.

The political cartoon of the day shows how Horace Greeley, one of Clay's most influential Northern supporters, tries to drive the party wagon downhill toward "Salt River" (a contemporary idiom for political doom). At the same time, a Brother Jonathan or Uncle Sam figure steers in the opposite direction, toward the White House. Greeley whips his horse, a scrawny nag with the head of Henry Clay, with a switch or small branch; the uphill-bound horse has Taylor's head, and its driver wields a carriage whip. The cart is laden with papers marked "Tariff," "Bank," and "Internal Improvements," traditional catchwords of Whig politics.

GREELEY: "It's of no use to talk to me, for Mr. Clay says he would rather be right than to be President, and that is the policy I am adopting now."

"Whig Harmony" (1848). The Wilmot Proviso was hotly debated and became a focal point in the struggle about whether newly admitted states should be slave states or free.

BROTHER JONATHAN: "Do slack up a little there, Horace, till we get over a chock that some one [*sic*] has put before the wheel."

The "chock" that the cart has run into is a rock marked "Wilmot Proviso," placed in the road by Congressman David Wilmot. The question of the validity of the proviso became an important issue in the 1848 campaign and a stumbling block to candidates like Taylor who courted Southern support. The proviso was never passed by the Senate.

The authorship of the proviso itself was disputed. Wilmot claimed that the proviso was his alone; however, Ohio Democrat Jacob Brinkerhoff stated that he was the author. The controversy was never completely resolved.[52] In fact, much speculation centered not only on authorship of the proviso, but also on motivation for drafting it. Brinkerhoff argued that whereas he was the author, Wilmot was chosen to introduce the rider as cover for Brinkerhoff's well-known anti-slavery positions.[53]

Wilmot persisted in claiming authorship of the proviso named for him, and explained in an 1847 speech that he originated the idea alone and had consulted with several anti-slavery Democrats before introducing the rider. The individuals Wilmot spoke with included Democrats Martin Grover, Jacob Brinkerhoff, Hannibal Hamlin, George Rathbun, Preston King, and James Thompson.[54] Wilmot qualified his claim of exclusive ownership the following year, explaining that "several gentlemen collected together to agree upon the form and terms of the proposed [free soil] amendment.... After various drafts had been drawn and altered, the language in which the amendment was offered was finally agreed on."[55]

The first time the rider was attached to another bill was August 8, 1846. This bill passed in the House but failed in the Senate. The division was almost completely along sectional lines, with seventy-four Southern representatives and four Northern voting to table the amendment, versus 91 Northern representatives and three Southern voting to advance the bill.[56]

Despite its strong anti-slavery language, the proviso cannot be summarized as a move against Southern and pro-slavery interests alone, as it also contained a political element. Supporters of Martin Van Buren, intent on establishing themselves on the majority side of the slavery issue among Northern voters, favored the proviso as a move to attract Northern states' support among anti-slavery voters.[57]

The same outcome—approval in the House and rejection in the Senate—occurred when the proviso was reintroduced in 1847. A third attempt made the proviso part of a treaty bill, but it failed for a third time. Southern Democrats wanted the proviso removed from the bill so that newly acquired territories would allow slavery. The debate continued until 1847, when Congressman Preston King of New York reintroduced the Wilmot Proviso once again, but with expanded language specifying that slavery was to be excluded to "any territory on the continent of America which shall hereafter be acquired."[58]

This question of whether or not to allow slavery in the Western territories escalated and drew sharp lines between the pro-slavery Democrats and anti-slavery Whigs (and later, Republicans). The Wilmot Proviso was a clear turning point that focused attention on the issue, marking the point where the Democrats became identified as the party of the slave-dominated South. In this period Democrats representing the South

> lost the hard core of their original doughface[59] support. No longer could they count on New England and New York Democrats to provide them with winning margins in the House. Not only had many old allies turned their backs on the South, many had joined the opposition and added their voices to the growing crusade against the Slave Power.[60]

The schism among Democrats caused by the Proviso was a deep one that not only split the party but created a new political problem as well:

> Southern Democrats, for whom slavery had always been central, had little difficulty in perceiving exactly what the proviso meant for them and their party. In the first place the mere existence of the proviso meant the sectional strains that had plagued the Whigs on Texas now beset the Democrats on expansion, the issue the Democrats themselves had chosen as their own. The proviso also announced to southerners that they had to face the challenge of certain northern Democrats who indicated their unwillingness to follow any longer the southern lead on slavery. That circumstance struck at the very roots of the southern conception of party. The southerners had always felt that their northern colleagues must toe the southern line on all slavery-related issues.[61]

The ramifications were widespread. In June 1850, delegates from nine slave states met in Nashville, Tennessee, and threatened secession if Congress approved the Wilmot Proviso or any other measure limiting slavery in the new territories. Represented at the Nashville Convention were delegates from Virginia, Georgia, Alabama, South Carolina, Mississippi, Arkansas, Texas, Florida, and Tennessee. However, the delegates were not able to put forth an outright vote for secession.

However, in November 1850 a more extreme group of delegates met in Nashville again. This group voted to affirm the right of states to secede. Although this vote did not have any immediate impact, it fed the growing divide between Southern Democrats favoring slavery and Northern Whigs opposing it. Among these Southern delegates was Jefferson Davis of Mississippi, the future president of the Confederacy. The issue of whether or not to expand slavery articulated in the Wilmot Proviso continued for the next decade and became a core issue leading to the Civil War:

> Thus the contest was joined on the central issue which was to dominate all American history for the next dozen years, the disposition of the Territories. Two sets of

extremists had arisen: Northerners who demanded no new slave territories under any circumstances, and Southerners who demanded free entry for slavery into all territories, the penalty for denial to be secession. For the time being, moderates who hoped to find a way of compromise and to repress the underlying issue of slavery itself—its toleration or non-toleration by a great free Christian state—were overwhelmingly in the majority. But history showed that in crises of this sort the two sets of extremists were almost certain to grow in power, swallowing up more and more members of the conciliatory center.[62]

The proviso was not the only legislation that aggravated the divide between North and South or between free and slave states. However, it opened the question of sectionalism and pointed out how irreconcilable the issue was and would remain.[63] Ironically, the debate centered not on existing slave states but on whether or not future states would be admitted as slave states:

> Instead of being challenged where it prevailed, slavery was challenged where it did not exist. Instead of proclaiming the goal of emancipation, the opponents of slavery began the long battle in a way which prevented them from admitting the goal even to themselves. Certainly it was not dreamed of in the philosophy of David Wilmot.[64]

Wilmot himself was opposed to the expansion of slavery, not so much as an anti-slavery politician, but more as an advocate of white labor versus the competitive nature of a slave economy. In this respect, he identified with the wing of the Free Soil Party opposed to allowing any non-white settlement of Western territories. Wilmot explained that his proviso was developed for this reason:

> I have no squeamish sensitiveness upon the subject of slavery, nor morbid sympathy for the slave. I plead the cause of the rights of white freedmen. I would preserve for free white labor a fair country, a rich inheritance, where the sons of toil, of my own race and own color, can live without the disgrace which association with negro slavery brings upon free labor.[65]

Even with Wilmot's admission concerning his motives for the Proviso, this became an issue drawn out on pro-slavery and anti-slavery lines. On March 3, 1847, every Northern Whig in the Senate voted in favor and 22 Northern Democrats voted with the South in opposition to the proviso. Although various versions passed in the House, the Senate voted against the proviso each time it was introduced and it never became law.

The Wilmot Proviso did not mark the end of the discussion, but the beginning of debate on an elevated level. The next phase, beginning with the Compromise of 1850, occurred four years after the initial introduction of the proviso. Upon introduction, this new bill had been viewed by many as the ultimate solution to the issue of slavery in the new territories, with hopes that it would prevent escalation of the dividing issue. To many the debate concerning the Wilmot Proviso "marked the turning point, the time when aggressive slavemasters stole the heart and soul of the Democratic Party and began dictating the course of the nation's destiny."[66]

The Compromise of 1850

After failure of the Wilmot Proviso, a bipartisan effort to settle the slavery debate was undertaken. In September 1850, a set of five bills passed by Congress aimed at settling the disputes between slave and free states and the question of how slavery should be treated in new territories. The two senators behind these bills were Whig Henry Clay of Kentucky and Democrat Stephen Douglas of Illinois.

In January 1850 Clay offered eight resolutions, hoping that collectively they would satisfy both Northern and Southern sides in the escalating debate. These were later fine-tuned into five resolutions, setting up the start of a six-month period of great debate, one of the more notable in Congressional history:

> For the next six months Congress deliberated over Clay's proposals, in one form or another, and ended by enacting most of them in an important legislative settlement which history has dubbed the Compromise of 1850. The story of these deliberations, and of the great debate which ran through them, has become one of the classic and inevitable set pieces in American historical writing. The gravity of the crisis, the uncertainty as to the outcome, and the brilliant effects of oratory in the grand manner all combined to create scenes of stunning dramatic effect.[67]

On May 8, Clay presented an omnibus bill for all five resolutions, containing the following terms:

- California would be admitted to the Union as a free state.

Henry Clay offered a set of eight resolutions that were collectively called the Compromise of 1850. The bill did not pass in Congress after Whig Party opposition.

- Utah and New Mexico would be admitted but without provisions regarding slavery, so that the populations of those new states would be able to decide for themselves whether or not to ban slavery. The Wilmot Proviso was not applicable under this bill.
- In the District of Columbia, slave trading was banned, but not ownership of slaves.
- A new Fugitive Slave Act required federal officials in all states and territories to cooperate in the return of escaped slaves to their masters.
- Boundaries were set for the state of Texas and, in exchange, the federal government agreed to pay Texas's debt of $10 million. Texas also gave up its claims to New Mexico.

The omnibus bill as presented did not pass, mainly due to a majority of Whig senators in opposition. Stephen Douglas was able to get passage of the bill later that year. A coalition of Northern Democrats and Southern Whigs favored the bill, and those from border states especially favored the strengthened Fugitive Slave Act included in the final version of the bill.

The Compromise of 1850 delayed the Civil War for 10 years. However, the political divide continued and worsened. The Whig Party fell apart and was replaced by the new Republican Party, which further drew the lines for an eventual conflict. Republicans dominated in the North and Democrats in the South. Among the more controversial provisions in the compromise was the harsh Fugitive Slave Act, further dividing North and South. This provision had been included to gain Southern votes, but it created deep resentment in the North. During this period, economic changes also fed a growing uneasiness in the South. As the North industrialized in the coming decade, the South continued to rely on agriculture and slave labor. By 1860, the distinction between the industrialized North and the agricultural South added to the already growing tensions.

Addressing the issues of state boundaries, territorial policies, and slavery, the Compromise of 1850 did not resolve disagreements concerning slavery, but it did delay the armed conflict that inevitably grew from the issues

Fugitive Slave Act of 1850

Among the provisions of the Compromise of 1850, the Fugitive Slave Act was the most controversial, and it created the greatest animosity in the North. This updated version of the Fugitive Slave Law of 1793 required federal officials to actively assist in capturing and returning escaped slaves to the state or territory from which they had escaped.

Beyond enabling federal officials, the new law also authorized the formation of citizens' posse bands to hunt down escaped slaves. Escaped slaves were not allowed to offer testimony at a hearing to determine their status. As a consequence, freedmen accused of being escaped slaves were not allowed to provide direct evidence in their own defense and could be transported into slavery based solely on the property claim of someone in a slave state or territory.

The pro-slavery section of the Compromise of 1850 was seen as necessary to obtain Southern votes and pass the bill. Partly in reaction to this pro-slavery provision, Harriett Beecher Stowe wrote *Uncle Tom's Cabin* in 1851–52 (first published in serialized form in *The National Era* and then in book form in March 1852). This was a bestseller immediately, with 300,000 copies sold in its first year. The book highlighted the evils of slavery, especially for the treatment of recaptured slaves and the tragedy of slave families separated by their masters. The book strengthened anti-slavery sentiment in the North while enraging pro-slavery citizens in the South.

The Fugitive Slave Act of 1850 was especially objectionable to Northerners who were required under the law to assist in hunting down escaped slaves. Abolitionists called it the "bloodhound law," a reference to the dogs used in tracking runaways. In response to the Fugitive Slave Act, many Northern states passed personal liberty laws requiring jury trials before escaped slaves could be returned and, in some cases, outlawed the use of state officials in aiding escaped slave manhunts. When escaped slaves were indicted in federal court, some state juries declined to convict the accused.[68]

As with so many of the laws passed with the intention of settling the disagreements about states' rights and the expansion of slavery, the Fugitive Slave Act of 1850 accelerated the social divide between the two sides. In 1854, passage of the new Kansas–Nebraska Act only made matters worse.

Kansas–Nebraska Act of 1854

Two new territories, Kansas and Nebraska, were opened in 1854, but not without continuing controversy over the question of slavery.

In 1854, the Kansas–Nebraska Act was passed to create the two new territories. This act also opened up settlement lands to the west. However, the new law specified that territories would have the rights of "popular sovereignty," meaning the citizens could choose whether or not to allow slavery by popular vote of the citizens. This provision made the 1820 Missouri Compromise obsolete, adding to the continuing controversy and causing great chaos and even armed conflict. Immediately, the new territories were flooded with settlers hoping to gain a majority in this popular vote, including both pro-slavery and anti-slavery advocates.

This outcome was probably not foreseen by its originator, Stephen Douglas (D–IL), who intended to populate new regions to support the long-planned transcontinental railroad. However, the great influx of settlers from both sides led to a series of violent confrontations which have been called "Bleeding Kansas." Also referred to as "Bloody Kansas" or the "Kansas Border War," the conflict began in Kansas territory and spread into neighboring regions of Missouri. The term "Bleeding Kansas" was invented by Horace Greeley, the editor of the *New York Tribune*.

Although Bleeding Kansas has been cast historically as an issue concerning only the debate over slavery, this was not the central issue. Settlers were more interested in acquisition of land rights in Kansas, but poor planning led to considerable confusion about availability of land. Much of the land had been surveyed and no acreage was available even six months after passage of the Kansas–Nebraska Act.[69] Anti-slavery interests saw the new act as "part and parcel of an atrocious plot" to extend slavery as far west as possible, effectively nationalizing the practice.[70]

On the pro-slavery side, this was a states' rights issue. Proponents argued that citizens had every right to move to new territories and bring their property with them. In slave states, slaves were legally defined as property, so popular sovereignty provided free choice to settlers. The anti-slavery interests, known as "free soilers," argued that wealthy slaveowners would purchase the best lands and work those lands with slaves, robbing non-slaveowners of the chance to succeed in the new territories. To many, Bleeding Kansas was not only a slavery issue but directly related to the larger issue of states' rights.

In many respects, Bleeding Kansas was a precursor to the Civil War a few years later. It became apparent in the conflict created by provisions of the Kansas–Nebraska Act that the slavery issue could not be compromised or settled short of war, and the ultimate solution would have to be either complete emancipation or complete acceptance of the institution. Neither side was willing to concede.

An especially racist editorial cartoon of the era called "The Freedman's Bureau," tried to make the case that laws doing away with slavery would place a high cost on white citizens, aggravating further the divide between the two sides that often became violent and, notably in Kansas and Missouri, led to widespread cases of voter fraud.

The pro-slavery settlers who moved to Kansas from Missouri were named "border ruffians." These settlers attempted to dominate the vote over the question of slavery. They won 37 out of 39 delegates in the new territorial legislature. However, voter fraud was widespread and a Congressional committee audit revealed 1,729 fraudulent votes versus only 1,114 legal votes cast. Only small minorities in some locations were legal residents, but larger numbers of pro-slavery votes were cast by border ruffians from Missouri.[71]

Citing the widespread fraud, territorial Governor Andrew Reeder declared the results void in five voting districts and called for a special election on May 22, 1855. However, even after this new election, pro-slavery interests held an advantage of 29 to 10 representatives. A Congressional committee investigated again and, in 1856, issued a report declaring that if the election had been limited to residents, Kansas would have elected a free state legislature. The investigating committee declared that the Kansas legislature lacked legal power to pass laws. Despite this conclusion, the pro-slavery legislature met in July and invalidated the results of the special election, seating pro-slavery delegates originally elected in March. A second legislature formed and wrote a new constitution for the territory, resulting in one territory with two bodies: one pro-slavery and the other anti-slavery. On January 24, 1856, the free state government established in Topeka was declared insurrectionist by Democrat President Franklin Pierce.

Violence between the two sides escalated into outright warfare. In July 1856, President Pierce sent 500 soldiers to Topeka and, under threat of force, demanded the dismantling of the free state legislature. In August, thousands of pro-slavery men formed an army to support the federal troops and oppose anti-slavery residents. Before the violence ended in 1859, over 50 people had been killed. However, the animosity between the two sides spilled over and continued into the Civil War.

Senator Douglas had originally declared that the Kansas–Nebraska Act and the granting of the right of popular sovereignty would reduce tensions over the issue of slavery. However, the new legislation reversed the law set in the 1820 Missouri Compromise and brought the debate to new heights. It also led to political consequences for the Democratic Party and its pro-slavery policies. Before the 1854 election, Democrats held 93 Northern House seats. The election reduced the number to only 22 seats.[72]

One direct outcome of the Kansas–Nebraska Act was creation of the Republican Party, organized to create a formal opposition to the law. The first policy articulated by the new party was intended to stop the expansion of slavery. At approximately the same time, the Whig Party was on the decline, especially in the South. A split between Northern and Southern Whigs led to the demise of the party, and many ex–Whigs joined the new Republican Party based on its strong anti-slavery position.

The controversy over the expansion of slavery went far beyond the new law to include debate over the meaning of equality in the Constitution itself. For example, Senator John Pettit (D–IN), arguing in favor of slavery, declared in 1853 during arguments about the new law that the claim that all men are created equal was not a truth that was self-evident, but rather was "a self-evident lie."[73] Another pro-slavery senator was David Atchison (D–MO), who would only support the new law if slaveowners were allowed to emigrate. He declared he would rather see Nebraska "sink in hell" than allow it to be overrun by anti-slavery free soilers.[74]

The two sides had strongly held beliefs, and the pro-slavery side resorted to fear tactics to win the argument. A political cartoon from August 1856 brought the Democratic platform to light regarding free soilers (those who supported creation of free territories and states and opposed slavery). It depicts a giant free soiler being held down by James Buchanan and Lewis Cass standing on the Democratic platform marked "Kansas," "Cuba," and "Central America." Franklin Pierce also holds down the giant's beard as Douglas shoves an African American down his throat.

The Kansas–Nebraska Act was passed by the Senate on March 4, 1854. Less than two weeks later, the House of Representatives referred the

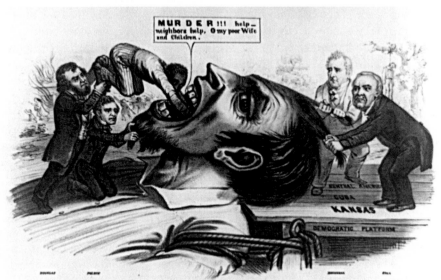

FORCING SLAVERY DOWN THE THROAT OF A FREESOILER

"Forcing Slavery Down the Throat of a Freesoiler" (1856). Political cartoons graphically made the point that Freesoilers would suffer if politicians forced the issue of slavery in newly admitted states.

bill to committee and when it came up for a vote, the bill passed by 113 to 100. President Pierce signed the bill into law on May 30. This by no means ended the debate; dispute continued and was not settled in Congress or the courts, but led inevitably to the Civil War before the issue could be resolved.

The Ostend Manifesto

Beyond the many attempts to legislate a middle ground for slavery and its expansion, some forces favored expanding the slave culture through land acquisition. One of the most ambitious of these plans was for the purchase of Cuba. As a possession of Spain, Cuba and its slave trade would have expanded the Southern slave power and added to the South's political influence.

This idea for expansion of slaveholding influence was first proposed seriously by the Knights of the Golden Circle (KGC). Founded in 1854 by George W.L. Bickley, this so-called secret society and its "Golden Circle" plan included annexation of Cuba and other Caribbean islands, all of Mexico and Central America, and the northern areas of South America, all to become new slave states. The plan, although impractical from a political point of view, was intended to establish clear domination in the United States of slave states over free states. Under this plan, Mexico alone would be divided into 25 new slave states. The plan would be accomplished through secession from the United States and invasion of the areas targeted.[75]

A modified version of this expansionist goal was expressed in a document called the Ostend Manifesto (also called the Ostend Circular), named for the city of Ostend, Belgium, where meetings took place among American ministers from October 9 to 11, 1854. The attendees were Pierre Soulé (Minister to Spain), James Buchanan (Minister to Great Britain), and John Y. Mason (Minister to France).

The underlying cause was for the purchase of Cuba from Spain, including plans to seize Cuba if Spain refused to sell. President Franklin Pierce was pro–Southern, and his sentiments in support of slavery were well known. Along with his Secretary of State William L. Marcy, Pierce favored the plan to expand U.S. territory while also accomplishing the goal of creating more slave states. The Ostend Manifesto was prepared by Soulé, Buchanan, and Mason on October 18, 1854, and forwarded to Washington. The Manifesto declared in part that "Cuba is as necessary to the North American republic as any of its present members, and that it belongs naturally to that great family of states of which the Union is the Providential Nursery."[76]

THE DEMOCRATIC PLATFORM.

"The Democratic Platform" (1856). A cornerstone of the 1856 Democratic
Party platform was support of states' rights and support for continuation
of slavery.

Upon publication of this document, the stated goals were strongly
condemned by politicians in the Northern states, as well as by Spain,
France, and Great Britain. The outcome was abandonment of annexation
and the dream of an expanded slave power. Horace Greeley of the *New
York Tribune* called the document a "manifesto of the Brigands." The attempted expansion became a focus for opponents of the slave power and
its expansion.[77]

Buchanan ran for president two years later and won. The election of
1856 was especially focused on the debate between free and slave states
and on states' rights, and Buchanan remained committed to the slave
power and to expansion of the U.S. beyond its Southern borders. A racist
cartoon of the times highlighted the election issues and ridiculed Democrat candidate James Buchanan as saying, "I am no longer James Buchanan, but the platform of my party."

The slavery and states' rights debates had gone on for years, and each
attempt through legislation to settle the debate only led to further conflict and a deeper divide. By the late 1850s, the Civil War had become
unavoidable.

3

The Greatest Political Evil[1]

T here has never been harmony or agreement among politicians of the United States. From the very beginning, a fundamental difference of opinions was present during discussions about how to organize a country and where power should lie.

For some, a strong central government with the power of supremacy was the ideal, and for others, states' rights (even the right to nullify federal law) were preferred. This chapter demonstrates how this debate evolved and became the theme for the first 100 years and beyond. The Founding Fathers did not imagine how severely the country would be split. These differences (federal power versus states' rights) led to the development of political parties and, ultimately, divided the country over one issue: slavery.

The history of political parties and what they stand for has been misrepresented and distorted over time. The initial debate over central government power versus states' rights led to the creation of disparate political parties; this difference of opinion led to a divide not only in terms of politics, but also in an economic sense (industrial North versus agrarian South). As parties came and went, the polarization led to the status in the years immediately before the Civil War.

The Democratic Party was focused in the years up to 1861 on a pro-slavery platform, and the Republican Party originally formed on the single issue of opposition to slavery.

The struggle between political parties and politicians is not new in America; in fact, it began as soon as the government was first formed. The emergence of political parties and the conflict between presidents and Congress define the nature of the U.S. political system and government. However, the founders did not anticipate the emergence of political parties and in fact believed they would be a destructive force.

During the early decades of the U.S. and leading up to the Civil War, the issue of slavery was the primary dividing point among politicians and was at the center of how political parties formed and developed their platforms; it was singularly the most critical issue of the times. However, what was conceived by the founders as a one-party system quickly moved to a split between two groups based on disagreements about the proper size of the federal government and on the question of states' rights, which itself focused on slavery and whether federal or state legislation should prevail.

Thomas Jefferson noted as early as 1798 that a political division between executive power and legislative power was emerging in the U.S. political scene. He wrote about the split between Federalists and Whigs:

> Two political Sects have arisen within the U.S., the one believing that the executive is the branch of our government which the most needs support; the other that like the analogous branch in the English Government, it is already too strong for the republican parts of the Constitution; and therefore in equivocal cases they incline to the legislative powers: the former of these are called federalists, sometimes aristocrats or monocrats, and sometimes Tories, after the corresponding sect in the English Government of exactly the same definition: the latter are stiled [sic] republicans, whigs, jacobins, anarchists, dis-organizers, etc., these terms are in familiar use with most persons.[2]

At the time, the system of political governance in the U.S. was termed the First Party System, referencing the emergence of two major forces at work and their philosophy of how political power should be divided between federal and state governments and between branches of the federal government. These forces became the first two political parties as well.

The First Party System

Between 1792 and 1824, the First Party System dominated U.S. politics. The two major parties at the time were the Democratic Republican Party (later called the Democratic Party), characterized by the political philosophies of Thomas Jefferson and James Madison, and the Federalist Party, based on the philosophy of Alexander Hamilton.[3]

It was not always the case that the political scene was dominated by the two parties. This came about as different governing philosophies were expressed. The major distinctions between the two groups—Democratic Republicans and Federalists—is summarized in the following:

> During the first decades of the new nation's existence, political parties were neither formally organized nor recognized. Nonetheless, it had become clear as early as 1792 that two competing visions of the country's future were emerging. Federalists favored a strong central government, a financial system that promoted merchant capitalism, and a pro–British foreign policy. Democratic-Republicans insisted on the primacy of state governments within the federal system, the agrarian base of a republican polity, and a pro–French foreign policy. Each side also had a correspondingly divergent view of the social order, with Federalists emphasizing the

maintenance of hierarchy, stability, and order while the Republicans advocated the expansion of egalitarian principles to larger and larger groups of white males.[4]

So it was that the emergence of separate parties became inevitable, based on vastly different visions of how the country should be governed. This often is simplified as competition between federal and state governance, but much more was involved, including ideas about finances, foreign policy, and even basic rights of citizens.

In coming decades, separate governing philosophies polarized the country geographically as well, with the industrialized North and agricultural South unable to agree on states' rights versus federal power. Unavoidably, the issue of slavery (on moral, political, and cultural bases) gravitated toward separate and irreconcilable points of view. The more the government (legislative, executive, and judicial) attempted to remedy the disagreements, the more these differences intensified. The theory of governance was not reconciled with the practice of governance, with the former expressed as ideas about the "proper" form of government and the role of the people:

> The birth of the Jeffersonian Republican Party by 1793 intensified, albeit slowly, public discussions about the proper sort of government for America as well as the place of ordinary people within that government. Federalists had expected to be able to shape the public sphere according to notions of deference. Because of their talent, virtue, and independence, they alone could provide the necessary paternal leadership for the fragile nation. They envisioned a public sphere in which the rational arguments of gentlemen, devoid of illiberal and local interests, could foster enlightened discussion, resulting in the wisest policy for all the people. Jeffersonians largely rejected that model, arguing that since no one could escape personal interest, the public sphere should be completely open to expression of individual opinion. The sovereign people could then select arguments—like buying wares at a market—that appealed to their own interests.[5]

The distinction between the two parties included economic and social interest groups, with Federalists tending to find greater support among businesspeople and the Democratic Republicans more popular among farmers. However, the dominant issue of the day was divided between Democratic Republicans, strongest in the South and opposed to federal control over slavery and other matters, and the Federalists, favoring a strong central government and legislative power over determination of slavery's legality. In the 1830s, the Democratic Republicans changed their name to the Democratic Party and were led by Andrew Jackson's political philosophy, dominated by the so-called "Jacksonian Democrats." This Southern-based group was "proslavery at heart."[6]

The overriding debate over slavery continued to be defined along the lines of opposition between the Democratic Republican Party and the Federalists. At the beginning of the split into two parties, the Federalist side included George Washington and Benjamin Franklin in addition to Hamilton. The "anti–Federalists" (later called Democrats) opposed a strong central government and were most concerned with preserving and strengthening states' rights (which included the right to determine the issue of slavery without interference by the federal government).

Over time, political views of the two sides evolved and were clarified, leading to distinctions between the federalist ideal of how the U.S. could function and the Democratic support of states' rights and slavery:

> In recent years, Hamilton and his reputation have decidedly gained the initiative among scholars who portray him as the visionary architect of the modern liberal capitalist economy and of a dynamic federal government headed by an energetic executive. Jefferson and his allies, by contrast, have come across as naïve, dreamy idealists. At best according to many historians, the Jeffersonians were reactionary utopians who resisted the onrush of capitalist modernity in hopes of turning America into a yeoman farmers' arcadia. At worst, they were proslavery racists who wished to rid the West of Indians, expand the empire of slavery, and keep political power in local hands—all the better to expand the institution of slavery and protect slaveholders' rights to own human property.[7]

The definition of slavery as a states' rights issue was both economic and political, with concern for accomplishing and maintaining a balance of power between slave and free states (and the resulting level of influence and power in the federal House of Representatives). The modern two-party system later evolved on the basis of disagreement about slavery, with Democrats favoring slavery and Republicans opposing it.

The Federalist Party

The Federalist Party, the first U.S. political party formally created, was also termed the First Hamiltonian Party. Its central theme favored a strong federal government even at the expense of states' rights. This philosophy controlled the government from 1792 to 1801. With the election of Thomas Jefferson, the champion of the Democratic Republican view, states' rights became dominant. During this period, pro-slavery interests were reflected in both the executive and judicial branches.[8]

Jefferson and his supporters opposed a strong federal government. In fact, the Federalists never regained power after Jefferson's term. The only Federalist president was John Adams. However, even with their short-lived existence, the Federalist political ideal left a lasting impression and later the same ideals led to formation of the Republican Party. Even 30 years after their brief time in control, the Federalists influenced the

Supreme Court through the leadership of Chief Justice John Marshall. The fourth and longest-serving chief justice of the Supreme Court, Marshall shaped the legal and political landscape of the United States between 1801 and 1835; his rulings continue to influence the Court and other branches of government today.

Previously a leading politician in the Federalist Party, Marshall also served as Secretary of State in the Adams administration. His accomplishments included setting the standard that the Supreme Court is responsible for judicial review. Under this principle, the Court has the power to invalidate laws passed by state legislatures and to overrule executive actions if deemed unconstitutional.

Marshall's first important decision was *Marbury v. Madison* (1803), in which the Court declared parts of the Judiciary Act of 1789 to be "unconstitutional." This was a precedent case that solidified the power of the Supreme Court. In another of Marshall's opinions, *McCullough v. Maryland* (1819), federal supremacy over the states was affirmed. In this ruling, Marshall wrote that the states lacked authority to tax federal institutions. The implication was that the states had no authority in matters claimed to be under the jurisdiction of the federal government. The states were not allowed to pass laws that contradicted or violated federal law. This ruling expanded to include the status of state challenges to laws concerning the status of slaves once removed from their home state and the federal jurisdiction involved (Fugitive Slave Laws). The supremacy of federal law over state law was further reinforced by Marshall in the case of *Cohens v. Virginia* (1821). Marshall wrote that federal courts had the power to hear appeals of state court decisions and to overturn those decisions in both criminal and civil cases. Virginia had argued that their courts could not be overturned by the federal courts because they lacked jurisdiction as an appeals court. Marshall ruled against Virginia.

Marshall's rulings affected the legal status of slaves up to the time of the Civil War. Although Marshall had himself owned slaves, he was opposed to the institution of slavery and, before his tenure on the Supreme Court, had represented Robert Pleasants, an abolitionist wanting to enforce his deceased father's will, which freed his slaves. Actions such as freeing slaves were not legal when this will was drafted, but Marshall argued successfully and the former slaves were freed. As a reaction, a Virginia justice named Spencer Roane developed the rationale for ownership of slaves as a property right.

Marshall was named in 1823 the first president of Richmond's American Colonization Society, an organization founded to promote resettlement of American slaves to Liberia. In 1825, Marshall reiterated his view in the Supreme Court case of a captured slave ship, the *Antelope*. He wrote in his opinion that slavery violated natural law, even though he also upheld the rights of slaveowners for one-third of the *Antelope*'s human cargo.

The decisions made by Marshall are examined in greater detail in the next chapter. Marshall's decisions as a leading Federalist and chief justice of the Supreme Court were central to the Federalist Party's philosophy. This was the genesis of what today is termed classical conservatism:

> Thanks to the framers, American conservatism began on a genuinely lofty plane. James Madison, Alexander Hamilton, John Marshall, John Jay, James Wilson, and, above all, John Adams aspired to create a republic in which the values so precious to conservatives might flourish: harmony, stability, virtue, reverence, veneration, loyalty, self-discipline, and moderation. This was classical conservatism in its most authentic expression.[9]

Among the Federalist Party's platforms, the conservatism of these founding fathers strongly opposed slavery, although they compromised in order to gain unanimous agreement to terms in the Constitution and formation of the country. This demonstrates the difficulty of disposing of an immoral institution such a slavery, especially when so many founding fathers were themselves slaveowners. Over time, the Federalists lost political influence. The remnants of a weakened Federalist Party eventually formed the new Whig Party, led by Daniel Webster and Henry Clay. Other former Federalists abandoned the Federalists' ideal and joined with the Jacksonian Democrats, including future Supreme Court Chief Justice Roger B. Taney.[10]

The Emergence of the Whig Party

As the Federalists' influence waned and its members moved primarily to the newly established Whig Party, states' rights proponents gained strength within the Democratic Republican Party. Leaders of this party originally were Thomas Jefferson, James Madison, James Monroe, and Andrew Jackson.

Founded in 1799, the Democratic Republican Party was dissolved in 1828 when its name was changed to the Democratic Party. The purpose in forming the party was to oppose the Federalists organized and controlled by Alexander Hamilton and John Adams. However, the terms "Democratic" and "Republican" have been used by each of today's major parties at times during their past. The Democratic Republicans were called the "Republican Party" and the "Jeffersonian Republicans" before 1798. Most of the party's strength was located in the South, where the states' rights issue favored state control over slavery.

Opposing the Democrats and their support of states' rights was the

Whig Party, the successor of the Federalists based on a strong central government. Its leaders were Henry Clay and Daniel Webster. The Whig Party survived a mere 21 years from formation in 1833 until its merger into the newly formed Republican Party in 1854. Formed to oppose the policies of Democrat Andrew Jackson, the Whigs were particularly opposed to Jackson's policy of forcibly removing Indians from the states and territories and pushing them westward. Their stance was in sharp contrast to the Jacksonian Democrats:

> Democrats stood for the "sovereignty of the people" as expressed in popular demonstrations, constitutional conventions, and majority rule as a general principle of governing, whereas Whigs advocated the rule of law, written and unchanging constitutions, and protections for minority interests against majority tyranny.[11]

The demise of the Whigs, like its formation, was over the issue and controversy of slavery. Within the Whig Party, there was no strong agreement on this issue, which was more readily passed over. In fact, Whig political campaigns succeeded only when the issue of slavery was not raised, but ignored. Those opposed to allowing slavery in newly admitted territories resided primarily in the North and later gravitated to the new Republican Party. Those in the South who favored allowing slavery in new territories were more likely to join the Democratic Party. So, as Federalists evolved into Whigs and then into Republicans in the North, the South continued to favor stronger states' rights policies. This polarization between the parties defined the landscape of American politics leading up to the Civil War and beyond.

The states' rights argument was centered on rights of slaveownership, but the Jacksonian Democrats' position went far beyond the legalistic belief concerning whether or not the federal government had the right to dictate property rights. The Whigs were not entirely innocent in this regard; however, Democrats were especially vocal in their racism:

> Democratic politicians relentlessly held blacks up to ridicule, denounced them for the urban crime rate, and accused them of lusting after white women. That, indeed, was the stock-in-trade of one Jacksonian politician after another. Leading the pack were doughface Democrats, who invariably portrayed themselves as patriots trying to save the country and the white race from Federalist traitors, British conspirators, and "nigger-loving" Yankee agitators who promoted abolitionism, racial amalgamation, slave insurrections, and sectional conflict.[12]

In addition to the conflict of ideas based on slavery and states' rights, a further divide evolved along economic lines. Whigs tended to appeal to affluent Northern professionals and business owners in larger cities. Democrats held greater appeal among the poor, who tended to reside in small towns and on farms, primarily in the South.[13]

While differences between Democrats and Whigs were easily defined, at least concerning opinions about slavery, both shared a common flaw by focusing on the gaining of voters' support rather than on promoting ideology:

> The Democrats had a generalized and mildly populistic orientation; the Whigs an equally mild orientation toward property values. These differences gave some real meaning to party distinctions. Yet, in the Anglo-American political tradition, the parties expressed themselves diffusely, in attitudes and tonal qualities rather than in doctrine or dogma.... By encouraging men to seek a broad basis of popular support, they nourished cohesiveness within the community and avoided sharpening the cutting edge of disagreement to dangerous keenness.[14]

This "dangerous keenness" often emphasized party loyalty over more lofty positions, such as an anti-slavery sentiment. Party loyalty often won out because, as a practical matter, politicians knew they needed votes. This often meant avoiding any position that would lose votes for a candidate.

The Free Soil Party

As the influence of the Whigs dissolved, the Free Soil Party was formed in 1848. However, this party lasted only until 1854, when it—like the Whig Party—merged into the new Republican Party. The Free Soil Party was the successor of many Whigs, but also attracted former members of the Democratic Party. Although the singular issue was opposition to the expansion of slavery in the new western territories, the underlying motives were not the same for all of the Free Soilers. Some were opposed to slavery as an institution, but most disputed the majority of Democrats and wanted to stop slavery from expanding. The central theme of the Free Soil Party was to stop the "aggressions of the slave power."[15]

To some this meant outright opposition to slavery, but to others it meant a desire to keep newly opened Western territories free of non-white citizens, either slave or free. While the Republican Party later claimed the distinction of being the first national party to oppose slavery, the Free Soil movement had a similar position within its mix as early as 1848. The disparity among Free Soil members and the inability of the party to unite in a common theme is what caused its rapid demise. However, their underlying purpose was not always to abolish slavery as the Republicans later were organized to accomplish:

> The formation of the Free Soil party in 1848 by New York Barnburner Democrats, radical anti-slavery Whigs, and the bulk of the Liberty party, marked a distinct turning point in the development of the American anti-slavery movement. For the first time an anti-slavery candidate and platform won the support of many thou-

sands of Northerners, and both major parties saw their Northern wings sundered by the issue of slavery.[16]

The term "barnburners" refers to the allegory of a farmer burning down his own barn to get rid of an infestation of rats, which describes the willingness among many Free Soilers to destroy the Democratic Party in order to get rid of slavery. The natural evolution for the Free Soil Party was to dissolve as a consequence of its internal debate and merge into the Republican Party, where opposition to slavery as an institution—not as a racist ideal—was a core platform. The Free Soil Party was a combination of many different points of view, combining anti-slavery morality with anti-black racist sentiment.

Some members of the party had economic motives, believing that a free society was superior to a society whose economy was supported by slave labor. A smaller number of Free Soilers wanted to ensure a white society in the new territories, excluding black members or other minorities. The majority were in the former camp, characterized by its political theme, "Free Soil, Free Speech, Free Labor and Free Men." The combination of moral, political, and economic motivations prevented the Free Soil Party from becoming a cohesive force in the political spectrum.

The debate within the Free Soil movement was a primary reason for its short history. Their inability to unite on a strong platform led to a vacuum, which the new Republican Party later filled with a clear, unqualified opposition to the expansion of slavery. The fate of Free Soilers was a split, with the anti-slavery group moving toward the Republican camp and the more racially political Free Soilers moving closer in position to the Democrats.

All the competing interests were variable, with crossover in philosophy and belief, notably about the question of whether slavery should be allowed to expand. However, what eventually resulted from the debate was a highly polarized two-party political system. While numerous issues defined these two sides, slavery was the most divisive and defining of all. In fact, the racism that grew out of slavery was readily apparent during the period of westward expansion. For many, this reality has been simplified to define only two groups, anti-slavery and pro-slavery. However, the issue is far more complex and the historical chronicling of the debate is incomplete:

> Racialism as a force in American history has been too little emphasized by American historians. Constitutional, political, and economic factors have been stressed in explaining the coming of the Civil War. But the power of folk prejudice to paralyze statesmanship has not been adequately examined. Perhaps this is because American historians have taken bias for granted; and perhaps they have been embarrassed by it.[17]

This pervasive undertone in American life is reflected in politics as well as elsewhere. It would not be realistic to claim one side guiltless and the other guilty as there were so many variations in the debate over slavery up to the Civil War. However, an examination of political parties as they were organized prior to the Civil War does point to the polarization of pro- and anti-slavery forces (with varying motivations) and the economic and moral factors expressed through legislation, court cases, and, of course, political leaders and parties.

No other issue defines the polarization of the parties as much as slavery. Motives were economic and political as well as moral; as events unfolded, it became clear that no legislative or judicial actions were likely to solve the problem other than complete abolishment or acceptance of the institution. This defining force created the two parties—Democratic and Republican—and also set the course for settling the issue through the Civil War.

The Free Soil movement not only complicated the debate by adding the conflict between racism and political motives. It also split the Democratic Party into three distinct factions: Hard Shell Democrats (full support for Southern slavery rights), Soft Shell Democrats (those seeking compromise with anti-slavery forces), and Free Soilers. As a consequence of this three-way split, the Democratic Party could no longer rely on support from Democrats in the North as they had in the past, especially if the party put forth Hard Shell candidates. Northern Democrats at the state level began voting against pro-slavery Southern interests.[18]

Founders' Concerns About a Party System

At the time the Constitution was written in 1787 and ratified in 1788, most of the founders did not anticipate a multi-party system and believed that such a system would be harmful to the republic. One of the first serious conflicts between the Federalists' view and that of states' rights followed passage of the Alien and Sedition Acts of 1798. Under the Alien Act, the president was granted power to deport aliens he believed to be a threat to the country. Under the Sedition Act, false or malicious statements against the government were criminalized. Several opposition newspaper editors were jailed or fined and several supporting the Democratic Republican Party were forced out of business.[19]

A response to these controversial laws was the drafting in 1798 of the Kentucky and Virginia Resolutions (together known as the "Resolutions of '98"), which declared at the state level that the Alien and Sedition Acts were unconstitutional and, more significantly, that the states had the power to nullify federal law. Associated with this was state-level opposition to the Fugitive Slave Act. The debate between Federalists favoring centralized power (including power over legislation concerning the return of escaped slaves) and proponents of states' rights dominated the political scene. The debate over states' rights, generated by the Alien and Sedition Acts and the Fugitive Slave Law, was not resolved by any means by the year 1861.

The states' rights debate was aggravated in 1803 under Jefferson's first term when the Louisiana Purchase was completed, doubling the size of the United States. The debate over slavery was central to this acquisition of land. Anti-slavery politicians were concerned that slavery would be permitted in the new areas, territories, and states acquired. As a consequence, slave states would gain greater power in Congress as representation—based on the Three-Fifths Compromise—increased the number of newly formed slave states and their representatives. This concern led to a political compromise to maintain a balance between slave and non-slave states so that neither side would be able to dominate the politics of the U.S. in the House of Representatives.

The Federalists gradually lost power after Hamilton's death and were not able to elect a strong leader over coming years. The party "had collapsed as a national political force."[20] They were not able to win the presidency ever again, and were replaced eventually by the Whig Party. Their last presidential candidate was Rufus King in 1816 and, after the failed campaign, the Federalist Party ceased to exercise any political influence. Remaining Federalist leaders such as Daniel Webster and Henry Clay formed a new National Republican Party, which was renamed the Whig Party by 1833.

The Era of Good Feelings

The period of Monroe's presidency, from 1817 to 1825, has been termed the "Era of Good Feelings." That phrase was first used by Benjamin Russell of the *Columbian Centinel* newspaper in 1817.[21] The period often is described as one of relative harmony in politics. However, the period actually was characterized by significant discord among the parties, so the term may also be used ironically to mean the exact opposite.

Despite the "Era of Good Feelings" brand, a great deal of turmoil within the Democratic Party developed as leaders began adopting policies previously favored by the Federalists. By 1820, the debate over slavery ended any image of good feelings among the political parties. The Missouri

Compromise did not settle the conflict between states' rights and federal law—it only made matters worse. Those arguing for state sovereignty insisted on strict construction of the Constitution, whereas those favoring federal dominance argued that federal law had precedence over all state laws. The nationalism of the Democrats in this debate had itself led to the rise of Jacksonian Democracy. This movement occurred during what is called the Second Party System, led by Andrew Jackson, and the claim of the Democratic Party to stand for the rights of the common man. Jackson was the first clearly identified Democratic president, even though the party had at first named Thomas Jefferson as its originator. Before 1820, the

President James Monroe was associated with the Era of Good Feelings, which was characterized by conflict and discord between the major political parties.

Jackson version of the Democratic Party strongly favored legalizing the vote to most white male adults, but not to women or blacks. The new Jackson-controlled party also favored an executive branch stronger than Congress.[22]

Democracy and Andrew Jackson

The Democratic Party of modern times was clearly defined at its origin as "Jacksonian." Its policies and philosophy were based on the political positions of Jackson and other leading Democrats. This evolution also marked the onset of what has been called the Second Party System, lasting from Jackson's election in 1828 up to the Civil War. A core position among Jacksonian Democrats was support of voting rights for all white males, a concept referred to in the day as "universal white male suffrage."[23]

The pro-slavery position of the Jacksonian Democrats was part of a larger states' rights philosophy and based on a distrust of big government, wealth, and centralized power:

> The Democrats represented a wide range of views but shared a fundamental commitment to the Jeffersonian concept of an agrarian society. They viewed a central government as the enemy of individual liberty and they believed that government intervention in the economy benefited special-interest groups and created corporate monopolies that favored the rich.[24]

In addition to promoting suffrage for adult white males, Jacksonian Democracy supported manifest destiny, a belief that white Americans had a destiny to settle the West to the Pacific Ocean. This was tied directly to the issue of whether or not slavery should be allowed in new territories and states.

Andrew Jackson (daguerreotype by Mathew Brady, 1844) became the leader of the Democratic Party as a supporter of universal white male suffrage.

The Second Party System

Historians have defined the era from the late 1820s through the end of the 1850s as the period dominated by the Second Party System. The two parties dominating politics of the time were the Democratic Party of Andrew Jackson, Martin Van Buren, John C. Calhoun, Martin Van Buren, James K. Polk, and Stephen Douglas; the Whig Party was led by Henry Clay, Daniel Webster, and William H. Seward.

The election of 1824 was the last election in which parties did not nominate candidates directly. Four candidates emerged in the primary voting: Henry Clay, Andrew Jackson, William Crawford, and John Quincy Adams. None of these obtained an electoral college majority, so the selection of president and vice president went to the House of Representatives. Andrew Jackson had won the largest portions of the popular vote and electoral college. Even so, the House chose John Quincy Adams as president, and Adams named Henry Clay as his Secretary of State. Jackson saw this as a deal made between Adams and Clay behind the scenes and called it a "corrupt bargain."[25]

Jackson had his revenge four years later when Adams failed to win reelection and Jackson became the seventh U.S. president with vice presidents John C. Calhoun (1829–32) and Martin Van Buren (1833–37). Jackson's 1828 victory was seen by many as the advent of the modern political party:

> Jacksonians believed the people's will had finally prevailed. Through a lavishly financed coalition of state parties, political leaders, and newspaper editors, a popular movement had elected the president. The Democrats became the nation's first well-organized national party ... and tight party organization became the hallmark of nineteenth-century American politics.[26]

As the organizer of what became the Democratic Party, Van Buren later won the presidency on a platform of states' rights regarding slavery and stated,

> I must go into the Presidential chair the inflexible and uncompromising opponent of every attempt on the part of Congress to abolish slavery ... and also with a determination equally decided to resist the slightest interference with it in the States where it exists.[27]

It appears that Van Buren intentionally set up what has been called the "Jackson coalition" of the Democratic Party to favor and even protect Southern slaveholders and their interests, a theme that came to define the entire party up to the beginning of the Civil War.[28]

While the Democratic Party was clearly and strongly united in its policies in the slave-holding South, the Whigs were a coalition of Northern Republicans opposed to slavery and Southern Nullifiers (those believing the states had the right to nullify federal laws considered unconstitutional) demanding states' rights over federal influence. This coalition weakened the Whigs in comparison to the unified stance of the Democrats, who supported the federal power to override the states on questions of slavery and other issues. The Jackson administration strengthened the federal government permanently:

> By creating a national government with the authority to act directly upon individuals, by denying to the state many of the prerogatives that they formerly had, and by leaving open to the central government the possibility of claiming for itself many powers not explicitly assigned to it, the Constitution and Bill of Rights as finally ratified substantially increased the strength of the central government at the expense of the states.[29]

The inability among the Whig factions to unify their positions concerning slavery led to the party's demise by 1854, much as a similar internal conflict had destroyed the Free Soil movement. That year, passage of the controversial Kansas–Nebraska Act directly led to the formation of the Republican Party. The act allowed slavery to spread by providing popular sovereignty as a means to determine the status of new territories and states, a decision that led to a rush of proponents on both sides to gain dominance in the vote. The result was violence as the two sides fought to gain power through population numbers. Former Whigs (termed "Conscience Whigs" for their moral opposition to slavery) and Free Soil Party members formed the core of the Republican Party by 1858. Unified opposition to slavery was the driving force behind the new party, and it strengthened the movement up to the election of 1860.

The Kansas–Nebraska Act of 1854 sharply divided the two sides. It was supported by all slave-owning states of the South and Northern Democrats who supported slavery (Northern Doughface Democrats). Opposition, on both moral and economic grounds, was found almost exclusively in the Northern free states. The Kansas–Nebraska Act defined the sharp disagreement between free and slave, North and South, that inevitably led to the beginning of the Civil War. The act itself often has been cited as the event that not only led to formation of the Republican Party, but also made civil war inevitable.

During the Polk Administration (1845–49), the growing seriousness of the divide between the parties over slavery was seen as an irritation, but not as a priority. Polk referred to those who brought up the issue as unpatriotic. The irony in Polk's point of view is that he did not view slavery as the potential cause of disunion, but rather viewed the debate as the problem. He explained his belief that conflict over slavery (but not slavery itself) would have "terrible consequences to the country, and cannot fail to destroy the Democratic Party, if it does not threaten the Union itself."[30]

A Change in Political Climate

The newly formed Republican Party favored grants of free land to farmers and opposed allowing slaveowners to settle in those regions and dominate the economy with slave labor. One aspect of this policy was found in the Free Soil racist ideal of preserving new western territories for white people only. However, the majority in the new party was opposed to slavery on moral grounds. A unifying policy of the Republican Party was that free markets were superior to slave labor markets and would create strong and lasting growth in the future.

This unifying theme of anti-slavery was clearly the primary Republican Party platform. However, it spread beyond politics and included positions taken by churches. The Christian churches (Congregational, Presbyterian, Methodist, Scandinavian Lutheran, and Quaker) in New England and other areas agreed with Republicans in opposition to slavery. However, some Christian churches (Roman Catholic, Episcopal, and German Lutheran) sided with the pro-slavery Democratic Party. This split among Christian church groups further defined the underlying differences in political philosophy between Republicans and Democrats.

The anti-slavery churches were committed to purging sin from American society; the major sins were named as alcoholism, polygamy, and slavery. The involvement of churches in the young Republican Party also led to establishment of widespread networks used to sign up new voters. This grass-roots movement was a large part of the party's success.

Republicans from 1854 to 1860

The period leading up to the election of 1860 was marked by a clear division between the anti-slavery North and pro-slavery South; in fact, in many ways it was the only important issue on the minds of voters. The election was, for the first time, a decision among four candidates rather than the more traditional two characterizing past elections. Lincoln's chances were greater improved due to the split of opposition votes; the debate on the Democratic side between the Douglas and Breckinridge wings helped Lincoln to win a majority of electoral votes.

The outcome of the election was exactly along the lines that divided North and South in the Civil War. Lincoln, as a Republican candidate, won in nearly all of the Northern states with 180 electoral votes. Breckenridge won most of the South with 72; John Bell of the Constitutional Union Party came in with plurality in three border states with 39 electoral votes; and Douglas finished last with only 12 votes in only two states.[31] The 1860 election can also be described as a split between two separate groups, with Lincoln and Douglas on opposite sides in the North and Breckenridge and Bell in the South.[32]

Many Democrats had abandoned Douglas, despite his past popularity, over his stand (along with other Northern Democrats) against admission of Kansas as a slave state. The resentment toward Douglas prevented him from being able to make a strong showing in 1860. Even though he sided with the Republicans on the issue of Kansas, one Republican said, "A penitent prostitute may be received in the church, but she should not lead the choir."[33]

The results of the 1860 election were a great departure from past trends. In the 72 years since 1789, slaveowners had won the presidency for a total of 50 years, or 70 percent of the time. No parties had declared outright opposition to slavery until Lincoln did so. He was elected despite repeated threats from Democrats that his election would lead to secession. The Republican Party won on a full commitment to the position that freedom was the "normal condition" for all states and territories of the United States.[34]

This strong anti-slavery platform did not arise for the first time in 1860. It was first introduced in 1856, the first year a Republican (John C. Frémont) had run. In that year, Frémont had been defeated, but the Republican Party came back four years later with a platform that was more specific, but which also moderated some of the party's statements regarding slavery. The platform

> denounced disunionism, efforts to reopen the African slave trade, and the extension of slavery into the territories; but it contained no language comparable to the earlier castigation of slavery as a "relic of barbarism."[35]

As the new Republican Party defined itself largely on the debate over slavery, three primary groups emerged. The first group was called "the Radical Republicans" and opposed Lincoln's position because it would lead to war; however, the radicals were at the same time opposed to slavery like most other Republicans. The "Moderate Republicans" followed the

beliefs of Lincoln in opposition to the institution of slavery. Finally, "Conservative Republicans," led by Lincoln's Secretary of State William Seward, sided with Lincoln in his anti-slavery philosophy. Radicals were especially prominent in promoting voting rights and other civil rights for freedmen (former slaves), with opposition from so-called conservative Democrats in the South and liberal Democrats in the North.[36]

Prior to the Civil War, the radical movement consisted of politicians opposed to the political influence of the slave-owning states, the so-called slave power. Many had arrived in the Republican Party as former Whigs, including William Seward, who was at first favored as the most likely Republican candidate in the 1860 election. He was later appointed

Stephen Douglas (photographed ca. 1851) was the most prominent Democrat running in 1860, but he made a poor electoral showing against Lincoln.

to Lincoln's cabinet, and eventually agreed with Lincoln's views. The primary differences between them had been based on reasons for opposing slavery. Seward saw the political problems growing from ever-higher slave populations and increased numbers of representatives for those states, whereas Lincoln focused on the moral element of slavery and its inconsistency with the intentions expressed by the Founding Fathers.

Lincoln effectively merged the three sects of the Republican Party into a cohesive political group. He himself was a newcomer to the party, having run in 1854 for the Senate as a member of the Whig Party. After losing that election (at the time, senators were elected by the state's legislature), Lincoln clarified his position on slavery. In 1855, he wrote, "I do oppose the extension of slavery because my judgment and feelings so prompt me.... I now do no more than oppose the extension of slavery."[37]

At the convention, Lincoln finally emerged as the candidate based on the issue of slavery. He conceded at the convention that the Southern states had a constitutional right to continue the practice of slavery, but also believed the institution was morally wrong and should not be allowed to expand into new territories. This moderate position was appealing to the delegates, who selected Lincoln despite predictions favoring Seward. Lincoln won a majority on the fourth ballot to become the 1860 Republican presidential candidate.

The party had not come into being gradually; rather it formed as a reaction between 1856 and 1860 to the proposed expansion of slavery expressed in the Kansas–Nebraska Act. The Republican Party was based more on a strong moral opposition to slavery than to the more generalized political problems it created. The party came into existence officially on June 19, 1855, when a small group of slavery opponents met in the capitol and declared themselves the Republican Association of Washington, District of Columbia. Their initial plank contained only one issue and defined the purpose for forming the Republican Party: "There should be neither slavery nor involuntary servitude, except for the punishment of crime, in any of the Territories of the United States."[38]

In January 1856, Republican representatives of five states (Massachusetts, Ohio, Pennsylvania, Wisconsin, and Vermont) called for a convention the following month, to be held in Pennsylvania. The intention of this gathering was to nominate candidates for president and vice president in the 1856 national election. Lincoln attended this first Republican National Convention, where he came in second place as nominee for vice president. The convention took place in Philadelphia from June 17 to June 19, where former California Senator John Frémont was nominated as the presidential candidate with New Jersey senator William Dayton as candidate for vice president.

The election of 1856 saw incumbent Franklin Pierce replaced by a new Democrat, James Buchanan. The dominant issue in the campaign, once again, was slavery. The Democrats' platform was stated clearly: They stood for non-interference by the federal government into the matter of slavery in the states and territories. In sharp contrast, the Republican position condemned slavery as a form of barbarism and called for Congress to exclude its practice in the territories that would be admitted as future states.

Buchanan defeated Republican John Frémont with a plurality of popular votes and a majority of the electoral college. At the Democratic National Convention held in Cincinnati, Ohio, from June 2 to June 6, 1856, the delegates agreed on support for the Kansas–Nebraska Act in contrast to the Republican Party, which came into being specifically to oppose it. This singular issue defined the 1856 election. This election not only ushered in the new Republican Party, but drew a clear line between the two major parties on the issue of slavery.

The election was close. In free states, Frémont won just over 45 percent of the vote versus 41.5 percent for Buchanan, with the remainder going to ex-president Millard Fillmore running as candidate of the Know Nothing Party. The election was decided in the slave states, where Buchanan won 56 percent of the popular vote versus just under 44 percent for Fillmore, and only a small fraction for Frémont. Overall, Buchanan won the majority of electoral votes with 174.[39]

The Know Nothing Movement

As the election of 1854 set the course of politics until 1860, another party formed. This movement paralleled the new Republican Party and, in fact, momentarily looked like a likely replacement for the Whigs:

> The strongest organization opposing the Democratic party in the North and throughout the nation in 1854 and 1855 was the anti–Catholic, anti-immigrant American party. Dubbed the Know Nothings because members were instructed if questioned to say that they knew nothing about it, this secret political society underwent a phenomenal expansion beginning in 1853; in less than two years it had organized in every state and, claiming a national membership of one million voters, seemed destined to replace the rapidly disintegrating Whig party as the major opposition to the Democratic party in the country.[40]

The official name of this party was the American Party, and its primary platform was limited. It opposed the surge in immigration to the U.S., especially Catholic immigration. Virtually no prominent politicians joined this party or supported their views, including the argument most often put forward: If Catholic participation in politics grew, the U.S. would be controlled by the pope and the Vatican.

The Know Nothing movement never gained traction, due in part to its narrow focus on immigration and because the singular issue did not appeal to a wide section of Republicans. It was largely associated not so much with the political issues of the day, such as slavery, but more with nativist fears of Catholic immigration, which had begun in the 1840s at the time of the Irish potato famine.[41]

The anti–Catholic immigration stance was not associated with pro-slavery by any means. In fact, the American Party platform was specifically anti-slavery, but its focus on anti-immigration narrowed its appeal. The party did not last long and, after the election of 1856, the Know Nothing movement subsided as the ongoing debate over slavery dominated the political and cultural landscapes. The slavery debate was intensified in 1857 with the Supreme Court's landmark decision on slavery, *Dred Scott v. Sandford*. In this decision, written by Chief Justice Roger B. Taney, the Court ruled that blacks were not citizens of the United States and held no constitutional rights. This decision was denounced strongly by most Republicans, notably by Lincoln, who stated that

> the authors of the Declaration of Independence never intended "to say all were equal in color, size, intellect, moral developments, or social capacity," but they "did consider all men created equal—equal in certain inalienable rights, among which are life, liberty and the pursuit of happiness."[42]

After the Republican loss in 1856, the party began preparing for 1860. In 1858, it nominated Lincoln for the open U.S. Senate seat. On June 16, 1858, Lincoln spoke at the state capitol in Springfield, Illinois, and delivered his famous speech, expressing a belief that "a house divided against itself cannot stand. I believe this government cannot endure permanently half slave and half free."[43] This speech set the tone for Lincoln and his beliefs and carried over to 1860. However, in 1858, following a series of seven debates between Lincoln and Stephen Douglas, the Democrat-controlled Illinois state legislature chose Douglas for the Senate seat.

At this point, Lincoln seemed an unlikely presidential candidate, having won no national elections. However, his strong anti-slavery stance made him a national figure and set the stage for 1860. This election, like the one four years earlier, was focused on the single issue of slavery above all other issues, and the Democrats, as they had in the past, warned that if Lincoln were elected, the South would secede and civil war would be inevitable. For the Republicans, slavery was the core issue and opposition to its spread into newly established territories soon evolved into solid opposition to the institution as it existed.

The growing strength of Southern pro-slavery sentiments was expressed in an 1859 meeting of the Southern Commercial Convention, a group originally formed to promote economic growth in the South. At a meeting of the group in Vicksburg, Mississippi, a 40-to-19 vote approved a resolution stating, "In the opinion of this Convention, all laws, State or Federal, prohibiting the African Slave Trade, ought to be repealed."[44]

The Opposition Party and the Constitutional Union Party

Two different parties used the label "Opposition Party" during the years just before the Civil War. First was a party existing from 1854 to 1858, when the newly formed Republican Party was not yet organized or fully defined. Several former Whigs ran for office as members of this Opposition Party. In 1860 the remnants of this party merged with the Constitutional Union Party. The Republican Party originally was formed to oppose slavery, especially expansion of slavery to the western territories. However, the Opposition Party was a successor choice for many former Whigs not wanting to join with the Republicans or the Constitutional Unionists. The Opposition Party attempted to present a compromise between Southern Democrats and Northern Republicans.

These party splits were all based on the single issue of slavery and whether or not it would be allowed in newly established territories. Along the same division, a separate Opposition Party formed between 1858 and 1860 in the Southern states of Kentucky, Tennessee, North Carolina, and Virginia. The primary goal of this short-lived party was to represent a group of politicians who supported slavery and its continuation.[45]

Another successor of the Know Nothing movement was the Constitutional Union Party (1860–61). Former Whigs joined forces with the Know Nothing group and many Southern Democrats with the narrow focus of avoiding secession over the debate of slavery. As a unification of former Whigs and Know Nothing members, it ceased to exist as an effective political force after the election of 1860. During the Civil War, many former Southern members supported the South and adopted a pro-slavery opinion. Northern members tended to support the Union and opposed slavery. One singular contribution of this party was strong representation at the 1861 Wheeling Convention, which led to the breakaway from Virginia and formation of a new state, West Virginia.

The Election of 1860

The election of 1860, as predicted, led to the outbreak of the Civil War, the conflict that, more than any other, defined the United States from that point forward. As the election campaign began, the Democratic Party split into two parts, Northern and Southern. Failing to put forth a united platform or a single candidate, this split often is blamed as costing the Democrats the 1860 election. However, even if the Democrats had offered a single candidate unifying their Northern and Southern wings, the Republican ticket would still have won a majority of the electoral college vote, by 169 to 134.[46]

The split between the two sides of the Democratic Party did have an effect, however. The 1860 Democratic Convention was the longest in the party's history until 1924; a nomination required 59 ballots. Southern Democrats had walked out of the party's nominating convention in Charleston in April 1860. The remaining delegates (calling themselves National Democrats) reconvened in June in Baltimore, Maryland, where they nominated Stephen Douglas as their candidate for the presidential election. Douglas believed individual states (including those to be admitted in the future) should be allowed to determine for themselves whether or not to legalize slavery. This was in sharp contrast to Lincoln, who opposed expansion of slavery into territories or new states without exception. The Southern Democrats (calling themselves Constitutional Democrats) disagreed with both Lincoln and Douglas, and adopted a strong pro-slavery platform with John C. Breckinridge of Kentucky as their candidate.

Lincoln was by no means likely to face easy victory. The so-called rail candidate was immediately ridiculed in racist cartoons. One published in September 1860 depicted Lincoln carried by Horace Greeley and a black man, with the dialogue:

> **GREELEY:** We can prove that you have split rails, & that will ensure your election to the presidency.
> **LINCOLN:** It is true that I have split Rails, but I begin to feel as if *this* rail would split me, it's the hardest stick I ever straddled.
> **BLACK MAN:** Dis Nigger strong an willin, but it's awful hard work to carry Old Massa Abe on nothing but dis 'ere rail!

The phrase "riding the rail" was a reference to the Republican platform, which had pledged to not interfere with Southern states in their continuing practice of slavery, but opposed allowing slavery in the new territories of the West. The election was focused primarily on the issue of slavery, not so much in existing states but in new territories as the country expanded; this created the threat of secession that dominated the debate.

Abraham Lincoln (portrait from 1860) was widely ridiculed as a candidate in 1860, and was considered a long shot.

"The Rail Candidate" (ca. 1860). Lincoln was portrayed as "the rail candidate" in a reference to his homespun roots and anti-slavery position.

"THE NIGGER IN THE WOODPILE."

"The Nigger in the Woodpile" (1859). Among the editorial criticisms of Lincoln, a recurring theme was his agenda to free the slaves, an idea widely opposed by Democrats in the 1860 election.

As part of this movement, the suspicion among politicians in pro-slavery states was that Lincoln intended to end slavery throughout the country.

The platform caused even more racist cartoons, including one called "The Nigger in the Woodpile." It made fun of the platform's attempt to minimize its anti-slavery stance and showed Horace Greeley saying, "I assure you, my friend that you can safely vote our ticket, for we have no connection with the Abolition party, but our Platform is composed entirely of rails, split by our Candidate." Another figure, identified in the cartoon as Young America, replies, "It's no use old fellow! You can't pull the wool over my eyes for I can see 'the Nigger' peeping through the rails." Lincoln then remarks, "Little did I think when I split these rails that they would be the means of elevating me to my present position."

The racist attacks on Lincoln and the Republican platform demonstrate the depth of the division in the country and the suspicion of Lincoln and his intentions. Lincoln won under 40 percent of the popular vote but a majority of the electoral college vote. He did not win in any slave states. However, with a concentration of free-state votes in the North, he prevailed. Lincoln expressed faith during the campaign in the common sense of Southerners and argued that in no probable event will there be any very formidable effort to break up the Union. The people of the South have too much of good sense, and good temper, to attempt the ruin of the government, rather than see it administered by the men who made it. At least, so I hope and believe.[47]

Lincoln's expressed faith in the sensibility of the South was misplaced. As others had predicted, Lincoln's victory led to secession and the Civil War. Even before Lincoln was inaugurated, seven slave states declared secession and formed the Confederate States of America. Both Bell and Douglas had promised during the campaign that they would save the Union and prevent secession, but their arguments did little for either of them. Lincoln did not acknowledge the right to secede, but the mood in the South favored secession, even if that meant civil war.

4

"A slave, and not a citizen"[1]

T he history of the Supreme Court up to 1861 was dominated by Democratic Party control and outright racism on the part of many justices. This sad reality is a theme in this chapter, and several hypotheses are exposed as being true. These include:

1. Supreme Court justices were predominantly Democrats up to 1861. As a result, the rulings concerning slavery and related legal issues were the result of a Democrat-controlled court. Beyond 1835, all justices were Democrats.

2. All of the slavery-related cases (with only one exception) heard in the 1840s and 1850s favored slave states and slave-owners, usually with only one dissenting vote (in one case, there were two).

3. The court consistently ruled against present or former slaves, culminating in a decision that slaves could never gain the rights of citizenship. The history of the Democrat-controlled court has not been widely exposed and, consequently, is not widely known.

Party affiliation reveals that 59 percent of all justices appointed to the Supreme Court between 1804 and 1861 were members of the Democratic Party, and the slavery-related rulings reflect this majority over that period of more than a half century. From 1836 through to 1861, all of the justices were Democrats with only one exception.

In comparison, only one member of the Whig Party was appointed during this period. Benjamin Curtis served from 1851–87. Another 13 justices, or 38 percent, belonged to the Federalist Party and held terms between 1789 and 1835.

This chart reveals that Democratic control was clear. In the six decades between 1800 and 1860, Democrats were always in the majority. From 1800–10, six Federalist judges served; from 1811–1820, only two;

Supreme Court justices by party affiliation, 1789-1861

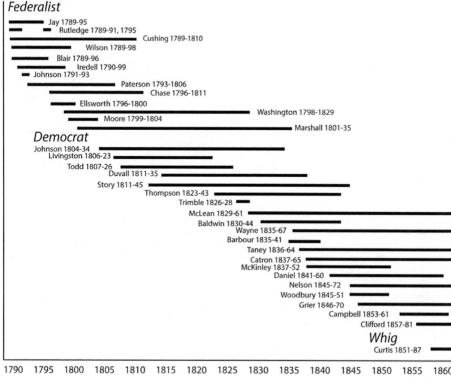

Based on data at http://supreme-court-justices.insidegov.com

Supreme Court justices by party affiliation, 1789–1861. The Democratic Party dominated the Supreme Court between 1806 and 1860. As a result, all of the slavery cases heard by the Court were decided in favor of slaveowners.

from 1821–1830, there were two Federalist justices in the Court; from 1830 until 1835, only one (Marshall); and from 1836 onward, there were no Federalists.

All but one of the Democratic justices were appointed by Democratic Party presidents (before Andrew Jackson's term, the Democratic Party was known as the Democratic Republican Party). The one exception was Tyler, who was a member of the Whig Party. During the period preceding the Civil War, the Court was nearly entirely nominated by Democratic presidents, and 59 percent of the justices were also Democrats. This history demonstrates how unbalanced the Supreme Court was, especially between 1836 and 1861, when a majority of pro-slavery rulings were made.

Slavery-Related Cases and the Supreme Court

Numerous slavery-related Supreme Court cases were heard from the initiation of the Court itself up to the beginning of the Civil War. The complexity of issues raised points out the inability of the Court to resolve the problems created by slavery.

At issue was not the morality of slavery itself, but a series of technicalities and constitutional interpretations raised by questions of state versus federal law. The states' rights debate was at the center of the eventual secession of the South, as well as the related question of whether slaves were people or property. The concept of nullification, the Commerce Clause of the U.S. Constitution, and the question of whether slaves could become U.S. citizens all grew from the ceaseless debate.

Even so, the Court did not resolve the thorny legal issues arising out of slavery in the Southern states. Each Supreme Court decision, very much like legislation passed by Congress, failed to resolve the conflict and only worsened the divide between pro-slavery and anti-slavery interests. Many cases ended up at the Supreme Court as the final source for decisions about questions of constitutional rights and the powers of the federal and state governments.

The U.S. Supreme Court is the only court established by the Constitution, and it was granted status of appellate jurisdiction over all lower federal courts and over all state courts when dealing with federal issues. This, at least, is a straightforward interpretation of how the Supreme Court is allowed to act. However, throughout its history, the Court has at times been an activist court and has become involved not only in law, but also in politics. This was especially true in the period from the Court's inception up to the Civil War, when numerous cases involving slavery came before the Court. Decisions were not specifically involved with whether or not slavery was allowed in specific states or territories, but in the status of escaped slaves or slaves who were transported from a slave state to a free state or territory.

The actions of the Supreme Court raised numerous issues and pointed out the complexity and far-reaching ramifications of slavery beyond its obvious problems. The moral objections to slavery often are used to simplify the issues as an aspect of North versus South or industrial versus rural. There was much more to the question. The Court placed itself in the position of determining the legality of policies concerning slaves escaping from slave states to free states or even of those transported *through* free states by their owners.

Among the issues lacking satisfactory resolution was that of where power should reside, whether with the federal government or with the states. The Court was asked to decide matters of nullification, a belief among some states that they had the right to override or nullify federal laws considered by the states to be unconstitutional. This belief unavoidably touched on issues of slavery, with the Court ultimately determining that the states did not have the power to override federal law. In this regard, the Court was instrumental in growing the power of the federal government and minimizing the power of state governments, not only regarding slavery but for many other issues as well.

The Nullification Battle

Does each state have a right to ignore, contradict, or reveal a federal law based on questions about whether or not that law is constitutional? The federal courts have consistently denied this right to the states. In fact, states "throughout U.S. history have attempted to use variations of the nullification doctrine to invalidate federal law. However, every attempt by states to nullify federal law was clearly rejected by not only the federal government, but also by other states."[2]

The state position is that the federal government originally was founded by the combined states, so the final determination of what is constitutional should rest with each state rather than centrally with the federal government. This so-called "compact theory" would allow states to reject or even to nullify any federal law it (the state) disagreed with; the theory also contended that such a decision would be outside of federal power.

The federal position points to the need for uniformity of law among the states, citing the Constitution's Supremacy Clause:

> This Constitution, and the Laws of the United States which shall be made in Pursuance thereof; and all Treaties made, or which shall be made, under the Authority of the United States, shall be the supreme Law of the Land; and the Judges in every State shall be bound thereby, any Thing in the Constitution or Laws of any State to the Contrary notwithstanding.[3]

The rationale for the Supremacy Clause was further explained by James Madison, which he described as vital. Without this clause, Madison argued, "it would have seen the authority of the whole society everywhere subordinate to the authority of the parts; it would have seen a monster, in which the head was under the direction of the members."[4]

Nullification was especially relevant to the debate concerning escaped or transported slaves between the states and territories. Although the Supreme Court tried repeatedly to settle the disputes concerning states' rights, decisions entered by the Court often created new legal quagmires and worsened the situation rather than amending or correcting it.

Over the course of time between 1789 and 1861, questions surrounding slavery were not resolved by the Democrat-controlled Court. Several of their decisions only polarized the free and slave states and promoted the gradual move toward civil war.

The "constitutional" aspect of the nullification debate goes to the origins of the U.S. government and raises the question of where power properly resides. The Court is unique in world government organizations in the sense that its findings are based on interpretation of the Constitution as well as on the understanding of federal and state laws. Alexis de Tocqueville commented on this characteristic of organization within the United States government, writing, "I am not aware that any nation of the globe has hitherto organized a judicial power on the principle now adopted by the Americans."[5]

Even though the ideal of this system was based on a belief in the Constitution and how it is interpreted, the Court has been more a political than an objective body interpreting law and, in many of its decisions, often has been motivated more by political opinion than by the law itself. Its ability to nullify laws, both federal and state, and to enter final decisions on issues makes the Court exceptionally strong as part of the three-part federal government, in many cases having greater power than either the executive or legislative branches. That power is more political than legal, despite how the Founding Fathers believed the Supreme Court would function. Alexander Hamilton speculated that the Supreme Court would be the weakest of the three branches because it held "no influence over either sword or the purse ... to have neither force nor will, but merely judgment."[6]

Hamilton appears to have not anticipated that the Supreme Court could or would become politically motivated in its decisions, nor that it would determine its position regarding interpretations of the Constitution. However, in the thousands of decisions rendered, those specifically relating to slavery demonstrate how easily the Court has grown and changed over its history.

From its early days, Supreme Court decisions often were based on interpretation of slavery laws as matters of personal property rather than of individual rights. The struggle between interpretation of the Constitution and moral stances has been present from the time the Court began entering decisions.

McCullough v. Maryland

The legality of slave importation was affected by the *McCullough v. Maryland* case of 1819, even though the case was not directly related to the legality of the slave trade. The Court cited national supremacy against the state of Maryland after the state enacted a tax on bank notes issued by non–Maryland banks.[7]

The Court cited the Necessary and Proper Clause of the Constitution as part of the federal government's right to pass laws not included in the list of express powers, granting the federal right "to make all Laws which shall be necessary and proper for carrying into Execution the foregoing Powers, and all other Powers vested by this Constitution in the Government of the United States, or in any Department or Officer thereof."[8]

Two key issues were the result of the Court's ruling. First, the Court assumed that the U.S. Constitution granted "implied powers" to Congress. Second, state laws could not limit or contradict the power of the federal government. Chief Justice Marshall wrote against Maryland's argument that they held sovereignty because they (the states) had ratified the Constitution:

> Lurking in the background of *McCulloch* ... were two other issues. One was unspoken but specific in nature and omnipresent in states' rights thinking. The other was general and historical in character. The specific issue was slavery, which came to be connected to Marshall's doctrine of implied powers by the debates over Missouri's entry into the union as a slave state in 1820 and 1821. Strangely, little was said explicitly about the slavery issues in the initial attack on McCulloch, but the connection was there to see.[9]

The Court ruled 7–0 against the state's arguments in this case.

The question of state versus federal sovereignty was raised once again in another constitutional legal question related to interstate commerce. In *Gibbons v. Ogden* in 1824, the conflict between state and federal rights to regulate slavery was the issue.

Gibbons v. Ogden

Another case not involving the legality of slavery was *Gibbons v. Ogden*, in which the question of interstate commerce was interpreted regarding movement of slaves between states as a right of commerce.

A New York law had granted exclusive rights to steamboat inventor Robert Fulton to use New York waters in steamboat operations. Other riverboat owners challenged this monopoly, arguing that the New York law was unconstitutional and out of compliance with the federal power to regulate matters of interstate commerce.

Attorneys for New York argued that the steamboat provision involved an exchange and transportation of goods, but did not extend to transportation of passengers. A second argument was made that the right of the federal government to regulate interstate commerce did not prevent the states from enacting laws over commerce, to the extent that those laws did not conflict with federal statutes. This power, the New York argument stated, included the power to prevent or prohibit commerce, because the "difference between regulation or restraining and interdiction, is only a difference of degree in the exercise of the same right, and not a difference of right."[10]

The Court's decision, rendered by Chief Justice John Marshall, included a definition of "commerce" to encompass navigation as well as transportation and migration of people. He wrote that the federal power over commerce "acknowledges no limitations." Marshall, in the 6–0 decision, concluded that because Fulton's competitors has obtained their licenses under the Federal Coasting License Act of 1793, the New York law favoring Fulton's monopoly was in conflict and thus was unconstitutional.[11]

The *Antelope*

In the case of the *Antelope*, the Supreme Court debated the legality of international slave trade. Under Chief Justice John Marshall, the issue involved the status of slaves who were repatriated to an area of Africa that today is Liberia. Some were named as property of Spanish claimants and were returned to Florida and slavery.[12]

Importation of slaves had been declared illegal since 1808. However, the 1808 legislation failed to include penalties for violations and did not spell out what would happen to illegally imported slaves. In 1819, an Act in Addition (the Anti-Slave Trade Act of 1819) granted the president authority to use the U.S. Navy to capture ships carrying slaves for the purpose of "safe-keeping, support and removal beyond the United States" for any Africans on board.[13]

Presidential authority granted by the Anti-Slave Trade Act of 1819 included the power to enforce the 1808 law banning importation of slaves and also allowed for the return of illegally procured slaves to Africa. Before this, the federal courts referred matters back to the states, some of which allowed public auction and enslavement of captured individuals.[14]

With the background of the 1819 act, the status of captured slaves was soon determined through the case of the *Antelope*. The cutter ship *Dallas* captured a slave ship, the *Antelope*, on June 29, 1820, off the coast of Florida. Aboard were 280 Africans, and the ship was on its way to the United States. Although the ship had been constructed in the U.S., it was later sold to a Spanish owner and renamed the *Fenix.* The Spanish government had licensed the ship to carry slaves from Africa to Cuba. The ship, its crew, and the cargo of slaves docked at Savannah at the end of June, and this was where the controversy began.[15]

A claim was filed asking for $25 per person taken from the ship, citing the 1819 Act in Addition. The claim named the King of Spain as rightful owner of 150 of the slaves and the King of Portugal as owner of the remaining 130. Countering this, the U.S. District Attorney for Georgia, Richard Habersham, filed a suit citing the Act in Additions and declaring that the Africans on the then *Dallas* were legally free, on the basis that they had been removed from Africa to be sold as slaves.[16]

The case went to the Supreme Court. Of the Africans, 120 survivors were returned to Africa in 1827 and 30 were ruled the property of Spanish claimants and were sent to Florida to be sold as slaves. In this case, the Supreme Court applied federal law to some extent, but also recognized international law in determining that some of the African "cargo" could not be freed under the 1808 U.S. law. Not only did this case involve international law, it also began the long struggle to determine whether slaves were property (cargo) or persons.

The Court's decision was split 3–3 and, according to the rules, this meant the Supreme Court did not reverse the lower court's decision. The decision, however, by no means settled the question at issue regarding rights of those captured to be sold as slaves. The debate between Florida's interpretation of law and the federal position led inevitably to the question of supremacy, or presidential power over state law, and the right of the federal government to take precedence over state law. *McCullough v. Maryland*, a case not directly related to slavery, nonetheless brought up the issue of supremacy and became precedent for future cases.

After 1835, the Court's makeup changed significantly with the appointment of Roger B. Taney as the new chief justice following the long term of Marshall. Taney was perhaps the most clearly political justice the Supreme Court saw in the 19th Century.

Roger B. Taney

Taney is a pivotal figure in establishing the legal view of slavery and justification for rulings during his tenure as chief justice from 1835 to 1864. Taney had been the country's attorney general (1831–33) and Secretary of the Treasury (1833–34) under President Andrew Jackson, who also appointed Taney as chief justice. Loyal to his president, Taney was described as a "supple, cringing tool of Jacksonian power."[17]

As Attorney General, Taney supported a South Carolina law prohibiting free black persons from entering the state, as well as a second law declaring that blacks could not be citizens of the United States.

Taney's nomination as an associate justice to the Supreme Court was not an easy one for Jackson. In 1835, on the last day of the Senate session, Whig forces blocked a vote on Taney's nomination and introduced a bill to permanently abolish the open seat. The confirmation vote succeeded but the motion to abolish the open seat failed. As a result, the seat was left open for the following year.

In 1836, with Democrats in control in the Senate, Taney was nominated as chief justice to replace the recently deceased John Marshall. The debate over the nomination lasted nearly three months before confirmation. For the next 28 years, Taney and fellow Democratic justices were able to completely control Supreme Court decisions. The many slavery-related cases were mostly decided with one or no dissenting votes. An exception was the *Dred Scott* case, which had two dissenting votes against seven votes agreeing with Taney's infamous ruling.

Roger B. Taney (photographed ca. 1855) the most controversial of Supreme court chief justices, clearly favored slavery and opposed Republican desires to end the institution.

Although Taney's legal opinions were clearly biased and political, his personal attitude toward slavery cannot be simplified solely by those decisions. He freed his own slaves and in one case described slavery as "a blot on our national character."[18]

On March 4, 1861, as chief justice, Taney administered the oath of office to the new president, Abraham Lincoln. During the Civil War, Taney was in conflict with Lincoln in several rulings, including an order opposed to Lincoln's suspension of writs of *habeas corpus* and stating that only Congress had that power; Lincoln ignored the ruling and continued ordering arrests.

Taney's legacy was determined largely by his bias in entering pro-slavery rulings. He was widely despised as a result, both in the North and the South, and ended his life in near poverty, passing away on October 13, 1864, at the age of 87. The following year, the House of Representatives approved a bill to fund a bust of Taney to be placed in the Supreme Court building alongside the previous four chief justices' busts. Senator Charles Sumner (R–MA) objected to the decision, vilifying Taney by stating:

> I speak what cannot be denied when I declare that the opinion of the Chief Justice in the case of *Dred Scott* was more thoroughly abominable than anything of the kind in the history of courts. Judicial baseness reached its lowest point on that occasion. You have not forgotten that terrible decision where a most unrighteous judgment was sustained by a falsification of history. Of course, the Constitution of the United States and every principle of Liberty was falsified, but historical truth was falsified also.[19]

In 1873, after the death of Taney's successor, Salmon Chase, Congress authorized funding for busts of both Taney and Chase.

Taney was the most controversial justice in the history of the Supreme Court, primarily due to the *Dred Scott* decision. However, often overlooked were his rulings in many other cases as well, beginning with the 1837 case of *New York v. Miln*.

New York v. Miln

In 1837, the Court's position regarding rights of commerce arose once again, as it had in Marshall's court in the *Gibbons* case. As the newly appointed chief justice on the bench, Taney had a history of racially motivated opinions. As Jackson's Attorney General in 1832, he had written an opinion concerning South Carolina's Negro Seaman Act. This was an 1822 law requiring the imprisonment of black foreign seamen while their ships were docked in Charleston Harbor. The law also specified that if the ship captains did not pay the cost of imprisonment for their sailors, the state had the right to sell the sailors into slavery.[20]

Of this law, Taney had written his opinion on May 28, 1832, stating that

> South Carolina or any other slave holding state has a right to guard itself from the danger to be apprehended from the introduction of free people of color among their slaves, and have not by the Constitution of the United States surrendered the right to pass the laws necessary for that purpose.[21]

With this backdrop of opinion opposed to the "danger" of mixing free blacks among slave populations, many of Taney's decisions reflected a similar bias. However, the topic at issue was not always slavery itself, but related legal questions. *Miln* was the first case before the Taney court that involved the Constitution's Commerce Clause. At issue was a New York City ordinance requiring captains of ships passing through city waters to provide a complete manifest and to then remove undesirable aliens. This naturally led to the related question of interstate movement of slaves and free black persons. The Court's opinion, written by Justice Philip P. Barbour, implied that the Commerce Clause had intended to regulate goods but not "persons." The majority of 6–1 concluded that states were legally within their rights to prevent "indigents" from coming into their territory based on reasoning that a state cannot be required to carry the cost of caring for those indigents.[22]

The Court's opinions based on the Commerce Clause raised the difficult issue of whether slaves were "persons" or "goods," and this only aggravated the ongoing debate over the entire problem with the legality of slavery once state lines were crossed. However, the Court did not limit its findings to problems between free and slave states. International law also entered into the Court's future rulings regarding slavery. One such case was that of *United States v. The* Amistad.

The *Amistad*

The Supreme Court case *United States v. The Amistad* was a freedom suit argued in 1841 resulting from a rebellion of African captives aboard the schooner *La Amistad* in 1839. As in the case of the *Antelope*, the issues raised regarding status of Africans were complicated by international law.[23]

The *Amistad* was off the coast of Cuba with Africans on board scheduled for sale in Cuba. The Africans were able to take over the ship. They killed the captain and the cook, and two crew members escaped in a lifeboat. The remaining crew was ordered to return to Africa but instead sailed north. The ship was taken into custody near Long Island by the revenue cutter USS *Washington*, commanded by Lieutenant Thomas Gedney. The ship was taken with its captives to New London, Connecticut, where Gedney filed a claim of property rights for salvage of the ship's cargo (in this case, African captives). This was the custom under Admiralty Law. Gedney's intention was to sell the slaves.[24]

Surviving crew members José Ruiz and Pedro Montez also filed a claim that the cargo of slaves was their property and should be given over to them. The U.S. Attorney for Connecticut filed a claim that the slaves and vessel were the property of Spain and should be returned to that country. The Africans also filed, saying they were neither slaves nor property and should be set free.

The view from Spain was that the African cargo constituted property, citing Pinckney's Treaty of 1795. This treaty, also called the Treaty of Madrid, defined terms of friendship and cooperation between Spain and the United States. The U.S. negotiator, Thomas Pinckney, came to the agreement with Spain's Don Manuel de Godoy. Spain demanded surrender of the Africans as murderers, rather than cargo, under the 1795 treaty. This was due to the onboard revolt in which two crew members were killed.

Evoking the 1795 treaty moved jurisdiction of the case to the federal level under the Constitution's Supremacy Clause. The case was argued before the Supreme Court by John Quincy Adams in 1841:

> The Africans were in possession, and had the presumptive right of ownership; they were in peace with the United States; the Courts have decided, and truly, that they were not pirates; they were on a voyage to their native homes—their *dulces Argos*; they had acquired the right and so far as their knowledge extended, they had the power of prosecuting the voyage; the ship was theirs, and being in immediate communication with the shore, was in the territory of the State of New York; or, if not, at least half the number were actually on the soil of New York, and entitled to all the provisions of the law of nations, and the protection and comfort which the laws of that State secure to every human being within its limits.[25]

John Quincy Adams (photographed by Mathew Brady in the 1840s) argued before the Supreme Court in the case of the *Amistad*, a slave ship taken over by slaves who sued for their freedom.

The Spanish government argued that fugitives from a foreign government were under that government's jurisdiction under the doctrine of freedom of the seas. The initial case had been heard in district court, which dismissed the property claims of Ruiz and Montez and ordered the return of the captives to Africa as free men. However, it upheld Gedney's claim of one-third of the cargo as salvage.

The U.S. Attorney for Connecticut appealed the finding immediately by order of President Van Buren, who agreed with arguments put forth by Spain. The case went to the Supreme Court. Attorney General Henry D. Gilpin argued that the Africans were the property of Spain and must be returned to their owners. Attorney Roger Sherman Baldwin, cooperating with John Quincy Adams in the case, had represented the Africans in the lower court case. Baldwin described the Africans as fugitives rather than property. Adams spoke next, criticizing President Van Buren and claiming the president had assumed powers in the case that were unconstitutional and beyond the powers of the executive. Adams argued that cited treaties, specifically Pinckney's Treaty, were not applicable in the matter. The treaty, Adams pointed out, referred to property and not to people. He also argued that the decision in the *Antelope* case should not apply in *Amistad* because precedent had been set prior to the U.S. prohibition of the slave trade.

On March 9, Justice Joseph Story delivered the majority opinion. Pinckney's Treaty was ruled inapplicable as the Africans were not legal property. They were further not criminals, as they had been kidnapped unlawfully. The ruling continued that when the *Amistad* arrived in Long Island, it was under control of the Africans, who had no intention of becoming slaves. As a result, the president was not required to return them to Africa.[26]

The Court's ruling affirmed most of the District Court findings with a notable exception. The Africans were declared free and the Court stated that they should be dismissed from custody immediately. The 36 survivors, upon release, were taken to Farmington, Connecticut, where residents had agreed to house them until they could be returned to their homeland. In 1842, the Africans, along with several missionaries, embarked on a journey back to Sierra Leone. In the years following the outcome of this case, the Spanish government petitioned the U.S. for compensation for the loss of the ship and the cargo of Africans. Resolutions presented to Congress to approve payment to Spain were supported by two Democratic presidents, James K. Polk and James Buchanan, who accused President Van Buren of having conspired with Spain about the matter.[27]

Although 36 Africans regained their freedom as a result of the *Amistad* case, the Court decision made a distinction of what constituted "property" under international law. The ruling established that free men had the right to resist enslavement, but if the Africans had been recognized under law as property defined by the 1795 treaty, they would have been returned to the Spanish claimants. For example, one African named Antonio had been the captain's personal slave. He was determined to be property and was returned to Cuba.

This case was the sole instance of a slavery-related decision in favor of recognizing slaves as persons and not as property. The Court ruled 7–1 in this case, with Justice Henry Baldwin the only voice opposed to the majority.

The difficult question of property rights led, inevitably, to the Court's decision that state findings could not override federal law. In the case of slavery, a state court could not legally or constitutionally contradict federal power. Citing the Fugitive Slave Act, the Supreme Court ruled in *Prigg v. Pennsylvania* that a state could not enter rulings inconsistent with the federal law having jurisdiction. For example, Pennsylvania was banned from violating terms of the Fugitive Slave Law of 1793. The Court left a window open, however, stating that despite the high Court's ruling, contrary outcomes were possible if state legislation allowed exceptions. This language led to passage of many personal liberty laws in Northern states while also complicating the debate over slavery and movement of slaves between free states in the North and slave states in the South.

"Unless prohibited by state legislation"

In 1842, the Supreme Court decided one of its most pivotal cases directly regarding slavery. In *Prigg v. Pennsylvania*,[28] Chief Justice Roger B. Taney and five other justices ruled that the Federal Fugitive Slave Act precluded a Pennsylvania state law that prohibited blacks from being taken out of Pennsylvania into slavery and overturned the conviction of Edward Prigg.[29]

In the majority opinion, the Supreme Court found that federal law is superior to state law, but at the same time the states are not required to apply their resources to enforce federal law. Five justices voted to limit the Fugitive Slave Act. In addition to Chief Justice Taney, Joseph Story (who wrote the majority opinion), Smith Thompson, James M. Wayne, Peter V. Daniel, and John McLean concurred. There were dissenting votes.

This was a case in which interpretation of the Constitution conflicted directly with state law. The specific section of the Constitution providing rationale to the Fugitive Slave Act read:

> No person held to service or labor in one state, under the laws thereof, escaping into another, shall, in consequence of any law or regulation therein, be discharged from such service or labor; but shall be delivered up, on claim of the party to whom such service or labor may be due.[30]

The State of Pennsylvania had passed a law on March 29, 1788, prior to the passage of the federal Fugitive Slave Act. The state law was named "An Act for the Gradual Abolition of Slavery." This law was amended to read, "No negro or mulatto slave ... shall be removed out of this state, with the design and intention that the place of abode or residence of such slave or servant shall be thereby altered or changed."[31]

On March 25, 1826, another law was passed in Pennsylvania reiterating that no "negro or mulatto" could be removed from Pennsylvania for the purpose of selling them or using them as slaves. Both state laws conflicted directly with the federal Fugitive Slave Act, which led the Prigg case being heard by the Supreme Court.

In 1832, Margaret Morgan, a black woman, moved to Pennsylvania from Maryland, where she previously had been a slave and was owned by John Ashmore. Although she had not been officially emancipated, she had lived as a free person in Pennsylvania. Ashmore's heirs claimed ownership and hired slavecatcher Edward Prigg to return her to their possession.[32]

Prigg abducted Morgan in Pennsylvania and took her to Maryland where she was sold as a slave. Also sold were her children, including one born as a free citizen in Pennsylvania. Prigg and three accomplices were arrested and charged with violation of Pennsylvania law. Prigg pleaded not guilty. However, the York County, Pennsylvania, Court of Quarter Sessions convicted him. Prigg then appealed to the U.S. Supreme Court with the argument that Pennsylvania state law could not supersede the Fugitive Slave Act.

Prigg argued that the U.S. Constitution invalidated the Pennsylvania law, which should be voided. Justice Joseph Story agreed and reversed Prigg's conviction, further declaring the Pennsylvania law unconstitutional. He wrote that the state law had denied the rights of slaveholders to recover slaves under the Fugitive Slave Act of 1793.[33]

Story also cited the Supremacy Clause of the Constitution. This clause was justification for overruling any and all state laws in conflict with federal law:

> This Constitution, and the Laws of the United States which shall be made in pursuance thereof; and all treaties made, or which shall be made, under the authority of the United States, shall be the supreme law of the land; and the judges in every state shall be bound thereby, anything in the constitution or laws of any state to the contrary notwithstanding.[34]

Story's ruling allowed for possible future opinions contrary to the Court's findings, noting in his opinion that "state magistrates may, if they choose, exercise that authority, unless prohibited by state legislation."[35]

That clause, "unless prohibited by state legislation," inspired legislators in Pennsylvania and other Northern states to draft and pass many personal liberty laws. These were meant to prevent state officials from pursuing runaway slaves and their children. The result of this was that the federal Fugitive Slave Act remained in effect and supreme, but it could be enforced only by federal law enforcement officials, not by state officials.

Unlike the legislatures in Northern states, many Southern legislatures and individual politicians viewed state refusal to uphold the federal law as a violation of the federal compact between the central government and the states. This Supreme Court decision and subsequent actions by Northern states unavoidable increased the divide between North and South on the slavery issue. Southern pro-slavery interests had for decades relied on federal protection of its often-cited property rights, including rights to recover fugitive slaves.

One consequence of the Prigg decision was development of a new law, the Fugitive Slave Act of 1850. This was part of a compromise admitting several more states to the Union, notably California. Although admitted as a free state, the Compromise of 1850 upheld the new federal Fugitive Slave Act. Federal officials were still required to take action to return fugitive slaves to their owners even in states (like California) where slavery was banned.

All law enforcement officials, including those at the state level, were required to arrest anyone suspected of being a fugitive slave from another state. A posse could be formed consisting of both law enforcement and ordinary citizens to capture, hold, and transport anyone accused of being an escaped slave from a slave state. The rule further prohibited an accused person from testifying at the hearing to determine their status. All that was required to arrest a person was a claim by anyone to ownership of the slave.[36]

The *Prigg* case and its aftermath, notably the Compromise of 1850, divided North and South more than ever before. Three years later, the Kansas–Nebraska Act raised the issue of slavery once again. What was the status of slaves once moved from a slave state to a free state? This was the question in the case of *Strader v. Graham.*

Strader v. Graham[37]

The Supreme Court determined jurisdiction of slaves who moved to a different state. Three slaves were transported by their owner from Kentucky to Ohio aboard a steamship named the *Pike.* They escaped and went to Canada. Under terms of the 1789 Northwest Ordinance, the Court ruled that the laws of Kentucky (where the journey originated) prevailed, rather than the laws of Ohio.[38]

Writing for the majority, Chief Justice Roger B. Taney summarized the issue of the case, writing that the question was: "Whether slaves who had been permitted by their master to pass occasionally from Kentucky into Ohio acquired thereby a right to freedom after their return to Kentucky?"

The background of the case extended a full 10 years. In 1841, the three slaves (George, Henry, and Reuben) left Louisville, Kentucky, aboard the *Pike* and traveled to Cincinnati, Ohio. They escaped to Canada and freedom. Their owner, Christopher Graham, tried to get them back but failed. He then sued Strader, the owner of the *Pike* for the value of the slaves, estimated at $1,500 each. After 10 years, the case made its way to the Supreme Court.

Citing the rights of slaveowners to use the state of origin's laws to recover fugitive slaves, the court ruled in favor of Graham and against Strader. In a similar case four years earlier, *Jones v. Van Zandt*, the Supreme Court had ruled 9–0 against a resident of Ohio for harboring an escaped slave named Andrew. Under Kentucky law, the plaintiff (Jones) claimed Andrew as his rightful property and sued the defendant (Van Zandt) for depriving him of the slave's labor and services; Jones asked for compensation for this loss. Van Zandt had refused to pay the requested $500. Jones was entitled to compensation for his loss, according to the ruling, once again defining slaves as property rather than as individuals.[39]

In the Strader case, as in the Jones case, the Supreme Court cited state law in the state of origin and ruled that anyone harboring a fugitive slave from another state was liable for the value of that slave. This was the ruling even if the defendant did not know the slave was a fugitive. In *Jones v. Van Zandt*, the defendant had simply given a ride in his wagon to a group of slaves walking down a road.

In *Strader*, the defense argued that the applicable law was a presumption of freedom in Ohio, where this occurred, which was not a slave state. The Supreme Court disagreed with this argument, and it was one of the grounds for the ruling in *Strader*. In other words, just because an individual was located in a free state did not mean that the applicable state law made that individual free. The slave had to be returned or, if that were not possible, compensation had to be paid to the slaveowner for the loss of "property."[40]

The complexity in the issue of slave transport between states was at the core of *Strader v. Graham*. Under the Constitution, the Court had ruled that a fugitive slave could be recovered, but the question of moving a slave to a free state had not been previously addressed.

The issues concerning conflict between slave and free states continued arising, both in law and court decisions. This led to what has been called the worst decision ever made by the Supreme Court. In *Dred Scott v. Sandford*, the Court ruled that slaves were not citizens of the United States and, consequently, did not have the rights of citizens.

Dred Scott v. Sandford

The most infamous decision made by the U.S. Supreme Court was *Dred Scott v. Sandford*. This landmark decision included the opinion that people of African descent could never be citizens, meaning they lacked standing to file lawsuits. The Court ruled in a 7–2 decision written by Chief Justice Roger B. Taney against Dred Scott in his desire to be named a freed slave. The same decision declared that Congress could not ban slavery in the territories, and that the Missouri Compromise was unconstitutional. Finally, the Court ruled that the federal government had no power to free slaves transported into the federal territories.[41]

The basic right of citizenship was further decided by Taney's ruling, including a citation to the Declaration of Independence and the assumption that the ideals expressed in the document were never intended to include African persons, even those born in the United States:

> But Taney seemed to go further than just denying blacks' citizenship—he denied that they possessed any rights at all. In reviewing the history of the writing of the Declaration of Independence and the Constitution, Taney held that the founders had not acknowledged or included African Americans in the people of the United States. Taney reasoned that the fact that so many of the founders held slaves proved that they had no intention of applying the "all men are created equal" language of the Declaration to African Americans—it was too glaring a contradiction.[42]

The case, brought to the Court in 1856 and decided on March 6, 1857, was an attempt to settle the debate over the rules governing the rights of slaveowners and slaves who were moved from slave states to free states or territories. Instead of settling the question, this decision made the Civil War inevitable due both to the Court's one-sided ruling over states' rights and the nature of slavery and its future.

Although the Dred Scott decision was nullified by the Fourteenth Amendment and the Civil Rights Act, both enacted in 1866, the 1857 decision polarized the politicians of the day, with a majority of Democrats in support of the Supreme Court and Republicans strongly opposed. This outcome had much to do with Abraham Lincoln's election in 1860. The decision has been classified as "unquestionably, our court's worst decision ever."[43]

Dred Scott was a slave given the slave name Sam and held in Virginia who was taken to Missouri by his owner, Peter Blow.[44] Scott was then purchased by an army doctor, John Emerson, who later went to Fort Armstrong, Illinois, where the army had ordered Emerson to post. Emerson later was reassigned to Fort Jesup, Louisiana, and he sent for Scott. On his way to Louisiana, Scott's daughter was born while traveling on the Mississippi River between Iowa and Illinois. The state of Illinois was a free territory as defined under the Northwest Ordinance of 1787, and when admitted as a state in 1819, the Illinois Constitution banned slavery as well. Iowa was also free. Born in a free territory, the daughter was legally a free person under both state and federal law. If Scott had sued for freedom in Louisiana, it is likely he would have won, as Louisiana courts had a history of acknowledging the laws of free states.

However, the suit was not brought in Louisiana. Emerson passed away in 1842 and his widow inherited all of his property, including the Scotts. In 1846, Scott tried to buy freedom for himself and his family, but Eliza Emerson refused. With legal assistance, Scott sued for freedom in Missouri later the same year. Precedent cited included previous state court decisions such as *Somerset v. Stewart.* The Somerset matter was decided prior to establishing the United States in Boston, Massachusetts, which was, at the time, a British Crown Colony. The case involved James Somerset, an African slave who had been

Dred Scott (photographed in 1857). The Supreme Court, under Chief Justice Taney, ruled in the Dred Scott case that slaves were not entitled to citizenship rights. The decision drew extreme public reactions but was not the catalyst for war it has come to be portrayed as.

bought by Charles Stewart when he was in Boston. Stewart later returned to England with Somerset, who escaped. He was recaptured later and imprisoned on a ship, the *Ann and Mary,* and taken to Jamaica where Stewart directed that Somerset be sold to a plantation. Suit was brought before the Court of King's Bench asking for a writ of *habeas corpus,* arguing that Somerset's imprisonment was not legal. The King's Bench Court ruled that

> no master ever was allowed here to take a slave by force to be sold abroad because he had deserted from his service, or for any other reason whatever; we cannot say the cause set forth by this return is allowed or approved of by the laws of this kingdom, therefore the black must be discharged.[45]

This case set precedent that a slave could not be forcefully sold under English Common Law. Another precedent sited in *Scott* was *Winny v. Whitesides,* an 1824 case heard in the Missouri Supreme Court. The ruling stated that a slave was free after being taken to a free state, and that by transporting a slave, the owner had forfeited his property rights: "We are clearly of opinion that if, by a residence in Illinois, the plaintiff in error lost her right to the property in the defendant, that right was not revived by a removal of the parties to Missouri."[46]

In this case, a slave girl named Winny had been taken by her owner, Phoebe Whitesides, from North Carolina to Missouri. On February 13, 1822, the St. Louis Circuit Court found for Winny, but Whitesides appealed and the case went to the Missouri Supreme Court. The ruling also was in favor of Winny, and the decision read in part that "if, by a residence in Illinois [Whitesides] lost her right to the property in the defendant, that right was not revived by a removal of the parties to Missouri."[47] This case set a turning point in state law:

> The case of *Winny v. Whitesides* (1824) marked the beginning of the "once free, always free" era in determining the outcome of slave freedom suits. The Missouri Supreme Court set the precedent that if a slave had been taken into an area that prohibited slavery, that slave was free—even if returned to a slave state, such as Missouri.[48]

A third precedent cited in Scott was that of *Rachel v. Walker*, a freedom suit. Rachel was a slave who petitioned the Court to declare her free once her owner had established residence in Missouri. Her owner was William Walker, a slave trader, who had purchased Rachel from her previous owner, an army officer. The Court ruled that the officer forfeited his ownership of the slave by taking her to a territory in which slavery was banned.[49]

At first, *Scott* appeared an easy victory based on strong precedent favoring the freeing of slaves once transported to free territories or states. In 1852, *Scott* was heard by the Missouri Supreme Court, which ruled that Dred Scott was to remain a slave and was legally the property of Eliza Emerson. The Court also declared that Scott should have sued for freedom in a free state. The case was appealed and it was not until 1857 that the Supreme Court issued its decision. The Court was asked to decide two issues. The first was a question of citizenship. If Scott were deemed to be a citizen of Missouri, that would enable him to sue a citizen of another state. If he were to be judged a slave and not a citizen, his right to sue would disappear. The second issue was whether residing in the state of Illinois or the Wisconsin territory had transformed Scott into a free citizen. This raised a third issue: whether Wisconsin's anti-slavery law was legal.

The Court could have refused to hear the issue of citizenship as it had done earlier in *Strader v. Graham*. In that case, the logical conclusion would be that the states had jurisdiction to declare a slave to remain a slave or to be free. The Court had to decide, as a first step, which of the issues it would rule on in the case. However, this question was complicated by James Buchanan, the president-elect in early 1857.

Interference by Buchanan affected both the timing of the case and the decision by the Court. Buchanan corresponded with his friend, Justice John Catron, and asked to have the Scott case heard before his inauguration in March 1857. Buchanan hoped the case would end the slavery debate before he began serving his term as president. Buchanan also asked Justice Robert Grier to join with the Southern majority on the Court and to find against Scott.[50]

On March 6, 1857, two days after Buchanan was inaugurated, the Supreme Court published its decision, written by Chief Justice Taney with six justices in concurrence. Dissent was voiced by only two justices, John McLean and Benjamin Curtis. As the only non–Democrat on the Court, Curtis (a member of the Whig Party) was so appalled at the decision that he resigned from the Court. This made him the only justice to have resigned from the Court as a matter of principle.

The Court had faced more than one issue in this decision. First, they had to decide whether the federal Circuit Court had jurisdiction to hear the Scott case. The appeal had come to the Supreme Court from the Circuit Court, so a question of jurisdiction had to be resolved as a first step. The argument against Scott was that as an African, Scott was not considered a citizen, so he could not legally sue in Circuit Court. Chief Justice Taney wrote that under terms of the Constitution, blacks were "beings of an inferior order, and altogether unfit to associate with the white race, either in social or political relations, and so far inferior that they had no rights which the white man was bound to respect." The majority opinion continued in stating that Scott was not a citizen and had no right to sue in federal court, and also that emancipated slaves could not become U.S. citizens. The opinion included the statement that if citizenship of slaves were to be acknowledged, it would grant "to persons of the negro race ... the right to enter every other State whenever they pleased...."[51]

In fact, the decision written by Taney and based on the principle of states' rights included a rationale that his conclusion was consistent with the Declaration of Independence:

> Taney has been strong on "states' rights," though that is not quite the same thing. But when he said that the Constitution excluded Negroes from citizenship, he read into it a proviso neither expressed nor implied by its wording, and a power encroaching on the primary attribute of the states by virtue of which they had federated the attribute of original citizenship. Taney's contention was lamentably weak, being nothing but inference from antecedent and external circumstances.... Hence [he said] the axiom of the Declaration of Independence, that all men are endowed by their Creator with inalienable rights, was not meant or understood when written as including Negroes. He said the Founders used "the ordinary lan-

guage of the day," and could not have meant "all men" when they said "all men," because if they did, their conduct as slaveholders was inconsistent with their words.[52]

The Court also determined that the Fifth Amendment forbade passage of any laws that would deprive a slaveowner's property rights merely because of a move to a free territory. A final issue was whether Scott's residency in Minnesota made him free based on Minnesota's status as a free territory (at the time part of Wisconsin territory). Taney's decision settled the question against Scott. Taney wrote:

> We are satisfied, upon a careful examination of all the cases decided in the State courts of Missouri referred to, that it is now firmly settled by the decisions of the highest court in the State, that Scott and his family upon their return were not free, but were, by the laws of Missouri, the property of the defendant; and that the Circuit Court of the United States had no jurisdiction, when, by the laws of the State, the plaintiff was a slave, and not a citizen.[53]

The *Dred Scott* decision added to the severity of the Panic of 1857. This financial panic was caused by overly rapid economic expansion worldwide. Several influences caused the U.S. panic, especially in the railroad industry. With westward migration, rail expansion had been underway for many years, but in 1857 work slowed down and hundreds of employees were laid off. With many economic fears creating the panic, the *Dred Scott* decision in March led to speculation that as western territories were added, they would likely allow slavery. The economic events of 1857 contributed to the first worldwide financial panic, and the *Dred Scott* outcome was seen in the U.S. with added severity due to the decline in railroad security prices. A prevailing opinion of the time was that added slave territories would create additional negative impact, both economically and politically. From a financial point of view, the *Scott* case demonstrated "that political news about future territories called the tune in the land and railroad securities markets."[54]

Two years later, the panic had subsided. President Buchanan began withdrawing paper currency. Recovery was slow in the North, however, as continuing uncertainty surrounding the debate over slavery increased once again. Attitude in the slave states included a belief that the Panic of 1857 would aid in keeping the institution of slavery intact while making the North "more amenable to Southern demands."[55]

Slaveowners in Southern states viewed the Dred Scott decision as a reaffirmation of states' rights and an accurate reading of the U.S. Constitution. According to Senator Jefferson Davis, the case answered the question "whether Cuffee[56] should be kept in his normal condition or not."[57]

Southern papers editorialized that the *Dred Scott* case had vindicated Southern slaveholding positions, and that the series of decisions of the Supreme Court of the United States in the Dred Scott case, is of more vital importance in reference to the settlement of the slavery question than any or all the other acts and proceedings upon this subject—legislative and judicial, State or Federal—since the organization of the Federal Government.[58]

In the North, however, the reaction was opposite. One newspaper editorial cited political corruption as underlying the outcome, writing in reference to the seven justices who had voted for the Supreme Court decision, that the case should be

regarded, throughout the Free States and wherever the pulse of Liberty beats, only as the votes of five slaveholders and two doughfaces upon a question where their opinion was not asked, and where their votes would not count.... Our readers will bear with us if we frequently bring this matter to their notice. Since the organization of the government, no event has occurred that will entail upon the country the consequences, which are involved in this partisan movement of the slavery propagandists. It is the first step in a revolution which, if not arrested, nullifies the Revolution of '76 and makes us all slaves again.[59]

Although the Missouri Compromise had been repealed earlier with passage of the Kansas–Nebraska Act, *Scott* buried that older law once and for all, and opened the door for the spread of slavery into newly admitted territories in the expanding West. With the conclusion that the Missouri Compromise had not freed Scott, the case had ramifications beyond the fate of one man. It effectively denied any slave or ex-slave legal standing to bring suit as a citizen, but the conclusion itself was muddled. Six of the nine justices agreed that Scott lacked citizenship, but did not fully agree with Taney's view that a free Negro would never be able to become a citizen.

Despite the view by the Supreme Court and especially of Chief Justice Taney that the decision would settle the debate about slavery once and for all, it had the opposite effect. Northern opposition to slavery was strengthened after *Scott*, while Democrats were split, with secessionists' interest in the South growing stronger and Union supporters in the North aligning with anti-slavery views held by a majority of the Republican Party.

Scott and his family eventually did win freedom, not through the courts, but privately. The sons of Scott's first owner, Peter Blow, bought the Scott family and emancipated them on May 26, 1857. Scott found employment in St. Louis, where he was treated as a celebrity. He passed away the following year from tuberculosis.

The *Scott* decision was not the final entry in the series of Democrat-controlled Supreme Court decisions. A final case prior to the Civil War reiterated the Court's position that state courts lacked the power to override federal law or decisions of the federal courts. In *Ableman v. Booth*, the Court ruled against Wisconsin in its ruling in a violation of the Fugitive Slave Act.

Ableman v. Booth

An abolitionist editor named Sherman Booth was arrested in 1854 and charged with violating the Fugitive Slave Act. Booth had incited a mob to aid in the rescue of Joshua Glover, an escaped slave being held by U.S. Marshal Stephen Ableman.

Booth asked a Wisconsin state court for a writ of *habeas corpus* and the court issued the writ, ordering Glover to be freed from custody. Ableman appealed to the Wisconsin Supreme Court, which ruled the federal law unconstitutional. Ableman then appealed to the federal courts; however, the Wisconsin court refused to acknowledge the jurisdiction of the federal courts, as the matter was claimed to reside within state jurisdiction. Meanwhile, Glover escaped to Canada and was outside the jurisdiction of the federal government.

The case went to the Supreme Court, where Chief Justice Taney wrote the opinion. He stated that the claim to supremacy by a state court was not constitutional, as states lacked the power to override federal law or court decisions. Taney reasoned that the framers ceded certain rights to the federal government and that "in the sphere of action assigned to it, it should be supreme, and strong enough to execute its own laws by its own tribunals, without interruption from a State or from State authorities."[60]

Citing the Constitution's Supremacy clause, Taney declared that in all cases under dispute of constitutional matters, the Supreme Court held appellate jurisdiction and final authority without exception, making it the last court of appeal when those disputes were at issue. As a result, Wisconsin lacked the legal authority to nullify federal court rulings or to declare federal law (such as the Fugitive Slave Act) unconstitutional. This case highlighted the political nature of the legal system and specifically the debate between federal and state power:

> The *Ableman* decision remains not only a constant and salient reminder of this nation's most trying time, but also a potent example of both the confrontational elements and the fragile nature of America's political system. The principle upon which it was based, the sovereignty of a central government, has been a controversial topic of contention since the Constitutional Convention of 1787, when delegates pursued the goal of a strong central government that did not encroach upon the power of the states.[61]

Although Booth's conviction was upheld by the Supreme Court, he was pardoned by President Buchanan in 1861 immediately before his presidential term expired. The *Ableman* case reiterated the federal position that states lacked authority to nullify federal law. Despite repeated efforts on the part of states to ignore or contradict federal laws such as the Fugitive Slave Act, the Supreme Court was consistent in upholding federal jurisdiction over state law.

Unintended Consequences

The Taney court had attempted to simplify issues of slavery between free and slave states or territories, casting the debate in the Commerce Clause or in the theory of supremacy. However, the series of rulings, especially *Scott*, also had unintended consequences.

In a Virginia case, *United States v. Amy,*[62] Taney served as judge in the U.S. Circuit Court for the Eastern district of Virginia and ruled on the case. Amy was a slave charged with stealing mail. Her owner hired a lawyer to defend her, and he argued in her defense using many points Taney had concluded in his opinion in *Scott*. Since slaves were not legally people, they could not be tried by a jury of their peers as required in the Constitution, since such a jury would have to consist of other slaves. The defense also argued that the Virginia court lacked jurisdiction in the case, stating that

> 1, if a negro cannot sue or be sued civilly, neither can he be tried in a cause where conviction would impose fine and deprivation of liberty; and 2, because if the negro has no personal rights, he cannot be saddled with any personal responsibilities.[63]

The use of points Taney had raised in *Scott* was effective as a defense in *Amy*, as the outcome showed. Taney agreed that Amy was not legally a person, as he had ruled in *Scott* and was legally an item of property. Logically, it followed that a slaveowner could not have property taken without being compensated for the loss. An article about Taney's ruling in this case pointed out that if the slave girl were not punished in some form, it would send a message that blacks could not be held accountable for crimes; a black criminal would need only to hire other blacks, like the "boy Cuffee and the boy Sambo" to commit crimes for them and escape punishment.[64]

This case glaringly revealed the inconsistencies in the *Scott* decision and in Taney's reasoning in that case. When carried to its extreme, a non-person who was classified as "property" could not be tried for a crime.

* * *

The institution of slavery arose repeatedly in the Supreme Court and in the several cases it decided. This range of decisions defined not only the legal status of slavery, but also restricted movement of slaves between slave and free territories and states. Cited as a matter of property rights, the decisions entered (notably in *Scott*, which defined slaves as non-citizens) did not resolve anything; these decisions only made the differences between the free North and the slave South more pronounced. The Court's decisions also emphasized the unresolved moral and economic problems brought about by slavery, and in part created the political climate between polarized Democrats (pro-slavery) and Republicans (anti-slavery):

> The reaction to the decision varied by region and political party, with it being criticized by northerners and Republicans, and praised by southerners and Democrats. The nation's intense reaction to the Dred Scott decision not only had an effect on politics in the late 1850s, but would also serve as one of several precipitates for the ultimate breakdown in American politics, the southern secession and Civil War.[65]

Before Buchanan left office, the nomination of Abraham Lincoln led to immediate secession by South Carolina. Buchanan responded by suggesting a new amendment to the Constitution, not to end slavery but to resolve the issue, to "terminate the existing dissensions, and restore peace and harmony among the states."[66]

Buchanan's suggested amendment did not include any specific ideas about how the desired harmony would be achieved. As the Supreme Court revealed in its history of decisions concerning slavery, the desire to resolve issues was not enough, and the chain of decisions worsened the conflict rather than resolving it. Buchanan left office with no resolution to the problem, and passed the thorny issue of slavery and the secession of South Carolina (with more states to follow) on to the next administration to deal with.

Slavery and Racism in Context

In the context of the times, were justices like Taney properly called "racist" in their judgments? Some of Taney's remarks, such as his writing of blacks as "beings of an inferior order," clearly are racist by modern definitions. However, at the time, and in the middle of the debate over the legal, economic, and moral opinions about slavery, the label of "racism" cannot simply be applied without further discussion.

Some historians subscribe to the belief that slavery caused racism by codifying racist attitudes toward slaves. A different point of view holds that slavery was an outgrowth of a racist attitude and perception of racial inferiority among blacks. A similar conclusion is seen in the treatment of other minorities in U.S. history, including Indians, Chinese migrant workers, and Irish Catholics who migrated in large numbers in the 1800s.

Opinions include distinctions between racial attitudes and economic need. For example, in Caribbean countries practicing slavery, the following distinction was made:

> Slavery in the Caribbean has been too narrowly identified with the Negro. A racial twist has thereby been given to what is basically an economic phenomenon. Slavery was not born of racism: rather, racism was the consequence of slavery. Unfree labor in the New World was brown, white, black, and yellow; Catholic, Protestant, and pagan.... Here, then, is the origin of Negro slavery. The reason was economic, not racial; it had to do not with the color of the laborer, but the cheapness of the labor.[67]

The question has been further raised that since European countries adopted white servitude to satisfy colonial expansion, why not also adopt white slavery? This raises the racial element in an analysis of slavery. As one author observed, "Although there is no evidence that Europeans ever considered instituting full chattel slavery of Europeans in their overseas settlements, the striking paradox is that no sound economic reason spoke against it."[68]

The distinction between selection of white Europeans as indentured servants and black Africans as slaves highlighted the sense among slave traders that members of other races were inferior and not deserving of treatment as equals:

> From the moment when Europeans took their slaves from a race different from their own, which many of them considered inferior to the other human races, and assimilation with whom they all regarded with horror, they assumed that slavery would be eternal, for there is no intermediate state that can be durable between the excessive inequality created by slavery and the complete equality which is the natural result of independence. The Europeans have vaguely sensed this truth but have not admitted it.[69]

The question of whether slavery grew from racism or vice versa remains complex. However, the key ingredient in this discussion is that no one can simply use the term "racist" is describing a particular jurist's decisions or statements. Given the context of thinking in the 19th Century, the treatment of slaves was by no means excusable. However, it can be better understood by recognizing that widespread attitudes during that period were very different than a modern understanding of race relations, and the rights of all people to be treated with equality and to benefit from citizenship and acceptance from all others.

*   *   *

The history of Supreme Court decisions confirms the hypotheses introduced at the beginning of this chapter. It is reasonable to criticize the many decisions made by the high court with emphasis on constitutional principles, even as the moral ramifications of those decisions were ignored.

Three hypotheses below provide further observations about the Democratic-controlled Supreme Court and its decisions.

1. *Control of the Supreme Court by a single party led to politically motivated decisions.* From 1835 through 1861, all justices on the bench (with one exception) were Democrats who had been appointed by Democratic presidents. The resulting decisions slanted clearly toward a political position in favor of slave-ownership and against any rights among slaves. However, of equal importance is the inescapable conclusion that as long as the Democratic Party dominated selection of justices to the Supreme Court, the outcomes of cases clearly were decided in favor of that political preference, a pro-slavery set of opinions.

2. *The obvious bias seen in Supreme Court decisions affecting slavery cannot be ignored.* This second hypothesis further confirms the first one. With only one exception, all of the slavery-related cases heard between 1836 and 1861 revealed the political motivations of both the Democratic presidents and the justices they appointed.

3. *The ultimate result of a series of pro-slavery decisions led to the* Scott *case, in which the Court ruled that slaves could never gain citizenship.* This extreme conclusion was, in one sense, inevitable. The Court had ruled in so many instances, based on the Commerce Clause and on the basis of supremacy, that slaves were property and that slaveowners had property rights protected by the Constitution. Pushed to the extreme consequence of this philosophy, the *Scott* ruling highlighted the glaring flaw in thinking that controlled the Supreme Court just as it controlled the Democratic Party.

PART II

Politics During the Civil War Years

5

Let Us Cross Over the River[1]

The year 1861, when the Civil War began, set up a defining separation in the North between pro–Union and pro–Confederacy forces within the Democratic Party. In that first year of the war, many developments pointed out the nature of the political forces at work. Secession was not fast nor easy for the South. A last-minute attempt at resolving the debate between the two sides and avoiding war, the Crittenden Compromise, failed to gain enough votes for passage in Congress. South Carolina led the secession movement and was quickly followed by another 10 states. Several border states (Missouri, Kentucky, Delaware, and Maryland) voted to not join the Confederacy. During the war, West Virginia split from Virginia and also stayed in the Union.

The state where the secession debate was most difficult was Virginia. With strong ties to the founders and to the presidency, many Virginians had divided loyalties, both to the Union and to the state. However, the state did finally vote to join the rest of the Confederacy. Among those Virginians facing a tough choice was Robert E. Lee, Lincoln's first choice to head the army set up to defend the capital.

Throughout this first year of the war, Lincoln viewed secession as an irrational movement and did not expect it to last. However, he ended up fighting a war on two fronts. The battlefields of the Civil War are well known in history, but the second war was fought with Northern "Peace Democrats" or "Copperheads," those who supported the South and the institution of slavery, and opposed Lincoln at every turn. The slavery debate was characterized by threats of anti–Union violence, especially in Maryland, and Lincoln's decision to suspend *habeas corpus*. Throughout the year and beyond, highly racist editorials in Copperhead-leaning newspapers set a tone for fear mongering and accusations aimed at Lincoln about his intensions and motives for pursuing the war.

In the minds of most Americans today, the war began on the morning of April 12, 1861, when forces of the newly declared Confederate State of America began shelling Fort Sumter in South Carolina. It was a promise kept: Southern leaders had warned for the past several months that if Lincoln were elected, it would lead to secession.

Lincoln had run on a platform opposed to the expansion of slavery, but he had carefully avoided an abolitionist stance, and even had pledged to allow continuation of existing slavery in Southern states without interruption. However, many in the South referred to the Republican Party as the "Black Republican Party," due to its underlying opposition to slavery and its expansion. During the 1860 election, Democrats warned of slave rebellion if Lincoln won. Others threatened secession:

Robert E. Lee of Virginia (photographed in 1864) was Lincoln's first choice to head the Union Army and defend Washington, D.C.

The first act of the black republican party will be to exclude slavery from all the territories, from the District of Columbia, the arsenals and the forts, by the action of the general government. That would be a recognition that slavery is a sin, and confine the institution to its present limits. The moment that slavery is pronounced a moral evil, a sin, by the general government, that moment the safety of the rights of the south will be entirely gone.[2]

The accusations against Lincoln's Republican Party in the South accelerated as the election approached, with warnings that people should not "be deluded ... that the Black Republican Party is a moderate party. It is in fact essentially a revolutionary party."[3]

On the day after Lincoln's election victory, the *Mercury* of Charleston, a paper that had supported secession for several months prior, wrote, "Yesterday, November the 7th, will long be a memorable day in Charleston. The tea has been thrown overboard; the revolution of 1860 has been initiated."[4] The election brought to a head the ongoing debate among the Southern states. Was secession the answer? Would the North go to war to hold the Union together? There was no consensus in the South on these questions. The month before the election, South Carolina had called for a

Southern convention, but few in the South were enthusiastic about setting up a united front. The slaveholder states hoped to maintain their position, fearing that Lincoln would force the issue.

The Secession Movement in South Carolina

South Carolina was a special case, as that state's legislators were willing to secede on their own whether or not other states went along. Every congressman from South Carolina announced support for secession in the event Lincoln won election.[5] Despite hesitation throughout the South, other states gradually followed. The sole issue in the debate was slavery and Lincoln's anti-slavery position. The great fear was not only that Lincoln would prevent the spread of slavery to newly admitted territories (as he had pledged during the campaign), but that he also would take action to outlaw slavery in all of the states. On December 17, 1860, South Carolina held a state convention, where, on December 20, an ordinance of secession was approved unanimously.[6]

Sentiment shifted rapidly. Once South Carolina acted, other Southern states also adopted secessionist measures. Although it appeared that each state acted independently, a coordinated effort was underway:

> Theoretically, each southern state was acting independently, but in fact there was already a network of commissioners who maintained liaison between the states, and the southern members of Congress, meeting frequently in caucus, served as a kind of ready-made coordinating body to assure that the disparate action of the several states would converge....[7]

By December 31, the coordinated effort was working. South Carolina voted to appoint commissioners to the other Southern states to begin creation of a provisional government, the new Confederate States of America.

A unifying theme for the new government was defense of "Southern rights," which translated to the right to own slaves and to control legal issues on the state level rather than at the federal level. A conflict arose immediately, with some Southern citizens favoring immediate secession and others favoring "cooperation" with other seceding states. A majority favored remaining in the Union, but only with guarantees that their states' rights would be honored. The cooperation arm of citizens favored negotiating an agreement with Washington as a means for keeping the Union intact. Secessionists were more firmly united in their positions, believing that the only way they would be allowed to maintain their states' rights (slavery) was through secession, and that cooperation would not be possible with Lincoln's administration. For many, the cooperationists appeared simply to be obstructing the inevitable secession and formation of a new country.[8]

As the Southern states voted on the issue of secession over coming months, the outcomes were very close in some states. In Georgia and Louisiana, for example, secessionists won over cooperationists by slim majorities only. A more decisive victory occurred in South Carolina, where the vote for secession was 77 percent of the total.[9] The secessionist movement passed, however, and on February 7, 1861, delegates met in Montgomery, Alabama, and adopted a new constitution. Two days later, delegates elected Jefferson Davis (who had served as Secretary of War in the administration of Franklin Pierce) as president of the new Confederacy.[10]

Vote results in the Southern states reflected greater approval in counties with the highest proportion of slaveownership. In this regard, secession itself became a slaveholder's vote, and was widely supported—on average, 72 percent in favor—although popular vote by itself is not the entire story. Some Southern states were excluded from these averages, including Florida, Texas, and Louisiana.[11]

Southern voting in the most recent presidential campaign had been largely Democratic. In fact, in the 1860 election, all of the South voted for the Southern Democrat candidate Breckenridge, with the exception of Tennessee, Kentucky, and Virginia, won by Constitutional Union Party candidate Bell. Douglas carried Missouri, and all of the Northern states went to Lincoln.[12]

In the North, the tendency for Southern Democrats to favor slavery often has been blamed on poor white citizens, who were called "hill folk," "rednecks," and "peckerwoods."[13] However, the pro-slavery movement was much broader, and wealthier plantation owners dominating the cotton and tobacco industries were major forces behind the entire movement. They had more to lose than the poor "hill folk," who were not likely to be slaveowners. The terms applied to poor white Southerners encompassed "white trash" under many slurs. A similar disparaging reference to poor white Southern folk, especially from Georgia, was "cracker."[14]

The Crittenden Compromise

Contrary to Northern claims about ignorant Southern voters, the secessionist movement was orchestrated and operated by political leaders in the deep South's Democratic Party, aided by sympathetic Northern Democrats. This movement began in support of slavery but evolved quickly into a debate over secession. It was not a harmonious discussion, however.

The Southern border states had close ties to the North, and politicians in those states attempted to reach a compromise to avoid secession.

After the 1860 election, lame duck President Buchanan suggested a new constitutional amendment to permanently legalize slavery in the Southern states. However, he had no clear idea in mind about how this could be accomplished. On December 18, 1860, Senator John Crittenden (Constitutional Unionist, Kentucky) proposed a compromise including Buchanan's suggestion, along with other provisions. The purpose of this so-called Crittenden Compromise was to reconcile the two sides and end the secession threat.

The proposal contained several parts:

- a constitutional amendment making Southern slavery a guaranteed right.
- restoring the boundary set in the Missouri Compromise, banning slavery north of the 36°30' line (approximately forming the border between Missouri and Arkansas; Kentucky and Tennessee; and Virginia and North Carolina.
- legalizing slavery in Washington, D.C.
- continuation of the Fugitive Slave Law along with the banning of continued African slave trading.
- reinforcing popular sovereignty in the states to decide whether to allow slavery in future states to be admitted to the Union.

Senator John Crittenden (photographed by Mathew Brady ca. 1865) proposed a compromise which included a constitutional amendment, hoping to settle the slavery question and avoid war.

The Crittenden Compromise failed because the two sides could not find areas of agreement on the terms. There was too much resistance to a constitutional amendment in the North as well as to the

Fugitive Slave Act, and the South was not willing to modify their position. On March 2, 1861, Representative Thomas Corwin introduced the Corwin Amendment in the House; Senator William Seward (R–NY) introduced the same bill in the Senate. The amendment was designed to avoid secession by Southern states.[15]

The Corwin Amendment text limited future abolishment of slavery but avoided the use of the word "slavery" consistent with the original wording used by the Constitutional Convention in 1787:

> No amendment shall be made to the Constitution which will authorize or give to Congress the power to abolish or interfere, within any State, with the domestic institutions thereof, including that of persons held to labor or service by the laws of said State.[16]

The guarantee of permanently legalized slavery was unacceptable in the North, as was the provision in the original Crittenden Compromise that this condition could not be later repealed or amended. President-elect Lincoln opposed the Crittenden Compromise and the Corwin Amendment; his opposition made ratification unlikely.

Repeated attempts at passing the new series of amendments, in original form or with changes, revealed the impasse between North and South. An editorial of the day summarized the situation and its hopelessness:

> Men at Washington think there is no chance for peace, and indeed we can see but little, everything looks gloomy. The Crittenden resolutions have been voted down again and again. Is there any other proposition which will win, that the South can accept? If not—there comes war—and woe to the wives and daughters of our land....[17]

The proposal and its adjustments were also the topic of discussion at the Peace Conference of 1861, held from February 8–27 in Washington, D.C. In attendance were 131 of the country's leading politicians. The Crittenden Compromise, with a proposed "border state plan" that would have exempted future territorial acquisitions from conditions in the Missouri Compromise, was rejected at this conference.[18]

The Struggle Toward Secession

The beginning of the Civil War is identified with the bombardment of Fort Sumter. However, this did not occur without a lengthy debate among politicians, some seeking to avoid secession and others willing to accept nothing less. Those Southern politicians focused on secession after Lincoln's election cited the Constitution as justification to form a new government:

We hold these truths to be self-evident, that all men are created equal, that they are endowed by their Creator with certain unalienable Rights, that among these are Life, Liberty and the pursuit of Happiness.—That to secure these rights, Governments are instituted among Men, deriving their just powers from the consent of the governed,—That whenever any Form of Government becomes destructive of these ends, it is the Right of the People to alter or to abolish it, and to institute new Government, laying its foundation on such principles and organizing its powers in such form, as to them shall seem most likely to effect [sic] their Safety and Happiness.[19]

The right of the people to abolish the government and replace it gave Southern states a sense of right in voting to secede, despite Northern accusations that it was an act of treason. The disputed interpretation was not reconcilable, and the matter rested ultimately on the South's claimed right to own slaves; this divided belief was accelerated by Lincoln's victory. He won, however, only in the North and carried no Southern states.

The Southern interpretation of the Constitution was by no means decisive, and debate continued even after the Civil War. Despite a disagreement over the legality of secession, which is not mentioned in the Constitution (although the Preamble did allow for the right to "institute new government" when the existing government "becomes destructive"), the movement continued and, within months following the 1860 election, 11 states left the Union.

On December 20, 1860, South Carolina voted for secession. An additional five states followed in January 1861. These were Mississippi, Florida, Alabama, Georgia, and Louisiana. Between February and June, another five states also seceded: Texas (February), Virginia (April), Arkansas and North Carolina (May), and Tennessee (June). Two additional states—Missouri and Kentucky—had votes of secession, but those votes failed.

The elderly ex-president, John Tyler, even as a Virginia native and slaveholder, ended up serving in the Congress of the newly formed Confederacy. However, he sponsored a last-minute conference of 12 border states with the purpose of avoiding war. The invitation to attend was ignored by the Southern states, and the only real interest in Tyler's idea came from Northern Democrats. In February 1861, 21 states were represented with 132 delegates in attendance. The only result was a suggestion for a new series of amendments to the Constitution, which were very similar to the Crittenden Compromise from the previous December.[20]

The largely ceremonial convention ended with a presentation to Congress of a new seven-part amendment. It had no chance for approval and the convention ended in early March. Even before Lincoln took office, this final effort at avoiding war failed and, in the South, state officials had begun seizing federal property. Those citizens and politicians opposed to secession but living in the South hoped the Union would at the last moment offer concessions on the question of slavery. However, the combination of Buchanan's unwillingness to take any action and the impending inauguration of Lincoln kept matters in suspense, allowing the new Confederacy to organize itself politically and militarily. The election itself was cited as reason to secede, and Lincoln's well-known positions on slavery encouraged Northern Republicans to refuse any compromise with the South:

> The Republicans, in short, without compromising their central principle, could now take a more flexible attitude about implementing it because they would soon have control of the executive department. But the implications of that control had in turn replaced the territorial question as the focus of sectional conflict. Secession had begun, after all, not as a response to anything done or left undone by Congress, but rather as a response to the election of Lincoln.... The outstanding sectional issues were now less important than the northward shift of political power—and southern reaction to it.[21]

What once had been a fierce disagreement about slavery in new territories now paled as focus shifted to the debate over secession itself and how North and South (Republican and Democratic) would function in a country split in two or going to war. In the North, focus moved from fear of Southern expansion of slavery into new territories to demands for maintaining the Union. In the South, focus moved from once-lauded states' rights (primarily the right to own slaves) to a rejection of the Lincoln presidency and the electoral victory consisting of Northern states only. Once secession occurred and the South formed a separate government and constitution, the only apparent solution would be a voluntary form of reconstruction. Stubbornness on both sides made avoidance of war impossible and the hope for compromise fade as a realistic possibility.

As unrealistic as peaceful or "voluntary" reconstruction was at the time, all sides—Lincoln's new administration, border state neutral politicians, and Confederacy officials—seriously considered the idea. Although it might have been possible, the intense opposition to Lincoln, nationalistic pro-slavery trends among Democrats, and unwillingness on both sides to compromise, especially among slaveholder states, doomed voluntary reconstruction as a viable alternative to war.[22]

Virginia's Debate

During Buchanan's final months in office, he was reluctant to take any action to protect forts under threat, notably Fort Sumter and Fort Moultrie in Charleston, South Carolina. Even among states voting to secede, this period between votes and the beginning of war was a time of struggle between conflicting loyalties. Even the vote to secede had been difficult, notably in the state of Virginia. So much of Virginia's legacy was tied to the founding. More than half of the period since 1790 (37 out of 71 years) had seen a Virginian in the presidency. The legacy of Washington, Jefferson, Madison, and Monroe (collectively 32 years), plus an additional five years of William Henry Harrison, Tyler, and Taylor, made Virginia truly the "mother of presidents," so secession was not a decision taken lightly in the Old Dominion.

As the debate in Virginia began, a majority of citizens opposed leaving the Union. Compromise was a preferred course, not only because of the ramifications of splitting the country, but also due to the historical and patriotic connection between the state and the founding of the United States. At the same time, a majority did not want to accept any form of federally-imposed limitation on slavery. The situation was summarized in reference to Lincoln's election as a turning point in the debate:

> Although a majority probably favored compromise, most opposed any weakening of slaveholders' protections. Even so-called moderates—mostly Whigs and Douglas Democrats—opposed the sacrifice of these rights and they rejected any acquiescence or "submission" to federal coercion.... To a growing body of Virginians, Lincoln's election meant the onset of an active war against southern institutions. These men shared a common fear of northern Republicans and a common suspicion of a northern conspiracy against the South.[23]

At the convention to determine secession for Virginia, the 152 delegates were evenly split between secessionists and unionists (30 each), with 92 undecided moderates. However, among moderates, secessionist leanings were outnumbered by those preferring compromise.[24]

The issue was heatedly debated. Henry Lewis Benning, delegate to the Virginia Convention from the state of Georgia (and later, a general in the Confederate Army, and for whom Fort Benning, Georgia, was named), incited fears about dire outcomes if and when slavery was abolished. He spoke at the convention:

> If things are allowed to go on as they are, it is certain that slavery is to be abolished. By the time the north shall have attained the power, the black race will be in a large majority, and then we will have black governors, black legislatures, black juries, black everything. Is it to be supposed that the white race will stand for that? ... We will be overpowered and our men will be compelled to wander like vagabonds all over the earth; and as for our women, the horrors of their state we cannot contemplate in imagination. That is the fate which abolition will bring upon the white race....[25]

Benning, who had been nominated for Congress as a Democrat in 1851, was elected two years later as a justice to the Georgia Supreme Court. His most noteworthy ruling was that states were not bound to obey rulings by the federal Supreme Court on constitutional issues. He believed the two levels of courts were "coordinate and co-equal." Benning attempted to convince the Virginia delegates to join with Georgia in secession. Ultimately, he succeeded.[26]

On May 23, 1861, the sentiment among delegates had shifted and secession was approved. The decision was ratified by a general vote of over 77 percent: 132,000 in favor to less than 38,000 opposed. The proposals adopted by the Virginia Convention clearly defined the state's position as well as that of the greater South:

> Proposals Adopted by the Virginia Convention of 1861: The first resolution asserted states' rights *per se*; the second was for retention of slavery; the third opposed sectional parties; the fourth called for equal recognition of slavery in both territories and non-slave states; the fifth demanded the removal of federal forts and troops from seceded states; the sixth hoped for a peaceable adjustment of grievances and maintaining the Union; the seventh called for Constitutional amendments to remedy federal and state disputes; the eighth recognized the right of secession; the ninth said the federal government had no authority over seceded states since it refused to recognize their withdrawal; the tenth said the federal government was empowered to recognize the Confederate States; the eleventh was an appeal to Virginia's sister states; the twelfth asserted Virginia's willingness to wait a reasonable period of time for an answer to its propositions, providing no one resorted to force against the seceded states; the thirteenth asked United States and Confederate States governments to remain peaceful; and the fourteenth asked the border slave states to meet in conference to consider Virginia's resolutions and to join in Virginia's appeal to the North.[27]

The decision to secede or remain loyal to the Union was not limited to the convention's delegates. Robert E. Lee was offered the role of general in the Union Army to command the defense of Washington, D.C. He replied to presidential advisor Francis P. Blair, who had made the offer in behalf of President Lincoln: "Mr. Blair, I look upon secession as anarchy. If I owned the four million slaves in the South, I would sacrifice them all to the Union; but how can I draw my sword upon Virginia, my native state?"[28]

Lee's struggle between loyalty to the Union and to Virginia was further expressed in his statement concluding that Virginia was first in his mind: "I shall never bear arms against the Union, but it may be necessary for me to carry a musket in the defense of my native state, Virginia, in which case I shall not prove recreant to my duty."[29]

Lincoln's Policies in 1861

To Lincoln, secession made no sense whatsoever. He had assumed that a slaveholding minority would not prevail against the larger numbers of pro–Union citizens in the Southern states. As with the beginnings of so many wars, the events leading up to secession and the Civil War were, in Lincoln's mind, illogical and without any hope of a good outcome:

> We have just carried an election on principles fairly stated to the people. Now we are told in advance, the government shall be broken up, unless we surrender to those we have beaten, before we take the offices. In this they are either attempting to play upon us, or they are in dead earnest. Either way, if we surrender, it is the end of us, and of the government. They will repeat the experiment upon us *ad libitum*. A year will not pass, till we shall have to take Cuba as a condition upon which they will stay in the Union.[30]

While Lincoln had never been as militant in opposition to slavery as many of his fellow Republicans, he was exceptionally militant about holding together the Union. The two issues were intertwined and the newly elected president was well aware of the many effects that disunion would likely have: the immorality of slavery, economic consequences in South and also in the North, and, in the immediate sense, the threat to Washington, D.C., with its close proximity to Virginia and the Confederate capital of Richmond, only 120 miles away.

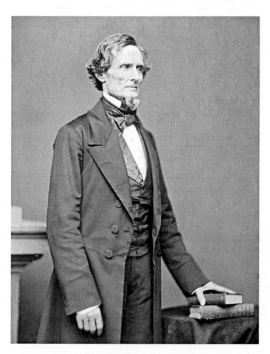

Jefferson Davis (photographed by Mathew Brady some time before 1861) was sworn in as president of the Confederacy in February 1861.

Before his inauguration, Lincoln had heard many rumors of planned disruptions in the capital, his assassination, and the South's plan to invade and take control of Washington before March 4, inauguration day. Military advisors warned Lincoln of a "widespread and powerful conspiracy to seize the capitol."[31]

Oddly, it seems, in hindsight, Lincoln played down the crisis of secession as well as threats of assassination or seizure of Washington, predicting that the entire matter would evaporate, stating, "Let it alone and it will go down of itself." This opinion ignored the widespread fears throughout the country that secession was all too real. He reflected logically about state sovereignty, asking: "By what principle of original right is it that one-fiftieth or one-nineteenth of a great nation, by calling themselves a State, have the right to break up and ruin that nation as a matter of original principle?"[32]

In February 1861, as Lincoln traveled across Ohio, Pennsylvania, and New York on his way to inauguration, the reality of secession began to sink in. On February 18, Jefferson Davis took his oath as president of the Confederate States of America in Montgomery, Alabama. Lincoln modified his remarks for the remainder of his journey, pledging a commitment to keep the Union together and avoid armed conflict if possible. He promised, "The man does not live who is more devoted to peace than I am. None who would do more to preserve it. But it may be necessary to put the foot down firmly."[33]

One of the first challenges Lincoln faced in his new administration was the disposition of U.S. forts in the South. In the interest of avoiding armed conflict, Lincoln delivered his inaugural address with deletions of passages pledging to reclaim federal property seized by Confederate forces. Wanting to avoid armed conflict, Lincoln continued to hope for a peaceful resolution, but was unyielding on his pledge to hold the Union together. Even with a modified inaugural address, however, the message clearly reinforced his pledge to not yield any forts. This position centered immediately on Fort Sumter. This was largely symbolic, as the fort held no strategic value. Its guns all pointed out to sea, thus offering no military value in the event of an invasion from land.

In the address on March 4, 1861, Lincoln spoke, as he had during his journey to Washington, of his intention to hold the Union together, but slavery was the major topic of his speech. He made a sort of peace offering, pledging to not interfere with the Southern states' rights to own slaves, either through legislation or armed conflict:

> I have no purpose, directly or indirectly, to interfere with the institution of slavery in the States where it exists. I believe I have no lawful right to do so, and I have no inclination to do so.... Resolved, that the maintenance inviolate of the rights of the States, and especially the right of each State to order and control its own domestic institutions according to its own judgment exclusively, is essential to that balance of power on which the perfection and endurance of our political fabric depend; and we denounce the lawless invasion by armed force of the soil of any State or Territory, no matter what pretext, as among the gravest of crimes.[34]

Lincoln's inaugural concessions were designed to maintain peace without accepting the idea that secession would be allowed. He closed with the statement,"We are not enemies but friends.... Though passion may have strained, it must not break our bonds of affection."[35]

COLUMBIA AWAKE AT LAST.

"Columbia Awake at Last" (1861). This political cartoon referred to the Union and the treason of secession.

Predictably, Republicans approved of Lincoln's inaugural tone and message, and Democrats largely heard coercion and threat in his words. The new president had stated clearly that he wanted to avoid war and favored "voluntary" reconstruction to keep the Union together. However, the day after the inauguration, Lincoln heard from Major Robert Anderson, commanding officer at Fort Sumter, that without reinforcements it would be impossible to hold the fort if Southern forces were to attack. When Lincoln consulted with his new cabinet, most members expressed the view that Fort Sumter would be lost and no actions could prevent such a loss from taking place. The pledge Lincoln had offered to not interfere with slavery in the South had made no difference. It was too late to send reinforcements, so the debate among the cabinet centered on whether to abandon Sumter or hold ground.

With the administration in office for only one month, a lack of clear policy regarding secession and the disposition of Fort Sumter characterized Lincoln and his advisors as indecisive and lacking direction. In early April, an expedition to reinforce Sumter was underway but this was seen in the Confederacy as an intention to use force against the South. On April 9, the Confederate government decided to launch an attack on Fort Sumter in response to what they saw as provocation. Mixed messages from Washington about federal troop withdrawal and reinforcement of the fort led the Confederates to believe Lincoln was planning to attack Charleston preemptively. Knowing of the planned expedition launched by Lincoln, the Confederacy decided to act before the ships could arrive in Charleston.

On April 10, Confederate General P.G.T. Beauregard was ordered to demand the surrender of Fort Sumter. Upon refusal, a bombardment began early on the morning of April 12, 1861. Two days later, Major Anderson surrendered the fort.

The battle of Fort Sumter set a tone for the next four years of war. "Columbia Awake at Last," a political cartoon of the day, described the conflict and its major players.

In the cartoon, Columbia (symbol of the United States) throat-punches a man (perhaps a caricature of Jefferson Davis) with the text "TREASON" and "SECESSION" on his pants and a Confederate flag on his hat. Davis is stopped short by Columbia's blow; his tongue extends out from his mouth, his eyes bulge, and he drops a knife, a gun labeled (Fort) "SUMPTER," and a corner of the U.S. Constitution he apparently tried to tear from Columbia's hand. In the background two other Confederates are startled and move back. A face of a founding father (George Washington, or possibly Thomas Jefferson) watches over Columbia's head.

The Rise of the Copperheads

As soon as the war began, Northern politicians in the Democratic Party divided their loyalties. War Democrats, led by Stephen Douglas, supported the president and favored reuniting the country. Peace Democrats refused to support the war and believed secession was legal. Neither side expressed opposition to slavery; in fact, many Democrats in the North supported making peace with the Confederacy and yielding to the demand that Southern states be allowed to keep their slaves. Peace Democrats were labeled as "Copperheads," a derogatory term implying that Peace Democrats were traitors.[36]

The Copperheads dominated the Northern Democratic Party for most of the war years. Their opposition to Lincoln's policies and support of the Confederacy included repeated calls for an immediate peace settlement. That would have included terms unacceptable to Lincoln, such as recognition of the Confederate State of America as a separate country and allowing the South to keep alive its institution of slavery. Despite the intended negative connotation of anti–Union Democrats as venomous snakes, those Peace Democrats accepted the title and proudly wore badges cut from the Liberty Head penny coin, the "Copper Head" badge.[37]

In some instances, the Copperhead movement went beyond favoring the Confederacy. Repeated efforts to resist the draft led to encouraging Union soldiers to desert. Some Copperheads became agents of the Confederacy and accepted payment for spying and reporting on Union military moves. However, the Confederacy was never able to accurately judge the levels of strength held in the North by sympathetic Democrats. Thus, the Copperhead support and calls for resistance within the Union Army were not effective, even with Confederate support for the effort.[38]

Despite Copperhead support for the South, Jefferson Davis was portrayed in Northern papers as drunk on the power of secession at the point of his inauguration as Confederate president.

The cartoon shows Davis as a skeleton holding a pirate flag and a torch labeled "desolation," and a slave at his feet. He sits atop a bale of cotton and a barrel of whiskey.

The conflict of sentiment continued throughout the war. However, several Northern newspapers were sympathetic with the Confederate cause and were labeled as Copperhead papers. One editor in particular, Edward G. Roddy of the Uniontown, Pennsylvania, *Genius of Liberty*, was outspoken in his criticism. He "circulated scurrilous charges that Lincoln was a tyrant and a tool of black slaves, members of an inferior race." Another Copperhead editor, Marcus Mills "Brick" Pomeroy of the *La Crosse Democratic*, "labeled Lincoln a bigot and butcher and encouraged an as-

THE INAUGURATION AT RICHMOND.

"The Inauguration at Richmond" (1862). Upon the inauguration of Jefferson Davis, Northern editorial cartoons portrayed him as drunk on power, enthroned on a bail of cotton atop a whiskey barrel, a slave at his feet, surrounded by ruin and desolation.

sassin to strike the president to the heart."[39] Pomeroy's editorials worsened over time. He described Lincoln in one editorial as

> fungus from the corrupt womb of bigotry and fanaticism [and a] worse tyrant and more inhuman butcher than has existed since the days of Nero.... The man who votes for Lincoln now is a traitor and murderer.... And if he is elected to misgovern for another four years, we trust some bold hand will pierce his heart with dagger point for the public good.[40]

The Copperhead movement had numerous supportive members in the Northern press. The *Metropolitan Record*, New York City's official Catholic newspaper, had initially supported the Union but became a Copperheads publication later during the war. The paper urged Irish readers to undertake armed resistance and, from July 13 to July 16, more than 100 black citizens were beaten or hacked to death and more than 100 black-owned businesses, as well as an orphanage for black children, were burned down. On August 19, 1864, publisher of the *Record*, John Mullaly, was arrested and charged with inciting resistance to the draft.[41]

One of the most organized Copperhead organizations was the Knights of the Golden Circle (KGC). Founded in July 1854, by George W. L. Bickley of Cincinnati, the original purpose of the organization was to create a "golden circle" of annexed territories in Mexico, Central America, and the Northern section of South America, a goal perhaps generated by the 1854 Ostend Manifesto. This golden circle would lay a foundation for newly admitted slave states. This would strengthen the slave power so that it could never again be challenged.[42]

The lofty dreams of the KGC did not represent all Copperheads. However, once the Civil War began, KGC members aligned their goals with other Northern Democrat goals, opposing Lincoln and favoring the aims of the Confederacy. The active Copperhead movement, including KGC members, began as early as 1861 to support Southern causes in the North and to oppose Lincoln and the anti-slavery movement. The numbers of Northern Democrats opposed to Lincoln cannot be known with certainty, but as the war progressed, the term "Copperhead" was associated in the North with treason. The deep racism of Copperheads increased as the war progressed as well, especially in 1862, when the Union was not winning and battlefield casualties made the war unpopular in the North. Popularity of the movement mirrored the course of the war: when the Union was winning, Copperhead support declined; when the South was winning, support rose.

By January 1863, when the Emancipation Proclamation was published, the Copperhead movement picked up momentum. Freeing slaves and giving them the rights of citizens was repugnant to the Northern Democrats who agreed with anti–Union sentiments. As a direct consequence, the polarization between the parties worsened and continued after the war for decades.

An argument can be made that Copperheads had at least as much influence within the Democratic Party as did the War Democrats who supported Lincoln. However, the lasting effect of Copperhead control over Democratic Party platforms and policies was evident in outcomes of presidential races in the 70 years following the Civil War. The Democratic Party

> was so tainted by the exploits of the Peace Democrats that only two Democrats occupied the Executive Mansion between 1868 and 1932, by which time most of the Civil War generation had died.[43]

Those two presidents elected after the Civil War were Grover Cleveland (1885–89) and Woodrow Wilson (1913–21). Other than the 12 years of these two terms, the presidency was dominated by the Republican Party. The reason cannot be simplified by pointing to the outcome of the Civil

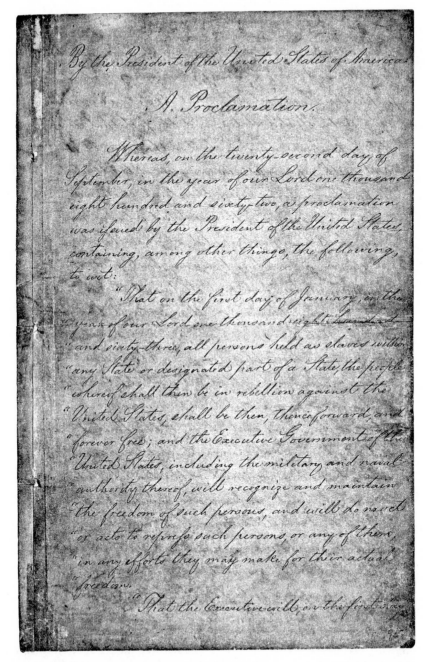

Page 1 of the Emancipation Proclamation (January 1, 1863). The Proclamation was cited as a cause of growing antagonism between Democrats and Republicans, even long after the end of the Civil War.

War; it is more related to the vocal Peace Democrats (Copperheads) and their undermining of Lincoln's war effort as well as actions during Reconstruction. The Copperhead movement was destructive to the Union and came to be seen as treason; it was equally destructive to the Democratic Party as a whole.

Controversy About Secession and Slavery

The Copperhead movement grew from widespread Democratic dissent not just in the South, but in the North as well. There was by no means universal agreement in the North about Lincoln's professed opposition to the spread of slavery.

On April 11, 1861, the day before the Confederate assault on Fort Sumter, an Ohio newspaper editorialized that the North would benefit if it would "throw off the shackles and stigma of negro equality." The editorial predicted that in this event, "all our calamities would disappear in a twelvemonth, and our national harmony would be re-established on a firmer and more lasting foundation than ever."[44]

After the assault and obvious beginning of war, sentiment in the North was largely patriotic and pro–Union. In New York, for example, after the attack on Fort Sumter was announced,

> wave upon wave of human beings, thousands, and thousands, upon tens of thousands, poured through the streets, for hours together, actuated by a sentiment, neither of joy, nor of triumph; but of inflexible determination that, whatever the cost may be, the Union shall be preserved.[45]

The strong support was not exclusive, but it was evident. Lincoln had called for 75,000 volunteers to step forward, but response was so great that many had to be refused because the Union Army was not prepared for an overly rapid mobilization. Volunteers, like their opposites in the South, expected a very quick war and easy victory. Attitudes among Northern soldiers and civilians betrayed a superior air, an example of urban versus rural. Such attitudes of bias and superiority are common at the beginning of all wars. For example, one Rhode Island man wrote of the rebels, "They can lie and steal to perfection, but I really do believe that they cannot fight—'Barking dogs never bite.'"[46]

Among Lincoln's supporters was prominent political rival of the past, Stephen A. Douglas. With strong support, his statements defined the difference between War Democrats (supports of the Union) and Peace Democrats (Copperheads, those opposed to Lincoln's war and in support of the Confederacy). Douglas stated specifically that anyone not supporting the war effort was a traitor; although Douglas did not include statements about slavery, he did say that the purpose of the war should be for a singular purpose: to reunite the country.[47]

Although opposition to Lincoln and his positions on slavery was common in the North, notably in newspaper editorials, response to events at Fort Sumter were supporting and patriotic for the most part. Even so, some newspapers predicted dire consequences. One editorial said about Lincoln and his administration, "The Abolition and disunion administration have attempted the coercion of the Confederate States. Such are the first fruits of Republicanism—the end no one can foresee."[48]

Editorials often were critical but tempered. Newspapers of the day tended to either support Lincoln and the war effort, or to editorialize critically but cautiously. In comparison, Copperheads in this first year of the Civil War were vocal and highly critical of the entire war effort. This attitude encompassed a hatred of Lincoln as well as support for secession and a belief that the South had the right to own slaves.

Copperheads referred to the Constitution as support for states' rights and secession. They were united in their belief that both presidents Jefferson and Jackson would have favored the South in its fight to maintain slavery and to resist interference from Lincoln. That political philosophy was opposed to a strong central government. Jacksonian Democracy was based on a relatively weak federal government, with greater power among the states—including power to own slaves and, if necessary, to secede. Often cited were Jefferson's writings, including a belief that states had the right to secede and override federal law if that law was unconstitutional.

Although many relied on strict constitutional interpretation and the philosophies of Jefferson and Jackson to support their anti-war positions, others (notably the dedicated Copperheads among Northern Democrats) played on fears of what would happen if and when slaves were granted freedom:

> Copperheads were notable for the depth and virulence of their racism. Like many Southerners, they regarded African Americans as inferior beings who were best off in bondage. Copperhead rhetoric throughout the war was filled with allusions to racial mixing that were designed to play on whites' deepest fears.[49]

Angry statements were commonplace, including pledges to drive out all Negroes and Republicans. Threats of Northern efforts to form military companies and kill "Black Republicans" were not uncommon. The term Black Republicans included any Republican politician opposed to slavery. A year before the war began, a professor of law in Virginia published a pamphlet rationalizing support for slavery and resistance in the South to Northern anti-slavery opinions:

Between the North and the South there is no real antagonism, but the Black Republican organization proceeds upon the assumption of one. It declares that between the free labor of the North, and the slave labor of the South an irrepressible conflict must take place until one gives way to the other.... Is there anything short of this, which would be a more serious aggression, whether we look at its immediate or future consequences, than the election of a Black Republican President?[50]

Once war began, many pro–Southern Copperheads joined or formed new units of the Knights of the Golden Circle (KGC). At this point, the KGC became a paramilitary group serving as a "rallying army for secessionists." With many loyal Northerners having volunteered to join the Union Army, several Northern cities and towns were unable to resist expansion of KGC units. A perception developed that this movement represented a threat to the safety of local citizens.[51]

Suspension of *Habeas Corpus*

Copperhead statements and activities led to Lincoln's decision on April 27, 1861, to suspend *habeas corpus*. This is the provision in law allowing those held without trial to demand release, or to challenge the reason for confinement. The Suspension Clause of the U.S. Constitution was cited by the president as justification for this decision. It reads, "The privilege of the writ of *habeas corpus* shall not be suspended, unless when in cases of rebellion or invasion the public safety may require it."[52]

Lincoln had been advised that anti-war forces in Maryland were planning an attack on railroad lines along a supply line between Annapolis and Philadelphia. As the North prepared for conflict with the South, this supply line was vital for the war effort. The threat culminated with an attack by a pro–Confederacy mob in Baltimore. Union troops were on the move to Washington, and federal troops then occupied the city to prevent further violence. He immediately suspended *habeas corpus* as a result.

The decision by Lincoln was challenged immediately in the Maryland U.S. Circuit Court of Appeals. Presiding Judge Roger B. Taney (chief justice of the Supreme Court) ruled that the suspension was unconstitutional, and that only Congress could legally suspend *habeas corpus*.[53] Taney made his ruling alone and without consulting other justices in the Circuit Court or hearing arguments by the government's side in the case.[54]

Lincoln ignored Taney's ruling, and further arrests followed. By September, the Maryland legislature was due to convene, but Lincoln ordered one-third of the General Assembly arrested, so the session had to be canceled. By February the following year, most of those detained under

Lincoln's suspension order were released from jail. However, throughout the war years, Lincoln used this power to arrest and detain several newspaper editors and politicians for expressing Southern sympathies. One ex–Congressman, Clement Laird Vallandigham (D–OH), was warned to cease expressing his support of the Confederacy, but continued doing so. He was arrested, but quickly released by Lincoln and banished to the Confederacy.

The issue in Lincoln's mind was a matter of necessity. He relied on his emergency powers under the Constitution:

> If the constitution of the United States vested in the executive, in time of war, absolute discretion as to the means to be employed to carry on the war, whatever evils resulted from the exercise of this discretion must only be added to the aggregate of misery of which a resort to arms is the cause, and so must be regretted, but sternly endured.[55]

Clement Laird Vallandigham (photographed by Mathew Brady ca. 1860), an ex–Congressman from Ohio, pledged loyalty to the Confederacy. Lincoln had him arrested and sent South, banished from the Union.

The dispute over the necessity of the suspension, as well as the president's authority to take that action, was more complex. Based on Lincoln's cited authority, arguments were put forth claiming that his constitutional authority could not be applied in times of civil war, but extended his right to suspension only during "normal conditions" within the country. Even so, the action was justified (despite Justice Taney's opinion) based on the necessity during war. Support of Lincoln's action is based on the rationale that "when war *exists*, and the arrest and detention of even innocent persons are essential to the *success* of military operations, such arrest and detention are lawful and justifiable."[56]

The president's power (or lack of power) extended as well to what to do with slaves in territories captured by Northern forces. Many forces operated on a time-honored tradition that captured "property" was contraband of war. As the South considered slaves to be property, this rationale made sense. However, once taken as contraband—meaning slaves became the "property" of the prevailing Union Army—the next step was to set those slaves free. However, this policy caused problems in border states that had not joined the Confederacy. The act of "field emancipation," as it might be termed, was abruptly halted by Lincoln, arguing that he alone had the power to determine what should be done with the contraband of slaves.

Lincoln's concern with this decision was not one of freedom or continued slavery, but for keeping the peace in those border states. Many were hybrid in nature, having not joined the Confederacy but continuing to legalize slavery. These included Delaware, Maryland, Kentucky, and Missouri. Lincoln's concern was that too liberal an application of the contraband principle could drive these border states to the Confederate side of the war. The events of 1861 regarding disposition of slaves in Southern territories later affected the decision by Lincoln to declare slaves free in the Confederate states. The wording was quite specific, and grew from the difficulty of policies within the border states:

> President Abraham Lincoln issued the Emancipation Proclamation on January 1, 1863, as the nation approached its third year of bloody civil war. The proclamation declared "that all persons held as slaves" within the rebellious states "are, and henceforward shall be free."
>
> Despite this expansive wording, the Emancipation Proclamation was limited in many ways. It applied only to states that had seceded from the Union, leaving slavery untouched in the loyal border states. It also expressly exempted parts of the Confederacy that had already come under Northern control. Most important, the freedom it promised depended upon Union military victory.[57]

Copperhead Editorials on Slavery

The Southern sympathizers in the North were fearful that the real purpose of the war was eventual emancipation of slaves. As war progressed throughout 1861, the vocal opposition to the Union accelerated. The Southern fears had justification, as results later revealed. The concern also extended to Union reliance on black soldiers as part of the war effort. One Copperhead-leaning newspaper editorialized that the Union should consider using black soldiers only if and when white men could not prevail in the war. Giving weapons to slaves, the editorial stated, "is disgraceful to the civilization of the age, and disgraceful to ourselves. The slaves are practically barbarians. Their instincts are those of savages."[58]

Repetitive sentiments were expressed throughout the war years. Some were merely critical of Lincoln and Northern anti-slavery; others played on racial fears. One example was found in 1861 in the *New York*

Freeman's Journal & Catholic Register, inciting racist fears in the North by describing the "beastly doctrine of the intermarriage of black men with white women.... Filthy black niggers, greasy, sweaty, and disgusting, now jostle with white people and even ladies everywhere."[59]

The *New York Times* was similarly willing to incite Northern citizens with editorial rhetoric. Continuing the fear-mongering of 1861, the Times later editorialized:

> We regret to learn from numerous sources that we are on the point of witnessing intermarriage on a grand scale between the whites and blacks of this Republic. It has, as most of our readers are aware, been long held by logicians of the Democratic school, that once you admit the right of a negro to the possession of his own person, and the receipt of his own wages, you are bound either to marry his sister, or give your daughter in marriage to his son. The formula into which this argument has always been thrown was this: If all blacks are fit to be free every white man is bound to marry a black: "Niggers" are blacks: Therefore every white man is bound to marry a "nigger."[60]

The progression of the war over four years is widely documented by historians in terms of battles won or lost, and of public sentiment during the period. However, at the same time, the struggle between Peace Democrats (Copperheads) and War Democrats (those loyal to the Union) continued without pause.

6

The Age of the Copperheads, 1862–1863

The year 1862 was a crucial turning point in the war, both in the fate of slavery and for Abraham Lincoln. Although the president had run on a platform of wanting to prevent the spread of slavery, his position began to change as events moved forward. However, in 1862, another attribute of the overall conflict became apparent. The Civil War was fought over not just one issue, but several. Slavery—and its possible spread westward—was a primary reason for conflict and, over previous decades, the country had not been able to resolve the disagreements about slavery on a moral, social, or economic basis.[1]

An examination of the complexities and causes underlying the conflict reveal that the war was not fought for only one reason. Slavery was one of several aspects of a larger social and economic dispute. The year 1862 was more than a series of battlefield victories and losses. It was the height of Copperhead opposition in the North, and it converted Lincoln and the Republican Party from an anti-secessionist to an anti-slavery policy. The year began the first full year of war, and with this transition in policy, but culminated with the divisive and historically important decision by Lincoln, issuing of the Emancipation Proclamation:

> The nature of the Civil War caused the Union government to shift, from an initial stand of noninterference with state institutions, toward policies of emancipation. As the war efforts of both sides grew to ghastly proportions, questions of constitutional authority gave way to measures on belligerent rights, contraband, confiscation, and Federal compensation. The government did not close its eyes to popular demand or individual actions. To some observers it was one thing to preserve the Union and another thing to emancipate the slaves. To others the preservation of the Union and the abolition of slavery were coterminous with one another.[2]

The debate over slavery, as expressed by Lincoln before the election, was not intended to do away with slavery altogether, but to stop its expansion into newly admitted states. Southern slaveowners saw this view as infringement on their property rights, and believed extinction or containment of slavery would destroy the Southern agrarian economy.[3]

The Evolution of a Struggle: 1862

The initial causes of the Civil War were focused on the singular issue of whether or not slavery would be allowed in new territories. As 1862 began, the complexities of the conflict became clearer and slavery itself became part of a larger set of disputes.

As the pace of battles picked up, this sectionalism of the South became focused. With the primary economics of cotton and tobacco, the South was profoundly different than the North, which over several decades had become industrialized and "modern" in the sense that more people lived in urban settings and worked in factories. In comparison, the South's economic differences further augmented the separation and sectionalism between the two sides. The fact that Lincoln won only in the North and carried no Southern states confirmed the perception that the United States was made up of two separate economies and mindsets. The Southern claim to states' rights included the argument that all states had a right to secede at any time—the Northern states and the federal government disagreed. This was as strong a dispute between North and South as the debate over slavery.

This separation came partly from the lack of need for mechanized technology in the South. Slave labor was cheap. The lack of need led to an attitude of protectionism in the South where free trade was preferred. In the North, however, the manufacturing economy was rudimentary compared to European industry, so Northern business owners favored tariffs on imported goods, including Southern-produced cotton.

The impact of the cotton economy was significant in the South's economic problems during the war. "King Cotton" expressed the South's hopes that Britain and France would ally with the South if cotton exports were stopped. The Union blockade of all Southern ports prevented an estimated 95 percent of all cotton shipments to Europe. However, even though cotton was as crucial in the 19th Century as oil was in the 20th, European world powers did not ally with the South during the Civil War. The blockade worked in choking the Southern economy while the North, with much greater assets, was able to finance its war efforts more successfully.[4]

Economic developments aside, opposition to the Union continued among Northern Democrats. Copperheads became more vocal as 1862 began, finding a voice of dissent and expressing support for the Confederacy cause. The Union cause was called "abolitionist" and pursuing reunification was described as "fanaticism and destructiveness."[5] The Copperhead's argument was based largely on the racial issue, favoring slavery in the South and opposing abolition. The level of discourse increased each time the Union lost a battle, and subsided with Union victories. The year 1862 split major victories between each side. For example, Union forces prevailed in the battles of Fort Donelson, Shiloh, and Antietam, while the Confederacy won the battles of Second Bull Run and Fredericksburg. Copperhead visibility tracked these battlefield trends.

Among their efforts, Copperheads tried to influence politicians in Illinois to pass a new state constitution. The plan was to ensure that pro–Southern Democratic politicians would dominate the state government. The proposal would have removed all military powers from the governor and barred all Negroes from living in the state. The pro–Union politicians prevailed, however, and the Copperhead-controlled plan failed. However, the Copperheads were gaining power and influence through the North, and the events in Illinois proved that support for the Union was not as strong as Lincoln had wished. In several Northern states, Copperheads organized by forming local arms of the Knights of the Golden Circle. These groups at times threatened physical harm to politicians and supporters of the Union.

The problem of Copperhead threats against Union supporters and abolitionist sentiments affected Northern citizens' attitudes toward the war. Contrary to initial enthusiasm and widespread volunteering, by the middle of 1862, the Union found itself short of men volunteering to join the army. In July 1862 Lincoln met with two of his cabinet members, Secretary of State William Seward and Secretary of the Navy Gideon Welles. Lincoln raised the topic of emancipation, primarily as a war measure and with the thought of allowing freed slaves to join the Union Army.[6]

A few days later, Congress passed the Militia Act. This new law specifically provided that black Americans would be allowed to sign up as soldiers. This was a first step toward emancipation, and it certainly was seen in that way among Southern politicians and slaveowners. A concern among Copperheads was that once Confederate territories were seized by Union troops, slaves could be conscripted to fight for the Union. The military advantage of allowing slaves to join the war effort was further justified since slaves were considered as free; thus, defeating the South served the Union's purpose as well as slaves' interests.[7]

Congress debated the proposal of letting black Americans serve in the army or as laborers employed in the war effort. The vote was largely along party lines. In the Senate, 26 Republicans, one Democrat, and one Unionist Party member voted yea. Voting nay were zero Republicans, five Democrats, and four Unionists.

On the same day that Congress passed the Militia Act, they also passed the Second Confiscation Act. The act followed the First Confiscation Act of 1861, permitting the Union to seize property from the Confederacy, including slaves. The 1862 law declared that all slaves held by Confederate forces or in territories were free. The act stated that for anyone committing treason, "all his slaves, if any, shall be declared and made free."[8]

Although the volunteer numbers did not meet Lincoln's goal, the decision to allow black Americans to fight for the Union was not a reflection of diminished support for the cause. For many 19th Century-communities, volunteering was considered an act of patriotism. More than in most wars, during the Civil War large numbers of volunteers enlisted due not only to pressure within the community, but also in response to bounties offered by towns, businesses, and the wealthy. The North had no shortage of soldiers in 1861 or 1862; the decision to increase the ranks with former slaves was also strategic. Conquered areas of the South no longer had slave labor to work the farms while their men were fighting for the Confederacy.[9]

Although this act of Congress is not often mentioned as significant in the time of the Civil War, it was. Combining the Militia Act and Confiscation Act for the first time allowed black Americans to fight alongside white soldiers, and also to work as laborers as part of the war effort. Congress had taken the step of embracing all citizens, including former slaves, in the effort to prevail over the Confederacy. This move has been described as "perhaps the most revolutionary feature of the Civil War."[10]

Copperhead Racism in the North

Many organizations in the North aided draft resistance and published statements opposing Lincoln and the war effort. The KGC was prominent among the Copperhead "secret societies" and, from August 1862 to the end of the year, many arrests of members occurred. Most arrests were of Democrats or newspaper editors sympathetic to the Confederate cause. As a majority of these arrests were of Copperheads, few objections were raised by the majority of Northern citizens, who supported the Union.[11]

Even making statements deemed to discourage voluntary enlistment was considered an act of treason, and this led to many arrests of KGC members and other Copperheads. One arrest in Illinois netted 10 KGC members, including two judges and a minister. Among those arrested, many had political motives, but others were focused on opposition to abolishing slavery:

Samuel H. Bundy [one of those arrested] allegedly said that "the object of the administration was to kill off the people of the South and liberate the slaves." The administration wanted to deprive the South of its rights, he said, citing as evidence the arming of blacks "to cut the throats of the Women & Children in the South." Dr. John M. Clementson ... said that the war's "true object was to liberate the niggers," according to one witness who said they heard both men speak at a barbeque. Nelson, the minster, said the war was brought on to elevate the black race and degrade the white.[12]

The racial distrust and outright bigotry was made more apparent once black freedmen began competing for jobs in Northern states. As the war progressed, this led to increased racial statements by Copperheads. Incidents of physical violence toward black workers were common in 1862. However, such outbursts were not unique to the war years, and had been going on for decades prior.[13]

During this year, Lincoln's attitude, driven in part by Copperhead resistance, gradually turned from his previous position favoring limitations on slavery, to one of abolishing it altogether. The president was aware of growing public support for this position, and recognized that the racially motivated violence was the work of a minority. The Copperheads did not represent the larger public sentiment. Lincoln began discussions with representatives of border states (Delaware, Maryland, Kentucky, and Missouri). Slavery was legal in these states, but none had joined the Confederacy. Lincoln was hoping to arrive at a plan for gradual emancipation and in his discussions with state representatives, several ideas were floated. Lincoln favored resettlement of freed slaves, either to areas of the Caribbean or to Africa. However, these discussions did not lead to any agreement, and talks were broken off in July.[14]

Not all previous or current slaves necessarily wanted to be resettled. The concept of emancipation implied for many the choice to live where they wished. The abolitionist and former slave, Frederick Douglass, wrote in response to Lincoln's resettlement proposal:

> No, Mr. President, it is not the innocent horse that makes the thief, nor the traveler's purse that makes the highway robber, and it is not the presence of the Negro that causes this foul and unnatural war, but the cruel and brutal cupidity of those who wish to possess horses, money, and Negroes by means of theft, robbery, and rebellion.[15]

The failure to reach agreement about gradually ending slavery led Lincoln to the idea of drafting an emancipation proclamation. However, on consultation with his cabinet and especially with Secretary of State William H. Seward, Lincoln held off. He waited for a major Union victory, providing political opportunity to issue a proclamation. In 1862, the war was not going well for the Union, so Lincoln kept his ideas about emancipation to himself.

Lincoln, in relying upon the advice of his Secretary of State, acknowledged the importance of timing of the political and military aspects of his decision. He later explained to artist F. B. Carpenter while having his portrait painted:

> The wisdom of the view of the Secretary of State struck me with great force. It was an aspect of the case that, in all my thought upon the subject, I had entirely overlooked. The result was that I put the draft of the Proclamation aside, as you do your sketch for a picture, waiting for a victory.[16]

During the same period, sentiment was growing in the North that Lincoln had changed his campaign position and now wanted the war to end slavery, not just to limit its spread. Copperheads had always suspected that this was the real agenda for pursuing the war. Northern Democrats argued that Lincoln had no constitutional authority to free Southern slaves. In several Northern states, KGC sects and less organized Copperhead groups began promoting plans for armed resurrection if and when Lincoln tried to declare slaves free.

Among soldiers in the Union Army, opinions were split. Many favored adding the cause of freeing slaves to the reason for the conflict; others had joined up to keep the Union intact and felt betrayed. A New Hampshire sergeant wrote home, "I came out here to fight for the Constitution & laws of our land, and for *nothing* else.... In case of an abolition war—*every* abolitionist should be *compelled* to come out here, and when here to be in the *front rank*—and then we would see how long their love for the Darkies would continue." On the other side, a soldier from Massachusetts wrote, "I think the fight is freedom or slavery. I thank God I have the priverlidge [*sic*] of doing what I can to proclaim freedom to all men, white or black."[17]

Lincoln's Decision: The Emancipation Proclamation

One of the most important battles of the war occurred at Antietam Creek, also known as the Battle of Sharpsburg, Maryland. More casualties occurred on September 17, 1862, than in any other American battle in any conflict, with more than 22,000 dead, missing, and wounded. This was a higher number of casualties than during the entire Revolutionary War.[18]

Lincoln had been waiting for a battlefield victory to announce his proclamation. Antietam, while tactically a draw and not a decisive victory, has been cast in history as a Union victory. The political decision for timing of the proclamation was based on the public knowledge of a significant Union victory:

> Antietam and its immediate aftermath signaled a sharpening of a debate about immediate wartime emancipation and the arming of black soldiers.... Without

something that could be called a victory at Antietam, Lincoln might not have judged that there was sufficient public support to proceed with emancipation.[19]

Lincoln was also troubled at the prospect that European powers might recognize the Confederacy and even offer military aid. Britain, in particular, had considered supporting the Confederacy in the interest of continuing to receive cotton exports. The Emancipation Proclamation and its timing accelerated an anti-slavery movement in Britain, ensuring that no military or diplomatic alliance would be possible. The South had hoped for such an alliance, and one consequence of Lincoln's proclamation was that Britain closed that door.

Pressure on Lincoln to issue a proclamation of general emancipation came from a delegation of Christian groups at least 10 days before publication. They argued to the president that military losses were a sign of God's disapproval of slavery, that Lincoln had the power to remedy the situation, and that it was a Christian responsibility to emancipate the South's slaves.[20]

Five days after Antietam, on September 22, Lincoln published the Emancipation Proclamation. During a cabinet meeting the same day, Lincoln asked his advisors for reactions to the draft of the document. Secretary Seward suggested that the proclamation should "not merely say the government recognizes, but that it will maintain the freedom it proclaims." Other cabinet members agreed and the change was added.[21]

However, the proclamation was worded carefully. Often cited as being a declaration that all slaves were free, it was not as broad. It declared slaves in Confederate states free, but did not free slaves held in border states or in the areas occupied at the time by Union forces.

The text of the preliminary Emancipation Proclamation included a provision calling upon Congress

to again recommend the adoption of a practical measure tendering pecuniary aid to the free acceptance or rejection of all slave States, so called, the people whereof may not then be in rebellion against the United States and which States may then have voluntarily adopted, or thereafter may voluntarily adopt, immediate or gradual abolishment of slavery within their respective limits; and that the effort to colonize persons of African descent, with their consent, upon this continent, or elsewhere, with the previously obtained consent of the Governments existing there, will be continued.... All slaves of persons who shall hereafter be engaged in rebellion against the government of the United States, or who shall in any way give aid or comfort thereto, escaping from such persons and taking refuge within the lines of the army; and all slaves captured from such persons or deserted by them and coming under the control of the government of the United States; and all slaves of such persons found on [or] being within any place occupied by rebel forces and afterwards occupied by the forces of the United States, shall be deemed captives of war, and shall be forever free of their servitude and not again held as slaves.... No slave escaping into any State, Territory, or the District of Columbia, from any other

State, shall be delivered up, or in any way impeded or hindered of his liberty, except for crime, or some offence against the laws, unless the person claiming said fugitive shall first make oath that the person to whom the labor or service of such fugitive is alleged to be due is his lawful owner, and has not borne arms against the United States in the present rebellion, nor in any way given aid and comfort thereto; and no person engaged in the military or naval service of the United States shall, under any pretence [sic] whatever, assume to decide on the validity of the claim of any person to the service or labor of any other person, or surrender up any such person to the claimant, on pain of being dismissed from the service.[22]

The exclusion of the terms applied to slaves in border states or in the areas of Virginia, Tennessee, and Louisiana. This exclusion was based on the legal argument that the proclamation was allowed only by Lincoln's war powers.

Consequently, the Emancipation Proclamation did not free a single slave.

Despite its limitations, the proclamation became the focus of a growing emancipation movement. Lincoln had entered his presidency and the war intending to hold the Union together. The Emancipation Proclamation was a turning point, in which the Union's goal was to end slavery completely and in all states. It led, eventually, to support for the 13th Amendment and its passage before the end of the war.

The proclamation was to be finalized and take effect as of January 1, 1863. However, before that would occur, Northern state governors met and expressed support for Lincoln and his aim in ending slavery. The Loyal War Governors' Conference was held in Altoona, Pennsylvania, on September 24–25, 1862. Twenty-one state governors from Union states met to discuss the war's progress, support for the president, and most of all, the Emancipation Proclamation. The result of this conference was a vote of 16–5 in support for Lincoln. Given the controversy of the proclamation, this expression of support was welcomed by the president.[23]

The significance of the conference has been overlooked by many historians. However, some have speculated that the timing of his issuing the Emancipation Proclamation was affected directly by concern over what outcome the attending governors might vote, as well as increasing Copperhead writings. One historian wrote that "in Lincoln's desk the Emancipation Proclamation would probably have remained had it not been for the increased activities of the Radicals and a new move from the governors."[24]

The speculation concerning timing of Lincoln's release of the famous proclamation and the meeting of Northern governors is not a certainty. At the time, the proclamation was accepted as a war measure and not as a political move or one timed to affect how the Northern governors might vote.

Reaction in the press was largely positive in the North, at times even excessively rhetorical in its praise. For example, one editorial called the proclamation "the most far-reaching document ever issued by the Government and its wisdom and necessity are indisputable."[25] Two days after the proclamation was made public, an editorial by Joseph Medill appeared in a newspaper that had been among the strongest supporters of abolition:

> The President has set his hand and affixed the great seal to the grandest proclamation ever issued by man... From this proclamation begins the history of the Republic, as our Fathers designed to have it—let no one think to stay the glorious reformation.[26]

On the same day, editor Horace Greeley wrote that the proclamation not only freed four million blacks from slavery, but also 20 million whites.[27]

Despite strong support from Union governors and many newspapers, the Emancipation Proclamation was not hailed universally as a positive step. While it galvanized Republican support, Copperheads were angered at the publication of the document and its significance. Despite resistance among Copperheads, approximately 190,000 black men volunteered for the Union Army, vastly increasing Union fighting strength. The refusal in the Confederacy to recruit and arm slaves placed them at a great disadvantage not only in the military sense, but also in world opinion. This was especially significant considering that the Emancipation Proclamation declared more than four million slaves to be free.[28]

Copperhead Reaction

The negative responses to the Emancipation Proclamation occurred immediately. For example, a week after publication, one newspaper wrote:

> We protest against this proclamation, in the name of the constitution, in behalf of good faith to

Horace Greeley. Newspaper editor Horace Greely noted that the Emancipation Proclamation freed not only four million blacks from slavery, but also 20 million whites.

the conservative millions of the northern and border states, and for the sake of the only means by which it has at any time been possible to restore the Union. We protest against it as a monstrous usurpation, a criminal wrong, and an act of national suicide.[29]

This was a mild response compared to many others:

A Circleville, Ohio, newspaper went so far as to urge that abolitionists be hanged "till the flesh rot off their bones and the winds of Heaven whistle Yankee Doodle through their loathsome skelitonz.... It is a pity that there is not more tormenting hell than that kept by Beelzebub for such abolitionist fiends." Horatio Seymour, running for governor of New York, denounced the proclamation as "a proposal for the butchery of women and children, for scenes of lust and rapine, and of arson and murder, which would invoke the interference of civilized Europe."[30]

Northern newspapers were by no means universal in their praise of the Emancipation Proclamation. One editorial posed the rhetorical question: "What interest has commerce in prosecuting a war upon such destructive and revolutionary principles?"[31] Copperheads also used the term "white supremacy" in arguments again the proclamation. They argued that the consequence would be a black invasion of the North.[32] An editorial in a New York paper stated, "This fools cap thunder would add 300,000 men to the rebel armies, and bring 30,000 Kentuckians to the side of Bragg. It is grandscale bunkum, swaggering bravado, which, alas! converted a war for the Constitution into a war against Southern rights and liberties."[33]

Many stories circulated as well about possible insurrection among freed slaves to the proclamation and responses from white citizens. One report from Amesville, Virginia, stated that

the white people of that region are in great terror of a slave revolt. Seventeen Negroes, most of them free, have been arrested on suspicion of being engaged in plotting an uprising of the entire Negro population. Copies of newspapers that printed President Lincoln's Emancipation Proclamation were found in their possession. All the Negroes know that such a proclamation has been made, and this terrorizes the whites. The seventeen Negroes have been taken to Amesville and lynched.[34]

Southern fears of an uprising were matched by Copperhead reactions. Copperheads, who for months had been suspicious of Lincoln and his motives for continuing the war, now pointed to the proclamation as proof that they had been right. No longer was this a war to hold together the Union and prevent secession, but rather a war for abolition and emancipation of the slaves. The Copperhead argument was centered on the claim that Northern white men and boys were dying on the battlefield to help Negroes, and this had been Lincoln's purpose all along. Lincoln's timing was a war measure, and Democrats in Union states, including those supporting Lincoln, were broadly opposed to the proclamation.

The debate over emancipation brought out the pro-slavery positions not only of Copperheads but also of those supporting Lincoln, the so-called War Democrats. The debate ended up splitting the party for years to come, centered on the question: "Shall we sustain the President, or is a revolution necessary?"[35]

Southern newspapers were in agreement with Northern anti–Lincoln editorials. One paper printed the full text of the proclamation, describing it as "a call for the insurrection of four million slaves, and the inauguration of a reign of hell upon earth."[36] Another paper in Richmond called the proclamation the "last extremity of wickedness," continuing that "Lincoln has crowned the pyramid of his infamies with an atrocity abhorred of men, and at which even demons should shudder." The piece concluded, describing the president as being "as black of soul as the vilest of the train whose behest he is obeying. So far as he can do he has devoted himself to the direst destruction that can befall a people." The following day, the paper went further, asking about Lincoln: "What shall we call him? ... coward, assassin, savage, murderer of women and babies: Or shall we consider them all as embodied in the word fiend, and call him Lincoln, The Fiend?"[37]

Reaction to the proclamation was widespread, not only among citizens and newspaper editors, but also politicians. In the election of 1862, Northern Democrats gained 32 seats in the House of Representatives (including those from Lincoln's home state of Illinois). Predictions, even among Republicans, cited the proclamation as evidence that Lincoln was a disaster for the party and that events would inevitably lead to the end of the abolition movement. However, even the Democratic gains in the House were small compared to larger gains for Republicans in California, Michigan, and Iowa, resulting in the party holding onto a majority of 101 to 81. In Iowa, Missouri, and Kansas, emancipation was a focus among voters, and in all three states, Republicans prevailed.[38]

The Democratic victories were close in most of their gains and, in the same election, Republicans added five Senate seats. Overall, the negative outcomes for Republicans were more than offset by positive gains, demonstrating a general mood of support for the war effort in Northern states. The strong support was expressed in editorials a week after the election, in one case referring to those not backing the president and his policies as "domestic traitors."[39]

In a lead-up to the election, Copperhead sentiments throughout the North were best expressed in the Democratic Party theme: "Every white laboring man in the North who does not want to be swapped off for a free nigger should vote the Democratic ticket."[40]

Copperhead opposition to the war and reaction to the Emancipation

Proclamation backfired immediately, as well as for many years after. Many Northern Democrats, loyal to the war effort, shifted their party affiliation. Copperheads came to be seen in negative terms, especially among enlisted men fighting for the Union. One soldier wrote: "It is a common saying here that if we are whipped, it will be by Northern votes, not by Southern bullets."[41]

Focusing on continued controversy in the North, Copperheads chose to ignore the reality that for the most part, support for the cause was solid. Bizarre plans were hatched in some areas, including a proposal to organize guerrilla warfare in the North against Washington and a plan to somehow gain alliances for the Confederacy with France and England. This would mean the Union would have to fight not only the Confederacy, but Europe as well. This plan ignored the shift in European sentiment in support of Lincoln following publication of the Emancipation Proclamation.

The error made by Copperheads was in assuming that Confederate battlefield victories in late 1862 would translate to a shift in Northern sentiment. In all instances when war goes poorly, citizens on the losing side tend to complain; this does not mean their loyalties go over to the other side. The wishful thinking among Copperheads blinded them to this reality.

Even so, battlefield wins for the Union silenced Copperheads for the moment, but Confederate wins led to greater and more vocal complaints. The December 13, 1862, attack by Union forces on Fredericksburg, Virginia, was a disaster for the Union, with 12,653 killed, wounded, and captured soldiers.[42] General Lee's Confederate forces prevailed, losing just 5,377 soldiers.[43] Response in editorials, not only to the battle's outcome but also to Lincoln's replacement of General McClennan a month prior, reflected the Copperhead sentiment in starkly racial terms, asking, could Lincoln

> ever make atonement for his unaccountable blunder? ... [to] satisfy the fanaticism of that herd who have pestered him since the election—the herd inflicted with the disease called "Nigger on the brain."[44]

Criticism in editorials and among soldiers was matched with jubilation in the South, where the Battle of Fredericksburg was taken as a sign that the Confederacy would prevail. The last part of 1862 had not gone well for the Union on the battlefield; in the North Copperheads became optimistic that Lincoln's war was doomed to fail and the South would have a final victory. The outcome was described as a "stunning defeat for the invader, a splendid victory to the defender of the sacred soil."[45]

As the year came to an end, Lincoln met with his cabinet to finalize the proclamation for publication on January 1. Each cabinet member was provided with a preliminary draft and invited to comment or suggest changes. On December 31, Lincoln rewrote the final version, including several changes cabinet members had offered. On the same day, the president signed a bill admitting West Virginia as a new state, having broken with Virginia. The effective date for admission was selected as June 20 of the following year.

As the year ended, the Confederacy was in dread of the possibility of a slave revolt. The belief among slaveowners persisted that Negroes were best controlled under the system of slavery, believing that freedom would lead to widespread chaos. The Confederate leadership became more resolved than ever to continue their fight, believing that the North was intent on destroying the white culture of the South by freeing the slaves.[46]

The South's greatest fear—loss of control over its large slave population—came into reality on January 1, 1863, when Lincoln signed the final version of the Emancipation Proclamation. Expanding on the preliminary declaration, the final version included the following language:

> Now, therefore I, Abraham Lincoln, President of the United States, by virtue of the power in me vested as Commander-in-Chief, of the Army and Navy of the United States in time of actual armed rebellion against the authority and government of the United States, and as a fit and necessary war measure for suppressing said rebellion, do, on this first day of January, in the year of our Lord one thousand eight hundred and sixty-three, and in accordance with my purpose so to do publicly proclaimed for the full period of one hundred days, from the day first above mentioned, order and designate as the States and parts of States wherein the people thereof respectively, are this day in rebellion against the United States, the following, to wit: Arkansas, Texas, Louisiana (except the Parishes of St. Bernard, Plaquemines, Jefferson, St. John, St. Charles, St. James Ascension, Assumption, Terrebonne, Lafourche, St. Mary, St. Martin, and Orleans, including the City of New Orleans), Mississippi, Alabama, Florida, Georgia, South Carolina, North Carolina, and Virginia (except the forty-eight counties designated as West Virginia, and also the counties of Berkley, Accomac, Northampton, Elizabeth City, York, Princess Ann, and Norfolk, including the cities of Norfolk and Portsmouth), and which excepted parts, are for the present, left precisely as if this proclamation were not issued. And by virtue of the power, and for the purpose aforesaid, I do order and declare that all persons held as slaves within said designated States, and parts of States, are, and henceforward shall be free; and that the Executive government of the United States, including the military and naval authorities thereof, will recognize and maintain the freedom of said persons.[47]

The Copperhead Response

Response was immediate. The anti–Lincoln press was especially vicious and racist in its ridicule of Lincoln and the Proclamation. One

Washington, D.C.–based publication held to their "initial interpretation that the Proclamation was of no use" and that "the proponents of slavery have nothing to complain of, as the final edict is powerless to destroy slavery outside the range of the Union Armies."[48]

Another Northern paper cited Clement Vallandigham, Ohio politician and acknowledged leader of the Copperhead Democrats in that state:

> The views of Vallandigham and the anti-war editors were underwritten by scores of local mass meetings and county conventions of the Democratic party. At one of the mass meetings which was held at Springfield, Illinois, the Democrats resolved that the Emancipation Proclamation was as unwarranted in military as in civil law; and that it was a gigantic usurpation, converting the war, properly begun for the vindication of the authority of the Constitution, into a crusade for the liberation of three million Negro slaves. Such a result, they said, would overthrow the Union and revolutionize the social organization of the Southern states.[49]

Resorting to alarmist urban myths, some papers wrote of unexpected outcomes for freed slaves. One tale was of "two Negro boys" who fled from slavery once the Proclamation was issued. However, the story continued, "the Yankees cut off the ears of the colored youths who did finally make an escape back to their master's plantation."[50]

Northern Copperhead reactions focused not only on Lincoln and the Proclamation, but also on negative messaging aimed toward the black population:

> The Democratic press continually reiterated its message of racism, concentrating especially on what they perceived as Negro cowardliness, stupidity and general worthlessness. This was done to reinforce in the minds of its readers their point that emancipation was a great blunder and to instill a distrust of Republican plans for future race relations that were based upon blacks being given greater rights and freedoms.[51]

The racist publications of the Northern Copperhead press were unrelenting. One Pennsylvania paper published lyrics for a song, to be sung to the music of an American folk tune of the day, "Wait for the Wagon."[52] In the newspaper parody, the song was renamed "Fight for the Nigger" and included the lyrics:

> I calculate of darkies we soon shall have our fill,
> With Abe's proclamation and the Nigger Army bill:
> Who would not be a soldier for the Union to fight?
> Now, Abe's made the nigger the equal of the white.
>> Fight for the nigger,
>> The sweet-scented nigger,
>> The woolly headed nigger,
>> And the abolition crew.[53]

Song parodies were favored among Northern Democratic publications. Another example:

> "De Union!" used to be de cry—
> For dat we went it strong
> But now the motto seems to be
> "De nigger, right or wrong!?"[54]

Fighting men in the Union Army were both troubled and disheartened. Some wrote home that morale had been high when they were fighting for the Union, but the sentiment of one soldier expressed the sentiment of many: "We have never been successful since the Emancipation Proclamation."[55]

Though the low morale was not permanent, neither was it universal. Many found a new source of pride and patriotism in gaining a new cause: freedom for all citizens, white and black. Many soldiers wrote home and used the word "freedom" as their cause for fighting. Copperheads in the North cited the disgruntled soldier as a new reason to criticize the war effort. Their criticism combined constitutional arguments with outright and heightened appeals to racism. They encouraged talk of dissent, including passing rumors of further secession in the Northwestern areas of the country. This idea of a "Northern Confederacy" had appeal among those Copperhead Democrats who wanted to see the Union split, but no serious second secession movement ever took hold outside of the South.

The Intellectual Arm of the Copperheads

The Copperhead movement is most readily associated with rhetoric against emancipation, and equally against Lincoln's policies. However, that racism often was masked in constitutional arguments and even in an attempt to elevate the debate to an intellectual level.

On February 9, 1863, famous telegraph investor Samuel Morse, along with other politically-minded men, met and formed the Society for the Diffusion of Political Knowledge. Other founding members included August Belmont, Samuel Tilden, Charles Mason, George T. Curtis, Manton Marble, and William C. Prime. Attempting to develop sensible arguments opposing Lincoln and the war, and supporting the institution of slavery, the organization deteriorated over time, becoming as racist as the larger Copperhead movement:

> Although the group initially set an intellectual tone in its pamphlets, the society had abandoned the high ground by 1864, when it was reprinting speeches as vituperative as anything else coming off the Copperhead presses.[56]

Morse, as spokesman for this "intellectual" version of the Copperheads, explained his beliefs during the war in a pamphlet published by his organization. He wrote:

> My creed on the subject of slavery is short. Slavery *per se* is not sin. It is a social condition ordained from the beginning of the world for the wisest purposes, benevolent and disciplinary, by Divine Wisdom. The mere holding of slaves, therefore, is a condition having *per se* nothing of moral character in it, any more than the being a parent, or employer, or ruler, but is moral or immoral as the duties of the relation of master, parent, employer or ruler are rightly used or abused.[57]

Samuel Morse. Samuel Morse (photographed ca. 1860), inventor of the telegraph, was an active supporter of the South and of slavery.

Morse was not a stranger to politics. As early as 1835, he had made a run for mayor of New York City on the Nativist ticket, whose primary position was as an opposition movement to immigration, Catholics, and abolitionists, which he called a form of "outside agitation." Morse's beliefs were further documented in a rationalizing of slavery as a positive force in the world:

> Are there not in this relation [of master to slave], when faithfully carried out according to Divine directions, some of the most beautiful examples of domestic happiness and contentment that this fallen world knows? Protection and judicious guidance and careful provision on the one part; cheerful obedience, affection and confidence on the other.
>
> Christianity has been most successfully propagated among a barbarous race, when they have been enslaved to a Christian race. Slavery to them has been Salvation, and Freedom, ruin.[58]

Morse cited Christianity in support of slavery, and wrote that opposing slavery was sacrilege against God's will. However, despite the failed attempt to create an intellectual rationalization for pro-slavery thought, the tide was turning against the Northern Democrats.

Pro-Lincoln Responses

The racism displayed in Copperhead writings, including the claimed intellectual arm of the Democratic Party led by Morse, created a backlash that worked against them. The intended support based on racial fear-mongering instead created a wave of denunciations by politicians, Unionist citizens, soldiers, and the pro–Union press. Among members of the army fighting for the Union, a sense was developing that by speaking out against the cause of the war, Copperheads were only prolonging the suffering. Many fighting men bitterly complained that the Copperhead arguments were identical to those of the Confederacy. The actions of Copperheads, perceived as harming soldiers, turned army sentiment largely pro–Union. This was true not only for those in favor of emancipation, but even among soldiers motivated to hold the Union intact. Copperhead actions were widely seen in the army as unpatriotic.

Many wrote letters home and talked about fellow soldiers' desire to return home and fight, or even kill, one or more Copperheads. Some believed the anti-war Democrats should be tried on charges of treason, and executed. One wrote that "it will not be safe for them to show their faces when the union patriots get back."[59]

The strongly held political beliefs among soldiers demonstrated that the conflict was not merely regional or cultural, and was not solely based on support for emancipation. Political activism was expressed by soldiers in the Union Army, many of whom were under the age of 26, despite limited education and agricultural backgrounds:

> Most of the Union Army was made up of young white men born in North America. Although soldiers generally ranged in age from 18 to 45, boys as young as 12 often served as cavalry buglers or drummer boys, and some men in their fifties and sixties enlisted as privates. Most of the Union soldiers were under 30.[60]

Even so, the political interest expressed by Union soldiers grew from a larger sense of the need to conform to the laws of the United States, and to resist secession as contrary to those ideals. As a result, soldiers—even those with limited education and exposure to the world of politics—tended to think of politics as a forum for resolving differences. Closely related to this was the idea that armed conflict becomes necessary to enforce the law when, for example, a part of the nation decides to split and form a separate country. Much has been written, even in modern times, asking about the root causes of the Civil War. One answer to this question is rooted in the political mindset in the North, more so than in the South:

To understand why war came we must first look not at secession but at the Northern response to it. In that response ... the concept of law and order loomed large. The concept is a complex one, contemporary political rhetoric notwithstanding. The order of a society depends on maintaining an enduring consensus about a people's fundamental goals and beliefs and hence on the success of the institutions created to secure this consensus.[61]

However, while many soldiers understood the war in terms of law and order, they were not as inclined to readily accept newly recruited black soldiers among their ranks. Having black soldiers among them for nearly a full year, some soldiers did not agree with the president's belief that black men were a significant, untapped resource for the war effort.[62]

Copperheads also argued that an aspect of emancipation was that the military service of former slaves would lead to demands for equality in civilian life. They presented many arguments to support their opposition to black fighting men, including the argument that they lacked the courage required of a military man. Some even cited Christian principles as reason to keep blacks out of the army: "If ever the Anglo Saxon American citizen forsake their manhood so far as to come on a level with the 'American citizen of African descent,' we will deserve to be forsaken by our Maker forever."[63]

Taking arguments even further, some newspapers editorialized about black conscription leading inevitably to a time when Negro women would be able to have white matrons and young, white virgins to perform their tasks as servants. This appeal to racial fears had no effect in the North, and despite the Copperhead appeal to their fellow citizens, few took the prediction seriously.

The Enrollment Act

Black conscription was not enough to fill the gap in Union enlistment. Men drafted in 1862 were coming to the end of their conscription period, and the original volunteers of 1861 had been fighting for two years. On March 3, 1863, Lincoln signed the Enrollment Act (also called the Civil War Military Draft Act) after the legislation passed in Congress. The new act created a draft requiring all able-bodied men between the ages of 20 and 45 to be available for drafting into the army.

Reaction to the new law turned violent. The New York Draft Riots extended from July 13 to 16, 1863, in Manhattan, and were the largest instance of civil unrest in United States history. President Lincoln dispatched several regiments from the army and additional volunteer troops to reestablish order.[64]

The riots were not simply out of objection to the draft, but out of resentment that wealthy men could avoid the draft by paying a "commutation fee" and hire a substitute to go in their place. A slogan evolved from this practice: "Rich man's war, poor man's fight." The rioters, mainly Irish working men, quickly turned their anger toward black citizens and the anti-draft riots turned into race riots. In addition to killing 120 people, the rioters destroyed several public buildings, Protestant churches, and the Colored Orphan Asylum in Midtown.[65]

One political cartoon of the day shows a wealthy man telling his companion, "Ah! Dearest Addie! I've succeeded. I've got a Substitute." Addie replies, "Have you? What a curious coincidence! And *I* have found one for YOU!"

Opposition to the Enrollment Act also arose in Congress among Copperhead elected officials. Samuel S. Cox (D–OH) attempted to add an amendment to the Enrollment Act by limiting the draft to white citizens only. However, this amendment failed.[66] Clement Vallandigham of Ohio said in the House that the Enrollment Act was meant "for coercion, invasion, and the abolition of negro slavery by force."[67] Democrat senator James A. Bayard of Delaware protested that the law was unconstitutional. He spoke in the Senate:

> I differ from honorable Senators as to what constitutes the life of the nation. In my judgment, the life of a free people consists in the preservation of their liberties, not in the extent of their dominion.[68]

The draft itself was far from successful. To encouragement voluntary compliance, the government offered a bounty in some areas. This led to a rush of "bounty jumping." Poorer men would accept payment to serve, enlist and claim the bounty, and then depart without showing up at the appointed date of muster. Some repeated the process many times, moving from one city to another.[69]

The numbers were less than satisfying for Lincoln's government. Draft dodging was widespread in 1863 and beyond, with an average of 20 percent of those drafted never appearing as ordered. In addition to simply not showing up, some cut off fingers or toes to make themselves ineligible. Many others moved to Canada, creating an immigration problem there. When the number of individuals who paid commutation or substitution fees to avoid serving is added to the number of draft dodgers, only 60 percent of draftees actually served. Of 76,829 called, only 46,347 men responded and became soldiers.[70]

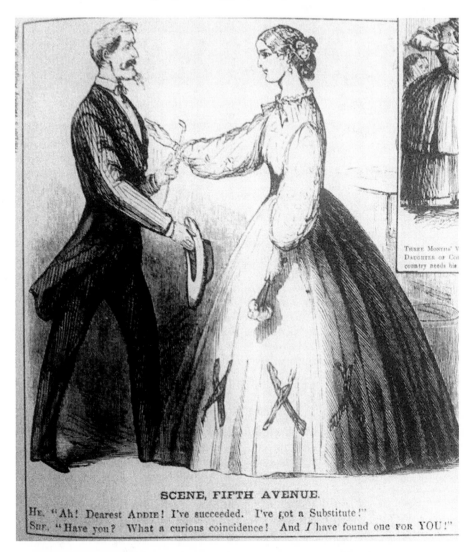

SCENE, FIFTH AVENUE.

He. "Ah! Dearest Addie! I've succeeded. I've got a Substitute!"

She. "Have you? What a curious coincidence! And *I* have found one for YOU!"

Wealthy Northern men were able to buy their way out of military service by paying substitutes. This cartoon shows a young man stating, "I've got a substitute!" to which his fiancée replies, "And *I* have found one for YOU!"

Since 1862, the Union had been actively recruiting former or escaped slaves into the Union Army. Ultimately, over 180,000 former or escaped slaves joined. In one editorial cartoon of the day, Lincoln is seen handing a weapon to a black man, saying, "Why I du declare it's my dear old friend Sambo! Course you'll fight for us, Sambo. Lend us a hand, old Hoss, du."

ONE GOOD TURN DESERVES ANOTHER.

Ab Old Abe   "WHY I DU DECLARE IT'S MY DEAR OLD FRIEND SAMBO! COURSE YOU'LL FIGHT
FOR US, SAMBO. LEND US A HAND, OLD HOSS, DU!"—*London Punch.*

"One Good Turn Deserves Another" (1862, a few months before the Emancipation Proclamation). An estimated 180,000 former slaves joined the Union Army between 1862 and 1865.

Growing Copperhead Strength

The Emancipation Proclamation had led to momentum in the Copperhead movement. Adding to this momentum was a series of battles won by the Confederacy and a Congressional bill allowing the president to suspend *habeas corpus*. The new law allowed the arrest and confinement of political opponents, editors, accused traitors, and others sympathetic to the South. This war measure was used by Copperheads to accuse Lincoln of violating the Constitution. There was some basis for this belief:

> Some individuals who were seized and incarcerated had obviously aided the Confederacy, but others appeared merely to have the administration's conduct of the war. Concern aroused by such prosecutions mounted when the government sanctioned trial by military commissions in noncombat areas. Because Democrats were subjected to such procedures, many party members concluded that the Republicans intended to stamp out all forms of opposition, whether loyal or disloyal.[71]

Among the prominent Copperhead political leadership was Clement Vallandigham, Ohio Democrat and vocal opponent of Lincoln and the Union cause. He had lost a reelection bid to Congress in the election of 1862, and, upon his return to Dayton in 1863, he continued anti-war speeches. At this point, the power of the suspension of *habeas corpus* came into play. General Ambrose Burnside, Union Commander of the Army of Ohio, responded by issuing a general order on April 13 declaring that anyone accused of treason against the Union was subject to immediate arrest and trial. Vallandigham pointed to Burnside's order as a violation of the First Amendment, and, in response, Burnside had him arrested. He was sentenced to military prison for the duration of the war, making him a Copperhead martyr. Lincoln subsequently had Vallandigham released and banished to the Confederacy.[72]

Reaction to the entire matter brought many to the defense of the Copperheads. One paper wrote that "if the people cannot discuss public measures, hear speeches, read such papers and documents as they desire, then all idea of a republican form of government is at an end."[73] From prison and prior to his exile, Vallandigham added to the controversy by writing to fellow Copperheads and editors. Well-organized Copperhead protests followed and the controversy led to Lincoln's explaining his actions as necessary in times of war, further justifying Vallandigham's arrest, explaining that in the interest of public safety, certain actions (including arrest) were justified which, in times of peace, would not be constitutional.

Although Vallandigham saw himself as a Copperhead martyr, when

Lincoln banished him to the Confederacy, it turned out that the South did not want to take him either. The Union Army reacted by placing their prisoner at a rebel camp near Murfreesboro, Tennessee. Vallandigham was exiled to Canada after rejection by both North and South. He spent the remainder of the war in Windsor, Ontario. Now a political problem for the North and distrusted in the South, Vallandigham had lost credibility, but his experiences encouraged other Copperhead factions in the North to continue protesting what they considered the government's illegal actions, including the Emancipation Proclamation, suspension of *habeas corpus*, and the arrest of dissenters.

The vocal opposition by Vallandigham and other Copperheads was accompanied by a series of battlefield casualties. General Lee defeated General Joseph Hooker at Chancellorsville. The loss was described by one New Jersey Copperhead newspaper:

> The Army of the Potomac has suffered another dreadful reverse.... [Pray to God to] stop the dreadful carnage and the inhuman merciless butchery which is desolating the land and disgracing civilization.[74]

In the same year, the Union prevailed at Vicksburg and Gettysburg, but the number of killed and wounded for the year was troubling. Although the Union armies won at Vicksburg and Gettysburg, these victories, combined with Chancellorsville, resulted in combined Union and Confederate casualties of nearly 116,500.[75] The Vicksburg win for Grant and the fall of Port Hudson that followed a few days later gave the Union a tremendous advantage: Mississippi was now in control of the North from Minnesota to New Orleans. This significantly improved the strategic map for the Union.

Despite the advantage newly gained by the Union, battlefield losses were seized upon by the Copperhead press and politicians to point out the flaws in Lincoln's war effort. Even so, the tide of public opinion, as well as opinion in the Union Army, changed during 1863. With black soldiers now serving alongside whites, the gradual approval of a fight for emancipation was a stark opposite of the Copperhead effort to discourage the Union cause.

Among Northern Democrats, not all agreed with the Copperhead agenda. However, many so-called Peace Democrats—those opposed to the Union's war effort—nonetheless supported soldiers fighting for the Union. In this less racist and less vocal group of Democrats, a voice emerged encouraging an armistice in the fighting, after which a peace conference should take place, including negotiating concessions made to the South. This was interpreted as agreeing to continue allowing slavery to be practiced.[76]

A Change in Sentiment

In the Union Army ranks, many soldiers once in favor of fighting for the Union but opposed to fighting to end slavery began to view the cause in a favorable light. Tensions developed between fighting men and friends or families at home, some of whom agreed with the Copperhead message in opposition to the war effort, as well as to emancipation. Soldiers, facing the threat of death or disease, resented the Copperheads and their message. They also believed Copperhead politicians offered vocal criticism without any risk of physical harm. This fed the growing resentment of fighting men toward the Copperhead effort.

The Emancipation Proclamation had stirred the Copperheads at the beginning of the year, but the Enrollment Act created widespread chaos. Many anti-war men eligible for the draft were particularly opposed to fighting to preserve the Union. The emigrating of many to Canada, paying of others to take their place, rioting and violent opposition, or simply dodging the draft were among the responses from the Copperhead Democrats in 1863. This resistance, paired with the war and the political aspects surrounding it, made the year a high point of unhappiness.

Resistance to the draft was especially strong in Ohio and Indiana, where enrollment officers were threatened and subjected to violence when they attempted to sign up drafted men. In Ohio, the conflict was so severe that 400 soldiers were sent into Holmes County, Ohio, after assaults and threats made it impossible to enforce the law.[77] In Indiana, enrollment officers were killed in several counties, ambushed by Copperhead draft resisters, who also formed militia groups to resist through armed conflict if necessary. They threatened confrontation if the government sent in soldiers to protect enrollment officers and other officials.

Consequently, many enrollment officers who had been threatened and assaulted resigned in fear for their lives, rather than face further harm. Attempts to replace them often met with refusal to serve as enrollment officers, because the violent reaction was well known. The deaths, assaults, and destruction of property made enrollment dangerous for those attempting to enforce the law. The need to send in soldiers to protect marshals and officers also took men away from the front lines, damaging the war effort. The Copperhead resistance was succeeding in this way, but it cost lives and, quite possibly, prolonged the war by encouraging the Confederacy. The anti-draft incidents encouraged many in the South to believe the Union did not have the heart to continue the war for much longer, despite the important battlefield victories the North had won during the year.

The Northern anti-draft and anti-emancipation efforts made by Copperheads were complicated by economic concerns. Copperheads continuously aggravated fears of unskilled Northern workers, claiming that emancipation would translate to a loss of jobs among the white population, who would be replaced by a large influx of new black workers. The Copperhead message was aimed at reminding low-skilled white workers that emancipation would lead to their being replaced.[78]

This led to the largest urban riots in U.S. history in New York City. The issues combined sentiment about the war in general, emancipation, the Enrollment Act, and economic fears:

> The New York draft riots of July, 1863, had their origin largely in a fear of black labor competition which possessed the city's Irish unskilled workers. Upon eman-

New York draft riots (1862, *The Illustrated London News*). Draft opposition included a racial element. In New York, Irish workers believed the draft was unfairly imposed on lower classes while the wealthy escaped service.

cipation, they believed, great numbers of Negroes would cross the Mason-Dixon line, underbid them in the Northern labor market, and deprive them of jobs.[79]

The conflict, combining the elements of wealthy versus poor, black versus white, and Union versus Confederacy, led to days of anarchy and violence. Black citizens of the city were convenient victims of the rage; many were murdered and their property burned. Many of those Irish workers believed not only that blacks were a threat, but also that the draft was aimed at lower classes while excluding the wealthy from service.[80]

By the end of the riots, the anti-draft sentiment had devolved into one of plunder and theft, and then outright racial attacks. Witnesses described the rioters as having "expressed themselves Democrats, believing this land is for white men & saying negroes shall not divide it with them."[81]

The riots finally died down, but only after soldiers were sent in from Pennsylvania and New Jersey to patrol the streets. The federal government feared that riots would spread to other cities and states. Many did occur, but were quelled immediately with participation of federal troops. To many, however, it began to seem that the real threat to the Union was not the Confederacy, but the Copperhead movement and its incitement of anti-black and anti-draft demonstrations and riots. The New York riots had the effect of strengthening Union sentiment against the Copperheads.

Resistance also took place on the political front. Copperhead candidates had run in 1862 with a view of building an anti-war coalition, but for the most part they were soundly defeated. Even so, the political opposition and impatience with the extent of what many believed would be a short war added to the Copperhead cause. The significant Union victories at Gettysburg and Vicksburg changed the minds of many, who began to believe the South could no longer sustain their war effort. The people of the North believed the war would end in the following year, 1864.

7

Copperhead Resistance, 1864–1865

The racial component of opposition between the two sides (Republican Unionists and so-called War Democrats on one side, Copperheads, also called Peace Democrats, on the other) defined the political conflict. In 1864, this conflict accelerated with the approaching national election. Some "Radical Republicans" hoped to replace Lincoln on the Republican ticket, while Democrats hoped for a victory that would lead to peace, meaning allowing the South to secede and keep the institution of slavery alive.

Possible Replacement Candidates for Lincoln

Two candidates emerged on the Republican side as possible replacements for Lincoln, but both failed to build momentum and, instead, destroyed their own chances through poor decisions and a general lack of enthusiasm for their efforts.

First was Salmon Chase, Lincoln's Secretary of the Treasury and one of the founders of the Republican Party. He had sought the Republican nomination in 1860 along with several others. Chase had a group of supporters for his nomination in 1864 as replacement for Lincoln. These "Radical Republicans" organized the writing and distribution of two pamphlets, both critical of the Lincoln administration and its conduct of the war and supporting Chase as a replacement nominee. The first was printed by Senator John Sherman, Republican from Ohio and brother of General William T. Sherman. This backfired badly. Many fellow Republicans saw it as inappropriate for a sitting senator to be directly involved in campaigning. Others saw the effort as a Copperhead plot. Sherman, upon hearing the negative response, distanced himself from the movement and referred top distribution of the pamphlet as a "fraudulent design" or possibly merely a mistake.[1]

The second pamphlet was distributed in February 1864. It was entitled the "Pomeroy Circular," named for one of its signers, Senator Samuel C. Pomeroy (R–KS). Pomeroy was chair of a committee supporting a Chase candidacy in 1864. This second publication had an equally adverse effect, serving only to bring the party together in support of Lincoln and oppose any moves at a replacement.[2] Any prospect of Chase as a candidate that year was over. In response, 14 state legislatures passed resolutions supporting Lincoln as the party's leader.[3]

Salmon Chase (photographed by Mathew Brady ca. 1860) was Lincoln's Secretary of the Treasury, and tried to gain the 1864 Republican nomination as a "Radical Republican."

"The document was still being privately circulated when the *Washington Constitutional Union* published it on February 20. The Associated Press transmitted the document nationwide two days later."[4]

The second possible replacement candidate was John C. Frémont, who had been nominated in 1856 as the first candidate in the newly formed Republican Party. The effort at bringing his name forward was doomed from the start. In May 1864, a convention convened in Cleveland to nominate him as a candidate. However, word was out that Copperheads had infiltrated the pool of delegates. Even so, a series of attacks on Lincoln characterized the Frémont effort. Frémont's supporters

had a particularly skewed view of their candidate's chances in early 1864. They predicted that Frémont would "succeed Lincoln by the largest majority ever given to a president." One set of pro–Frémont pamphlets described the president as being "not the emancipator, as the people ignorantly suppose; on the contrary he is the Pharaoh of the nation, who will not let God's people go." They dismissed the "cant about Lincoln's honesty" as being "always ridiculous," and asserted that the "country wants something more than a 'smutty joker' for president." Frémont's supporters in Kentucky intended to call a convention on Washington's birthday to nominate Frémont as an independent candidate to challenge both Lincoln and the

Democrats. Frémont was more formally nominated as the candidate of the "Radical Democracy" by a convention in Cleveland, Ohio, at the end of May.[5]

Frémont offered a compromise to Lincoln: Remove Montgomery Blair, Postmaster General, from the cabinet and he would withdraw his name from consideration. Blair had opposed Frémont's efforts as a Union major general who, on August 30, 1861, established martial law and declared freedom for all slaves in Missouri. Lincoln had rescinded that order. Ultimately, Frémont was relieved of command by Lincoln, a decision encouraged by Blair and his influential family. Now, in 1864, Frémont struck back, convincing Lincoln to ask for Blair's resignation. The demand worked. In addition to this political behind the scenes activity, Lincoln's nomination for a second term was all but assured based on battlefield successes in the second half of the year.[6]

A great part of the controversy in this crucial election year was the perception of Lincoln as a supporter and admirer of the radical wing of his party. He had been elected for his first term by arguing that he was *not* in favor of emancipation, but only wanted to limit the spread of slavery. By the time of the new election, it had become clear that he had either changed his mind or grown in office. By 1864, Lincoln had taken a firm stand against slavery, and the war, once focused on keeping the Union together, became a different matter. Lincoln was fully determined to win the war, reconstruct the Union, and free the slaves. As this transformation in policy and belief expanded, it was clear that Lincoln "sympathized with the Radicals and admired them as the genuine patriots and freedom fighters of the Civil War."[7]

Once Lincoln had survived the half-hearted attempts by some in his own party to replace him on the ticket, he was able to focus on the war effort directly. Victory was in

John C. Frémont tried to gain the Republican nomination in 1864 as well, but his attacks on Lincoln's character failed.

sight after three long years of struggle. The Confederacy and, in the North, the Copperheads, hoped for a defeat of Lincoln in 1864 as their last hope for establishing independence as a separate country and also prevailing economically and maintaining their institution of slavery. Even though the election of 1864, in hindsight, seemed inevitable in its outcome, at the time it was by no means certain. The election, as important as a decisive battlefield outcome in the minds of many, would define the winners and losers in the great struggle.

Even with a lack of alternative candidates, some politicians in Washington continued with their vocal opposition to Lincoln's wartime policies and to continuation of the war. This encouraged Northern Copperheads as well as leaders of the Confederacy. Any opposition to Lincoln was seized upon in the hope that a Democrat would win the presidency. As the battlefield situation became hopeless for the South, the only possibility for the secessionist effort was in a change of administration.

An example of anti–Lincoln rhetoric was that of Congressman Alexander Long (D–OH). He spoke in the House on October 5, 1864:

> I am reluctantly and despondingly forced to the conclusion that the Union is lost never to be restored.... In attempting to preserve our jurisdiction over the southern States we have lost our constitutional form of government over the northern.... I now believe that there are but two alternatives, and they are either an acknowledgment of the independence of the South as an independent nation, or their complete subjugation and extermination as a people.[8]

The response to Long's speech was widespread, but had an opposite effect than anti–Lincoln forces had hoped. Republicans rather than Democrats distributed copies of the speech during the election, seeing that it helped their cause while harming the Democrats' platform.

Southern Economic Problems in 1864

Northern support for a Democratic alternative to Lincoln ignored a stark reality: The South could not prevail in the war, solely on the basis of their failing economy. The entire Southern economy relied on cotton and tobacco, and these products in turn relied on slave labor.

Cotton prices in 1860, before the war, were about 10 cents per pound. By July 1864, the price had risen to $1.64 per pound due to profound inflation. Additionally, the Northern blockade prevented exports of cotton to Europe. Exports in 1864 were at only 2 percent of prewar levels.[9]

The blockade effectively ruined the South's economy. Even Confederate appeals to Great Britain did not end the blockade. The British were able to get cotton from India, and did not need to antagonize the Union. In

"The Rival Cotton Shops" (1861). The guard with a truncheon posted outside "Davis & Co." portrayed the Union's blockade of the South and resulting prevention of cotton exports, a major factor in the South's inability to finance its war effort.

one editorial cartoon, Great Britain ("John Bull") is shown being appealed to by the South to break the blockade. The individual at the window says, "Hi! Hi! John Bull, why don't you break the door open and come see a feller? I've got a lot of cotton inside!" John Bull replies, "Well, it don't look 'ealthy. I can get all I want for the present over the way; so I'll wait till yer open the door yourself, or that man with the club opens it for you—Au River." Reference to the "man with the club" was the Confederacy.

Because cotton represented nearly the entire economy of the Confederacy, the results of these changes were disastrous. The war was financed through printing more Confederate money, causing inflation in the thousands of percent. More than 60 percent of all Confederate revenue came from the printing of more money, growing the South's money supply by 20 times.[10]

The economic problems of the Confederacy were aggravated by the widespread counterfeit printing of their money. The Union dollar gained

Runaway inflation destroyed the South's economy, made worse by widespread counterfeiting of the "grayback" bills.

the name "greenbacks" during the Civil War, and Southern dollars were called "graybacks." Graybacks were crudely printed and easily duplicated. One counterfeiter was especially prolific. Samuel C. Upham of Philadelphia started in 1861 publishing novelty items, exploiting the war. In 1862, he began making counterfeit graybacks, selling his first batch of 3,000 five-dollar notes for one penny each. These were labeled as "facsimile" Confederate notes. Cotton smugglers trimmed off the notice and a thriving black market in Confederate currency took off.

Before long, Upham was marketing as many as 28 varieties of Confederate money and even advertising that he would buy authentic bills so he could duplicate them. He also published postage stamps issued by the South. Since the Union did not recognize the legitimacy of Confederate currency, Upham's Confederate money was not considered counterfeit, so there was no effort to stop his publishing enterprise. By the end of the war, Upham claimed he had printed more than $1.5 million in Confederate paper money, in denominations from five cents to one-hundred dollar bills.[11]

The distribution of counterfeit bills was widespread, and even though these bills accounted for only a small percentage of total Confederate money in circulation, they created great problems for the South. To this day, collectors of paper money see so many examples of counterfeit Confederate bills that the authenticity of graybacks is difficult to establish. Many collectors specialize in counterfeit Confederate money. The problem in 1864 was so severe that the Confederacy placed a bounty on the head of any captured counterfeiters.[12]

The Party Platforms

The situation in 1864 was dire. Even with Confederate victories in the field, the economic conditions in the South made it impossible to win the war strictly in military terms. Replacement of Lincoln with a pro–Southern candidate would be the only way to turn impending economic collapse into victory.

With this in mind, the Democratic Party nominated George B. McClennan at their convention in Chicago (August 29–31, 1864). The convention drafted a "peace platform" that was opposed by McClennan, who favored continuing the war. Contrast was drawn between Lincoln and his resolve to emancipate slaves and hold the Union together, and the peace platform calling for an immediate end to the war. The party made McClennan's position more difficult by nominating George H. Pendleton as vice president. Pendleton favored the platform of immediate peace, meaning allowing the Confederacy to secede and keep their slaves.[13]

McClennan stated in his acceptance speech that he favored peace with the Confederacy but only if those states agreed to come back to the Union.[14] Given the problem of secession and slavery as core issues of dispute, McClennan did not specify what he would do as president if the South refused to

George B. McClellan (photographed ca. 1861) was the Democratic nominee in 1864. He favored a "peace platform," allowing the South to continue slavery and secession.

rejoin or to relinquish their claimed right to own slaves. However, he did say he would make the first move, if elected, to make peace with the South.

This position at first appeared less than clear, but McClennan explained further in describing his policies as the future president. He explained:

> We should avoid any proclamations of general emancipation, and should protect inoffensive citizens in the possession of that, as well as of other kinds of property.... The people in the South should understand that we are not making war upon the institution of slavery, but that if they submit to the Constitution and the Laws of the Union they will be protected in their constitutional rights of every nature.[15]

This qualified statement appeared to cloak a promise to the South that upon agreeing to reenter the Union, the Confederate states would be allowed to maintain ownership of slaves. This, and the Democratic platform overall, was applauded widely by the Copperheads, whose positions had prevailed at the convention. McClennan's nomination was met with enthusiasm in the Copperhead press as well, with one editorial expressing a typical sentiment:

> The nomination of George B. McClennan, by the Chicago Convention, is the death-knell of the abolition party ... [a response to policies that] exalt a degraded, inferior race into equality with the white race....[16]

The Democratic Party position might have been able to win the election for McClennan as long as the war continued going poorly for the Union. But with the fall of Atlanta on September 2, Union victory was no longer in doubt. This was one of several significant victories by the Union over Confederate forces; and, just as suddenly, the gloom expressed by Republicans turned to confidence. At the same time, the Copperhead faction of the Democratic Party continued hoping for a political victory and, ultimately, success for the Confederacy. This position was a central theme used by the Republicans against the Democrats and their Copperhead faction.[17]

The "Chicago Platform" for the Democrats had as its central plank negotiation with the Confederacy to end the war *and* to dispel efforts toward emancipation. During the campaign, Democrats played to racist fears, accusing Republicans of favoring and advocating miscegenation, interracial relations with slaves or, if slaves were freed, with ex-slaves and Northern white women.

This playing on racial fears became characteristic of Copperheads and, by association, of Democrats as well. That same year, a convention of black Americans met in Syracuse and declared that the Democratic Party "belongs to slavery." A Democratic victory that November, in the words of the convention, would cause "the heaviest calamity that could befall us in the present juncture of affairs."[18]

The Democrats' declaration of principles seemed blind to the negative perception of its election plank. That plank included the position that preservation of the Union had failed, and that an immediate effort should be made to end the war:

> **Resolved,** that this convention does explicitly declare, as the sense of the American people, that after four years of failure to restore the Union by the experiment of war, during which, under the pretence [*sic*] of military necessity, or war power higher than the Constitution, the Constitution itself has been disregarded in every part, and public liberty and private right alike trodden down, and the material prosperity of the country essentially impaired, justice, humanity, liberty, and the public welfare demand that immediate efforts be made for a cessation of hostilities, with a view to an ultimate convention of the States or other peaceable means, to the end that at the earliest practicable moment peace may be restored on the basis of the federal Union of the States.[19]

A second plank referred to the government's "open and avowed disregard of State rights," a reference to the right of the Southern states to own slaves as property. That issue had been referred to in preceding decades as a conflict between federal policy and states' rights. However, the phrase "states' rights" had come to be associated with a strongly racist ideology:

> The struggle over the meaning of constitutional freedom revealed the ideological evolution not only in the Republican party but also in the Democracy. States' rights and white supremacy were still staples of Democratic ideology. But no longer as hardy as was the onetime Democratic adherence to the "Constitution as it is."[20]

The phrase was even more strongly cited as criticism of the Democratic Convention in a leading newspaper:

> There is no end to Copperhead charlatanry. Look at the front of Tammany Hall, or at almost any of the Copperhead banners swung over the street, and you see beneath the Janus-faced portraits of MCCLELLAN and PENDLETON, the inscription—"The Union as it was, and the Constitution as it is." This party device is given to the winds in the very face of the Chicago Platform, the most prominent feature of which is "an ultimate convention" for the amendment of the Constitution and reconstruction of the Union. It would seem as if these Copperhead managers take the American people to be idiots, without sense enough to heed these shuffling tricks.... If the party had the least moral earnestness, it would stick to the measure it has deliberately adopted. It would scorn to parade before the people this flagrant contradiction of it, "The Union as it was and the Constitution as it is," which means nothing else than No Convention. A party is lost to all principle, and is past shame, which can thus advertise its duplicity, so that it shall be seen and read of all men.[21]

The contrast between Democrats and Republicans in 1864 was stark. The Republican platform of June 18 demanded unconditional surrender from the Confederacy and also called for a new constitutional amendment ending slavery completely:

> **Resolved**, that we approve the determination of the Government of the United States not to compromise with Rebels, or to offer them any terms of peace, except such as may be based upon an unconditional surrender of their hostility and a return to their just allegiance to the Constitution and laws of the United States ... we are in favor, furthermore, of such an amendment to the Constitution, to be made by the people in conformity with its provisions, as shall terminate and forever prohibit the existence of Slavery within the limits of the jurisdiction of the United States.[22]

A comparison between the platforms of the two parties demonstrates the divide in perception of the future of the country. Democrats favored immediate peace, secession, and continuation of slavery; Republicans demanded unconditional surrender and an end to slavery through the constitutional process.

The Copperheads, desperate in the latter half of 1864 and recognizing that the election was their last hope, accelerated their rhetoric. One controversial figure of the times was publisher of the *Old Guard*, a New York-based paper, Chauncey Burr. In the paper's first edition in 1863, Burr had attacked Henry Ward Beecher for his abolitionist views, saying Beecher had made a deal with the devil. A supporter of slavery, Burr also predicted that abolitionist activities might "turn our country into an African jungle."[23]

In 1864, Burr continued this level of rhetoric against the Union. Serving as Copperhead spokesperson, Burr wrote that due to Lincoln's war policies, "the Constitution has been stricken down" and that "under the pretence [*sic*] of saving the Union, these bloody-minded scoundrels have been doing their utmost to destroy it."[24]

This and similar editorials did little to stem Lincoln's success in the election and in achieving victories on the battlefield. After more than three years of war and thousands of casualties, it became apparent for the first time just before the election that the Union would be preserved.

The Democratic Party position, upon being published, assured victory for Lincoln. Within two days from the end of their convention, the Union prevailed by taking Atlanta on September 2. Response against the Copperheads and, by association, against the entire Democratic Party, included charges of cowardice aimed at the politicians who drafted the party's platform. By this time, the South was virtually defeated already, both on the battlefield and economically. Even so, once the Democratic platform was published, the Copperhead press remained optimistic. One editorial summed up the opinion:

Proclaim the old watch cries of Peace, and Union, the Constitution and Freedom. Away with the gag, with all the manacles with which the present administration has endeavored to bind Liberty. Let the giant awake and burst his bonds.[25]

Conspiracy in 1864 by Copperhead Groups

The nomination and reelection of Lincoln was accompanied by conflicts between pro–Union and anti–Union forces in the North. As this conflict played out politically in 1864, thousands of soldiers returned home, with their three-year conscription expired. However, a large number reenlisted upon being given furloughs to return home briefly, often with the added incentive of a reenlistment bonus of several hundred dollars.[26] This group of furloughed soldiers represented only a small part of the total Union Army; only about 8 percent of the army was made up of drafted soldiers (2 percent) or paid substitutes (6 percent); the rest were volunteers.[27]

During this period when furloughed soldiers returned to their homes, violence against Copperheads and Copperhead-supporting newspapers occurred. Resentment among men who had risked their lives in battle was aimed toward those Democrats who remained behind and criticized the war. In previous months, resentment was confined primarily to letters sent home; now, with Union troops on leave, the Copperheads faced more direct violence.[28]

Antagonism toward Copperheads was caused for the most part by published criticism of the war itself and of Lincoln. At the same time, repeated rumors of Copperhead conspiracies to attack prisoner of war camps and free Confederate soldiers, to overthrow the government in Washington, and to take other actions to subvert the war effort kept the conflict alive on the home front. Such rumors are typical during times of war, but in the Civil War, word of Copperhead conspiracies was widespread.

The theme among Copperheads for making peace with the South only added to antagonism in the North. An editorial cartoon of the day showed a woman representing the Union fighting multiple snakes representing the Copperheads. The cartoon was entitled "The Copperhead Party—In Favor of a *Vigorous Prosecution of Peace!*"

The rumors added to distrust among soldiers on furlough, and also led to government investigations of rumors of Copperhead conspiracies. Due to the anti-administration rhetoric among Copperheads and sympathetic press, a belief emerged by 1864 that such plots did exist:

The Northern Democrat Party during the Civil War ... was of a double nature. On the one hand, its legitimacy as a quasi-formal institution would remain in the

THE COPPERHEAD PARTY.—IN FAVOR OF A *VIGOROUS PROSECUTION* OF *PEACE!*

"The Copperhead Party—In Favor of a *Vigorous Prosecution of Peace!*"
(1863). The Copperheads were Northern Democrats supportive of the South
and continuation of slavery.

last analysis unchallenged, so long as it kept its antiwar wing within some sort of
bounds. But by the same token there was the rough and ready principle that "every
Democrat may not be a traitor, but every traitor is a Democrat."[29]

The short-lived violence against Copperheads by furloughed soldiers was
an expression of a growing suspicion among Lincoln's supporters that
the Democrats and, most notably, their Copperhead arm (the so-called
Peace Democrats) were involved in treason. Although there is no evidence of widespread conspiracies, some activity along these lines has
been documented.

The organization known as the Order of the Sons of Liberty (OSL)
was founded by Harrison H. Dodd. This paramilitary secret society grew
out of the Knights of the Golden Circle founded by George Bickley. The
Knights had the goal of annexing large portions of Central America and
the Northern coast of South America and adding these vast areas to the
country as slave states. Dodd had a more focused vision with his OSL: to
subvert the Union's war effort.

Union military authorities were concerned about activities of the

OSL, especially rumors about planned attacks. One of these rumors was that Dodd was working on a plan for an attack on one of the largest prisoner of war camps in Indiana, Camp Morton. The attack was planned for August 16, according to the reports from the Indiana governor's office. Dodd had told Henry B. Carrington, adjutant general in Indiana, of his plans. Carrington reported the threat to the governor, who alerted the federal authorities. This would be followed by a statewide insurrection including seizure of Indianapolis, overthrow of the state government, and creation of an alliance between Indiana and the Confederacy. The Union Army raided Dodd's offices and seized hundreds of weapons and thousands of rounds of ammunition. Dodd was convicted of treason and sentenced to hang, but his conviction was overturned after the war by the Supreme Court.[30]

This incident demonstrated to the Union that serious plots existed during the conflict, and the seizure of weapons and ammunition supported the contention that the problem was more than rumor. It brought suspicion on the dozens of Democrat-based militia groups throughout the North, especially in the upper Midwest region. The degree of actual threat posed by these secret societies and militia groups is not known. Numerous reports by citizens about nighttime meetings of militia groups and plots brought the matter to federal attention, and many groups were infiltrated and monitored.[31]

In a related plot by the OSL, Indianapolis, St. Louis, and Louisville would all be captured, and the states in Indiana, Missouri, and Kentucky joined with the Confederacy. The OSL grand council wrote to Jefferson Davis describing the plan that August. Davis had previously sent operatives to Canada to recruit allies for subversive activities against the North. Secret societies like the OSL were of great value to Davis. His purpose was aligned with the secret societies of the North; he wanted to free Confederate prisoners, help sympathetic newspapers publish pro–Southern editorials, and offer direct support to militia groups like the OSL.[32]

Agents sent North by President Davis held discussions with Copperhead leaders about forming a Western Confederacy consisting of upper Midwestern states, similar to proposals put forth by the OSL (Illinois, Indiana, Ohio, Missouri, and Kentucky). The plan was not based on rational or likely strategies. It involved spontaneous uprisings among Confederate prisoners of war, aided by other escaped prisoners and Copperhead militia groups. Organizing this effort would have been a daunting task, and no specifics were developed. Even so, Davis hoped the plan worked and gave the OSL $500,000 to purchase weapons.[33]

The Confederacy was actively interested in foiling the Union's efforts and even in overthrowing the federal government. Its agents cooked up more plots. One was to overtake the Democratic Party with a coup at the July convention and ensure nomination of a pro–Confederacy candidate. Another was aimed at organizing New York's laborers to rise up and riot against the Union, but details were scant. Even so, Confederate agent Jacob Thompson was involved in representing Confederate President Jefferson Davis and financing Copperhead actions against Lincoln's administration:

> Mr. Thompson established his headquarters at Montreal on the 30th of May 1864, and opened an account with the Bank of Ontario in that city. Before *resorting to other and more extreme measures,* he endeavored to carry out Mr. Davis's primary ideas of negotiating "with such persons in the North as might be relied on to aid the attainment of peace." He sought, therefore, to secure conferences, not only with influential men representing the peace party in the Northern and Eastern States, but also with leading public men who were identified with the political party in power, and might be supposed to reflect the views of Mr. Lincoln and his Cabinet.[34]

Thompson also sent $25,000 to Benjamin Wood (D–NY) for the express purpose of buying arms in support of the planned New York labor riot against the Union. Wood was also publisher of the *New York Daily News,* a Copperhead newspaper. From 1863 to 1865, Wood used the paper to publish letters with coded messages aimed at the Confederacy. The $25,000 payment was reported in the press that August:

> The *New York Times* revealed on August 25 that the *Daily News* had cashed a $25,000 check from the Confederates in Montreal "and this is but one of many remittances from the same source for the sustenance of the *Daily News."* The August pay-off was later confirmed by Confederate agent John B. Castleman....[35]

Throughout the desperate battlefield situation faced by the Confederacy in 1864, Copperheads continued a rearguard action based on racial statements and pro-secession sentiments. For those Northern civilians weary of the war, peace was a desirable alternative. The Confederacy was interested in negotiating peace through its operatives in Canada. Horace Greeley, editor of the *New York Tribune* and a Lincoln supporter, was approached by Confederate agents, allegedly to encourage negotiations for peace. In fact, their real purpose was to encourage dissent in the North and to force a political compromise to end the war. Greeley, believing in the sincerity of the agents, wrote to Lincoln and warned that the time was ripe for peace and that a "northern insurrection" was likely unless Lincoln entered into peace talks. When Lincoln suggested to Greeley that he investigate to determine the validity of the proposal, Greeley was told by the agents that they were not actually authorized to speak for the Confederate government. The entire matter was dropped, and was a source of public embarrassment for Greeley.[36]

Confederate Efforts at Negotiating Peace

The Greeley incident enabled the president to focus his message: Peace was only possible through victory. This meant not only bringing seceding states back into the Union, but ending slavery entirely, without exception. Lincoln realized that behind-the-scenes negotiations probably were not sincere. However, to the extent that the Confederacy was willing to talk, they would insist on independence from the Union. In other words, the only way the South would agree to end the conflict would be adoption by Lincoln of the position stated in the Democrats' platform: recognition of the South as an independent country, where slavery was legal. Lincoln would not agree to those terms under any conditions.

Shortly after Greeley's botched meeting with Confederate agents, two Northern men traveled to Richmond and met with Jefferson Davis to discuss possible terms of peace. James F. Jacques, a preacher, and James R. Gilmore, a journalist, were not acting in an official capacity. Even so, Davis granted them an interview once the two men were allowed to travel through the lines. Although lacking authority to make promises, they told Davis that if the Southern states rejoined the Union, Lincoln would grant amnesty to everyone in the Confederacy. Davis was insulted by this, saying that no one in the seceded states needed amnesty because they had done nothing wrong. Davis further said that he was willing to "see every Southern plantation sacked, and every Southern city in flames." When the issue of slavery was raised, Davis said that the South was not fighting to preserve that institution: "We are fighting for independence—and that, or extermination, we will have."[37]

Unofficial peace feelers were made on both sides, recognizing that one way or another, the war would soon come to an end. In July, Lincoln reiterated his commitment to holding the Union together and ending slavery. Confederate agents in Canada were indignant and wrote that Lincoln's resolve would only extend the war and make peace harder to achieve. This declaration of challenge to Lincoln encouraged Copperheads. The press pointed to Lincoln's firm position as a united factor among Copperheads.

Throughout the war, Copperhead efforts had been supported and financed by the South through covert operations called "black propaganda" and approved by Jefferson Davis. Funding for Confederate operatives as well as Copperhead press editorials ran into the millions of dollars of Confederate funding. Both the Confederate State Department and War Department requested funding often for covert operations, and the Confederate cabinet approved those requests, notably during 1864. However, by later that year, efforts at subverting Northern support for the Union effort and Lincoln's policies were less focused on propaganda and more closely focused on attempts to negotiate peace. However, that peace—in the Confederate view—would have to include allowing the South to maintain independence as a separate nation.[38]

There were two central themes in the Confederate peace negotiations, both unacceptable to Lincoln. These were the South's belief that they had a right to secede and form a separate nation, and their claim of property rights, the ownership of slaves. Because there could be no compromise between the two sides, the dispute had to be settled militarily. The Copperheads exploited the war-weary North by demanding that Lincoln end the conflict and agree to the terms put forth by Jefferson Davis. This was a continuing source of aggravation to Lincoln as well as to the soldiers risking their lives on the battlefield. A sense of gloom and despair permeated the citizens of the North, now seeing the fourth year of war and hundreds of thousands of deaths and injuries to husbands and sons. Focus among Copperheads during late 1864 was on the election and the hope that Lincoln would not be returned to the White House.

The Political Climate in 1864

As long as battles went the South's way, Copperheads were encouraged and President Davis continued to hope for favorable outcomes from subversive activities and propaganda. But once Atlanta had fallen, the war was all but over in a military sense; the election was the only shred of hope left for the Confederacy and their Copperhead allies.[39]

Frustration with Lincoln was not confined to Copperheads. Many politicians in the Republican Party tried to organize a second convention to replace Lincoln on the ticket. Convinced he could not win in November, the convention was planned for September 28. Greeley, once a firm Lincoln supporter, was a driving force behind the idea of a new candidate, even that close to election day. Greeley

> persisted in attempting to set up a convention for an alternate presidential candidate, one who would defeat Lincoln in the election. "Mr. Lincoln is already beaten," Greeley wrote. "He cannot be elected. And we must have another ticket to save us from utter overthrow."[40]

Although nothing came of the idea for a challenge candidate to Lincoln at this late date, pessimism among one-time supporters grew until September. Republicans were fearful of a loss if the war could not be won. Some politicians encouraged Lincoln to conclude the war with the Confederacy before election day. In hindsight, Lincoln's reelection looks like a foregone conclusion; at the time, it was anything but certain.

The turning point was General Sherman's victory in Atlanta. The city was strategically significant as a railroad hub and supply line for the Confederate Army. Once Sherman prevailed, the Confederate's chances of victory fell to nearly zero. Once again, the last desperate hope for victory rested with the election, with Lincoln's defeat and replacement with a Democrat.

The sudden turn in fortunes favoring Union victory in the war and Republican victory in the election turned Northern despair earlier in 1864 into renewed enthusiasm:

> Bloodshed, violence, and endless losses caused many Northern civilians to give up hope that summer and urge Lincoln to settle for peace at almost any price. Lincoln's refusal to bargain with Davis and to give up emancipation in exchange for peace led to the perception in the North that Lincoln was to blame, nearly costing him his political career. The opposition, whose power had fluctuated in the previous three years, enjoyed the windfall of Northern dismay, and its strength grew to unprecedented levels. Military losses were largely responsible for the despair that summer, and a military victory erased it.[41]

Atlanta was a final defeat for the Confederacy. General John B. Hood was in command of Confederate troops defending Atlanta. When he was forced to retreat, he ordered that 81 ammunition cars be set on fire to prevent them falling into Union hands. The fire went out of control, leading to a widespread fire throughout the city. Folklore of the Civil War blames Sherman as the Union general who set Atlanta on fire. However, it was not the Union forces, but Confederate, that caused this disaster.[42]

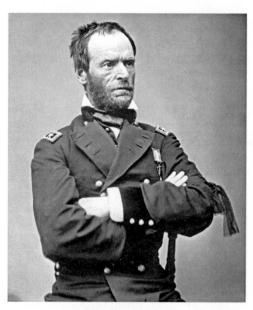

General William T. Sherman (photographed 1864). A turning point in the Civil War was Sherman's victory in Atlanta, the rail hub of the entire Confederacy.

Sherman wrote to President Lincoln on September 3: "Atlanta is ours, and fairly won."[43]

That victory ensured Lincoln's reelection. It was clear to all, especially in the North and among both soldiers and politicians, that the war was all but lost by the Confederacy. Without the essential supply lines, victory would be impossible. Lincoln prevailed, winning 212 of 233 electoral votes.[44]

The election was more than

a victory; it had ramifications for the entire party, not only in 1864 but for 20 years after. Lincoln's landslide victory included votes from 80 percent of soldiers in the field as well as nearly all of the electoral college:

> The election of 1864 was a disaster for the Democrats, and the peace wing found itself humiliated. Having counted upon public disaffection for the war to advance their cause, Copperheads lost when military fortunes and public sentiment turned on them.... Tarred as traitors, regardless of their actual positions on the war, Democrats were beaten at state polls in October and rounded thrashed in November. In fact, the stench of treason clung to the Democrats for years; nearly a generation would pass before another Democrat, Grover Cleveland, occupied the White House.[45]

Thinking ahead to postwar policies, Lincoln had replaced his first-term vice president, Hannibal Hamlin, with Andrew Johnson of Tennessee. Johnson, a Democrat, supported Lincoln's war effort and opposed Southern secession. Although a Democrat, Johnson joined the Republican ticket that year. Lincoln believed that adding Johnson to the ticket would help not only with his reelection, but also with Reconstruction following victory. Hamlin attended the Republican National Convention believing he would still be on the ticket, as Lincoln had not informed him of the decision. Even so, Hamlin remained loyal to Lincoln in his reelection bid and after. Had he remained on the ticket, Reconstruction might have been a smoother process. Johnson was abrasive and unpopular, not only for his personal style but also due to a drinking problem which all too often was exhibited in public, even at his inaugural ceremony in 1865.[46]

Political Responses to Lincoln's Victory

The reaction to Lincoln's victory among Copperheads, especially in the press, was immediate and vicious. Editorials by "Brick" Pomeroy of the LaCrosse, Wisconsin, *Democrat* were notably ugly in tone. "His hatred of Lincoln became an obsession," and he wrote in one editorial before the election: "May God Almighty forbid that we are to have two terms of the rottenest, most-stinking, ruin-working small-pox ever conceived by fiends or mortals in the shape of two terms of Abe Lincoln." He further wrote that

> the man who votes for Lincoln now is a traitor and a murderer. He who pretending to war for, wars against the Constitution of our country is a traitor, and Lincoln is one of these men.... If he is elected to misgovern for another four years, we trust some bold hand will pierce his heart with dagger point for the public good.[47]

Pomeroy also supported McClennan in the 1864 election through racist attempts at humor. He:

> suggested new words for the popular tune entitled "When Johnny Comes Marching Home." One of his vicious stanzas read:

The widow maker soon must cave!
   Hurrah! Hurrah!
We'll plant him in some nigger's grave!
   Hurrah! Hurrah!
Torn from your farm, your shop, your raft;
Conscript! How do you like the draft?
    And we'll stop that too,
      When "Little Mac" takes the helm![48]

The consensus among Copperhead newspapers had been that Lincoln had little chance of winning reelection and they, like the Copperheads in the public and in politics, had placed all hope with McClennan and the Democratic platform, favoring immediate peace, accepting secession, and continuing slavery in the South. They were encouraged months prior to the election by a series of Confederate victories. However, by election day, with Atlanta destroyed and Confederate troops on the run, the picture changed and Lincoln's position was strong once again. The anti–Union position continued to the end, however. Several papers published editorials during the campaign months, stating, "The Negro mania has been as mischievous in the conduct of the war, as it has been in and is in politics" (*The New York World*); another editorialized that the Union's military decisions were premised "not upon deeds of gallantry, but in devotion to the Negro-equality dogma of a political party" (*Philadelphia Age*).[49]

The Copperhead press was not alone in believing McClennan was destined to win the election. Lincoln himself thought throughout the campaign that he probably would lose. On August 23, 1864, expecting bad news on election night, he drafted a message, sealed it, and left it in his desk, intending to open it after the election. Lincoln understood, however, that a victory for the Democrats would dash his hopes to end slavery and hold the Union together. The president's short memo read:

> This morning, as for some days past, it seems exceedingly probable that the Administration will not be re-elected. Then it will be my duty to so co-operate with the President elect, as to save the Union between the election and inauguration; as he will have secured his election on such ground that he cannot possibly save it afterwards.[50]

Post-Election Conditions and the Thirteenth Amendment

Lincoln believed that the war's conclusion could only be complete if slavery were abolished permanently. His position was that even with military victory, all of the seceding states would have to agree to this condition before they would be allowed to rejoin the Union.

In June 1864, Democrats in the House had defeated Lincoln's first attempt at passing a new constitutional amendment. The Senate had approved the measure by 38 to 6 on April 8 that year. A second attempt at approval was made early in 1865, when the amendment came up again for a vote in the House of Representatives. The amendment passed 119 to 56. An editorial showing a celebration in the House after successful passage is shown below.

The language was clear:

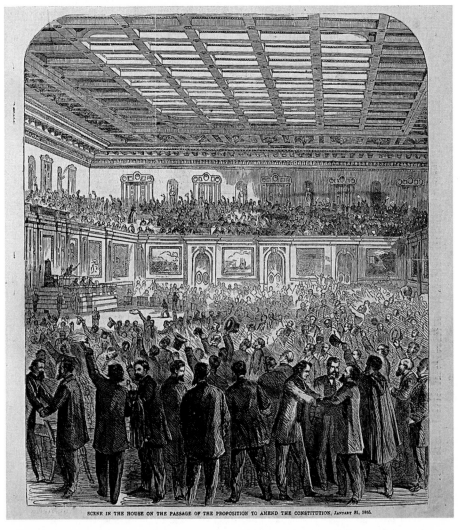

SCENE IN THE HOUSE ON THE PASSAGE OF THE PROPOSITION TO AMEND THE CONSTITUTION, JANUARY 31, 1865.

Slavery was finally ended with passage of the Thirteenth Amendment in early 1865.

Section 1. Neither slavery nor involuntary servitude, except as a punishment for crime whereof the party shall have been duly convicted, shall exist within the United States, or any place subject to their jurisdiction.

Section 2. Congress shall have power to enforce this article by appropriate legislation.[51]

Concerned that the Emancipation Proclamation could be overturned by a vote of Congress, Lincoln had worked diligently to get the new amendment approved:

Not content with rhetorical exhortation, Lincoln used his personal authority and considerable charm to influence Democratic and border-state congressmen whose votes were in doubt. Not since 1862 when he tried hard to persuade border-state congressmen to support his gradual emancipation plan, had the President been so deeply involved in the legislative process.[52]

The president had also recruited members of his cabinet to win over enough Congressional votes for passage, even promising appointments to desirable positions in the government. The effort succeeded and slavery was abolished permanently in the United States. The amendment was ratified by the states as well. All of the Northern states ratified by July 1865, and the Southern states followed, ratifying by December. The total, 27 of 36 states, signed on.

The legal effects were immediate. The new amendment nullified the Fugitive Slave Clause and the Three-Fifths Compromise of the original Constitution. However, the legal ban on slavery did not change conditions for black Americans in a substantial way. The infamous black codes followed in many states. These laws required black citizens to work for low wages with limited freedom. In many of the previous Confederate states, black citizens were not allowed to travel and were restricted to remaining on plantations where they worked. These codes also forbade assembly, bearing arms, learning to read, offering testimony in court against white citizens, and voting in local or national elections. The realization of true freedom was a long and painful process over the next 100 years.

As the war ended after such loss of life, the country began to move forward once again. Reconstruction was as painful a period as the war years had been, and even through the presidencies of Johnson (1865–69), Grant (1869–77), and Hayes (1877–81) the process moved slowly forward. Lincoln's decision in 1864 to replace Hamlin with Johnson as vice president had unintended consequences. Had Lincoln survived, Reconstruction might have been smoother under his leadership and with Hamlin in his administration. Johnson was perhaps the worst person to head up the Reconstruction effort, as later conflicts revealed. Johnson and Congress battled from the beginning, leading to the first effort at impeachment of a president.[53]

With the end of the Civil War and the president's assassination, even the president's critics mourned his loss. One of the more vocal wartime critics had been Kentucky Governor Thomas Bramlette. Following the assassination, Bramlette admitted: "He was right and we were wrong. The name and cause of Mr. Lincoln will go down to future ages as part of the record of our country."[54]

PART III

Politics During Reconstruction

8

Parties in Conflict—
The Johnson Administration

The Copperhead movement during the Civil War continued on after, despite the South's loss of the war and of its institution of slavery. They failed to set aside differences and move forward:

> Committed to a belief system that extended back at least a century, they could not keep up with the economic, social or political changes that the war and industrialization wrought. Beyond the obvious fact of emancipation, they seem not even to have recognized the massive shifts that had taken place between 1861 and 1865. Instead, by the end of the war they seemed to occupy a bubble world that had little connection within the society that was emerging. They preferred to harken back to a simpler era…. While they looked over their shoulders, the nation at large moved into the future.[1]

This summarizes well conditions in 1865. Copperheads, refusing to accept the reality of a lost cause, made Reconstruction more difficult and extensive and turned to a more sinister version of their previous resistance. No longer content with newspaper editorials, public statements, and fantastic plots for insurrection in the North, the Copperhead movement began a process leading to a more direct and violent form of resistance to emancipation and Union victory.

The first phase after the Civil War was political debate concerning the right to vote. No sooner had the war concluded than politicians began arguing over the benefits and consequences of black suffrage, with Republicans largely in favor of and Democrats almost unanimously opposed to expansion of rights to former slaves. To many, it seemed that Republicans were setting a dangerous course for themselves. Charles Walker commented in an editorial that "the Republican Party will be shipwrecked on the question of granting to blacks of the South the right of Negro suffrage."[2]

Beyond the vote, Copperheads continued citing states' rights as an argument against granting citizenship rights to former slaves—despite the outcome of the war. Refusing to accept defeat, Copperheads looked for other ways to win their case against what had been decided on both the battlefield and in the law. This began with criticism of the Thirteenth Amendment as an attempt to overthrow states' rights. The antagonism was seen as well in the political arena. President Johnson had been a vocal critic of the Peace Democrat movement as treasonous and had even called for punishment of Copperheads who had spoken against the Union during the war. The Copperhead press, even while Johnson was still vice president, had responded to Johnson's call for punishment, calling him an "ignorant, insolent, drunken sot."[3]

Andrew Johnson and the Post-War Era

The new president faced a conflict of loyalty. As a Democrat, he sympathized with the Democratic Party, including Copperhead sentiments. As Lincoln's running mate, he served as a Republican, if in name only.

Johnson relied on a series of presidential proclamations issued in 1865 and 1866 requiring state conventions and elections and reformed governments. Neither proclamation mentioned black suffrage. Johnson had opposed the Thirteenth Amendment even as vice president under Lincoln, and his active opposition to Republicans in Congress created immediate tension between executive and legislative branches.

Republican Andrew Johnson (photographed 1874) expressed support for Southern rights after Lincoln's assassination.

There was not much of a connection between Lincoln and Johnson. Having worked to replace Hamlin with Johnson for his second term, Lincoln met with Johnson for the first time since inauguration on April 14, 1865, the afternoon of the day he was assassinated. Johnson had made a special trip to the White House "to induce Lincoln not to be too lenient with traitors."[4]

This point of view, from the man who would be sworn

in as the new president in less than a day, diverged from Lincoln's desire to bring the country back together, and who believed that Reconstruction should be a period of healing and not of retribution. However, Johnson ran into immediate conflict with Radical Republicans who favored providing civil rights to former slaves. Johnson viewed the matter of black suffrage as a distraction and wanted to allow the Southern states to make their own determination about treatment of black citizens. Johnson was more closely aligned with Northern Democrats, who, like the new president, opposed black suffrage. To Johnson, and to many citizens in the North as well, priorities included putting the war in the past and reuniting the country. The black vote could wait, and in this opinion Johnson found support among most Democrats and many Republicans.

The New Administration and the South

Once he took office, Johnson continued his verbal attacks on the South, a tactic that Lincoln would never have supported. Johnson threatened land seizures of lands owned by Confederate leaders as a form of reparations. At the same time, he contradicted himself with such statements by responding to Democrats' fears about governmental policies, stating that black suffrage would not be managed by Washington, but would be decided by the states.[5]

Johnson had rationalized the decision to allow states to decide questions of the black vote, as he agreed with a majority of Democrats that former slaves were passive and easily controlled and that, if given the right to vote, would cast their votes as instructed by their former owners. This belief encouraged Democrats, both Northern and Southern, in the belief that the new president would not impose federal requirements upon the states.[6]

In fact, Johnson's positions convinced most Democrats that the president was committed to states' rights and favored "a white man's government" in the former Confederate states, according to Charles Mason. Mason, an attorney and influential Democrat, met with President Johnson in late June and believed the president was in complete agreement with the ideals of the Democratic Party. He described Johnson as "his political brethren."[7]

Mason's message was met with suspicion by fellow Democrats. At about the same time, trials for the conspirators involved in Lincoln's assassination concluded and all had been sentenced to hang. Democrats were upset that President Johnson had refused to soften or reverse the sentences, especially for Mary Surratt. Because of this, Mason's attempt to align the Democratic Party with Johnson were rejected strongly.[8]

The effort by Democrats to attach Johnson to their party—despite Johnson having run with Lincoln as a Republican—did not fail, and many in the party had attempted to flatter Johnson into an alliance with them. Johnson, a Democrat before being drafted by Lincoln, was easily swayed by such efforts. However, more extreme Copperhead interests, rejecting the diplomatic effort to declare the whole party as Johnson's, declared that the president could not be trusted and Democrats seeking his favor were exploiting the president for their own gain.

As a result of Johnson's attempts at pacifying both sides, the outcome was antagonism and distrust from everyone. His unwillingness to use federal power to enforce the new Thirteenth Amendment not only contradicted the entire aim of Lincoln's administration in the war, but also revealed his inability to exert leadership in advancing Reconstruction. As long as former Confederate leaders were to continue as political leaders in the South, the outcome would be that blacks would never be allowed to vote, despite the amendment's requirements.

Johnson's contradictory loyalties added confusion to the political scene. Wanting to escape the controversy surrounding black suffrage, he had reiterated his belief that it should be decided by the states. To Democrats, this sounded like he favored states' rights over the terms of the Thirteenth Amendment. To Republicans, it sounded like Johnson was at best neutral and at worst not in favor of black suffrage. His true feelings came out, however, after the Mississippi state convention concluded without taking a position on black suffrage. Rather than expressing disapproval, Johnson stated that he approved and sent a congratulatory wire to the state.

During state elections in 1865, referendums calling for black suffrage were defeated in several states, both North and South, and this was cited as a victory for the Democratic Party. The lack of strong presidential leadership throughout 1865 made the path of Reconstruction uncertain at best, and in favor of states' rights with anti-black suffrage at worst.

The Freedman's Bureau Bill

President Johnson created a clear impression that he opposed any legislative relief for former slaves. This policy contradicted the tone set by Lincoln in plans made during 1864 and 1865 to reconcile the country once the war had ended.

While Lincoln was still in office on March 3, 1865, Congress had passed a bill called "An Act to Establish a Bureau for the Relief of Freedmen and Refugees." This bill would provide medical help, food, shelter, clothing, and even land to those displaced during the war. It was a form of recovery and restoration that its authors viewed as necessary to reunite the country. Initially, the bill was intended to set up a bureau to operate for only one year and, since at the time the war was in progress, to possibly be extended after its initial year of operations. The bill was even more expansive, however. It would set up schools and manage lands confiscated from former Confederates. This overall concept of establishing a bureau had been debated in Congress since the year after the war began. However, it did not materialize in its final form until 1866.

Opinions concerning the Freedman's Bureau varied. Racist posters critical of Radical Republicans appeared, especially during the elections of 1866. One widely distributed poster, titled "The Freedman's Bureau! An agency to keep the Negro in idleness at the expense of the white man. Twice vetoed by the President, and made a lawy [*sic*] by Congress. Support Congress & you support the Negro Sustain the President & you protect the white man," showed a black man idling while one white man plows his

The Freedman's Bureau led to debate over whether the government in postwar America should take part in granting special privileges to ex-slaves.

field and another chops wood. Democrats running on white supremacy platforms employed posters such as this in their campaigns. Narratives included "In the sweat of thy face shalt thou eat thy bread" and "The white man must work to keep his children and pay taxes." The black man muses, "Whar is de use for me to work as long as dey make dese appropriations." Behind is a replica of the capitol with labels "Freedom and No Work" and "Negro estimate of Freedom!" and columns labeled Candy, Rum, Gin, Whiskey, Sugar Plums, Indolence, White Women, Apathy, White Sugar, Idleness, Fish Balls, Clams, Stews, and Pies.

The debate over the Freedman's Bureau centered on two issues. First was on which federal department should operate the bureau; second was a debate about whether the government should provide special privileges or benefits to one group over another. The initial law was passed by both houses of Congress and signed by President Lincoln on March 3, 1865. However, that version of the bill set up the bureau only until the war ended.[9]

On January 5, 1866, a new bill would have extended provisions of the Freedman's Bureau Bill, removing an expiration date and extending provisions to freedmen throughout the country rather than only in the former Confederate states. The revised bill also expanded the role of military governors in the South to protect the rights of former slaves. Republicans in Congress expected a presidential signature, whereas Democrats anticipated a veto. Johnson clearly was opposed to any protections in law for freedmen, and expressed his theories clearly after the House vote but before the bill was presented to him:

> Johnson granted an interview to a black delegation, reiterated his previous pronouncements against black suffrage, and suggested that the only solution to the nation's racial dilemma was black emigration.[10]

Conflict between the president and Congress, notably the Radical Republicans in Congress, led many to conclude that he would veto practically any Republican-approved bill that crossed his desk. Even so, the new legislation had bipartisan support. Both houses of Congress approved the revised bill, and it was sent to the president for signature. Surprisingly, Johnson vetoed the bill, citing several reasons. Most of all, Johnson explained, the bill interfered with states' rights to manage their own affairs without intervention by the federal government. He also reiterated previous objections to any bill providing benefits to one group while excluding everyone else.

An attempt to override the president's veto failed. A two-thirds vote would be needed, and Congress was not able to achieve that level. A moderated version of the bill was drafted to extend the bureau for two years, and was approved by Congress. The president received the bill in July and again vetoed it. Johnson explained in his veto message:

> The protection granted to the white citizen is already conferred by law upon the freedman; strong and stringent guards, by way of penalties and punishments, are thrown around his person and property, and it is believed that ample protection will be afforded him by due process of law, without resort to the dangerous expedient of "military tribunals," now that the war has been brought to a close.[11]

However, both houses of Congress were able to override the veto, and the Freedman's Bureau Act of 1866 became law on July 16. The stage for continuing antagonism between Johnson and Congress was set and would continue throughout his administration. The core of this conflict was found in policies concerning the Thirteenth Amendment and subsequent legislation.

Black Codes in 1865 and 1866

Once the war ended, Democrats in the former Confederate states attempted to make their case that the South was not opposed to rejoining the Union and moving forward. At the same time, however, the issue of emancipation continued to create friction in the same states.

The position expressed by the end of 1865 was that citizens in the South

> were anxious to resume their responsibilities as full-fledged citizens of the republic. As for the blacks, Southern whites knew their needs best and should be allowed to provide for the transition to freedom with a minimum of outside interference. Whatever racial turbulence existing in the South should be attributed to Republican agitators, whose objectives were personal and partisan gain.[12]

This position proved to be unfounded. Not only during Reconstruction, but for the next 100 years, a series of black codes and subversive activities aimed at preventing black citizens from attaining their rights demonstrated that for many in the South, one of the primary outcomes of the Civil War—emancipation of slaves—did not mean acceptance of blacks as equal, or deserving of the rights long held by white Southern citizens.

Immediately upon the end of hostilities, in fact, Southern spokesmen began insisting that Southerners (specifically referring to white Southerners) deserved recognition of their basic rights. These included the right to be left free of federal interference in what they considered state-level issues. To accomplish this claim to states' rights, several previous Confederate states, led by Mississippi, passed new laws enforcing provisions to exclude blacks from the vote and other civil rights. These black codes not only excluded blacks from the benefits of emancipation, but also restricted their movement away from the plantations where they had been owned as slaves. The codes prevented blacks from voting, buying property, owning guns, buying alcohol, gathering for worship, and learning to read. Citing "vagrancy" as one excuse for arresting blacks, the penalty was commitment to involuntary labor, effectively setting up a "convict lease" system.

In effect, the black codes were passed into law in response to the end of slavery, and were designed to maintain the effects of slavery. This convict lease system was

> a form of bondage distinctly different from that of the antebellum South in that for most men, and the relatively few women drawn in, this slavery did not last a lifetime and did not automatically extend from one generation to the next. But it was nonetheless slavery—a system in which armies of free men, guilty of no crimes and entitled by law to freedom, were compelled to labor without compensation, were repeatedly bought and sold, and were forced to do the bidding of white masters through the regular application of extraordinary physical coercion.[13]

The substitution of black codes for previous slave codes was only thinly disguised. In many previous Confederate states, the new laws were simply repeated verbatim from slave codes, with the word "slave" substituted with the word "Negro."[14]

A similar holdover was found in black codes in Mississippi, where blacks were allowed to rent land only within city limits, preventing them from running their own farm lands. Blacks also were required to present annual written proof of employment to prevent being charged with vagrancy. Any "runaway workers" were to be returned with the loss of wages for one year, a provision nearly identical to the fugitive slave laws. The Mississippi vagrancy law was so broad as to allow any number of minor offenses to fall within its definition. These provisions were written and defined to "include runaways, persons lewd in speech or behavior, those who misspent their earnings or neglect their works, and all other idle or disorderly persons." Another of the black codes in Mississippi provided that the state could take custody over former slaves' children if their parents were not able to provide for their support, and apprentice those children to former masters.[15]

South Carolina passed its own black code laws. Unlike Mississippi, whose legislature did not vote to ratify the Thirteenth Amendment, South Carolina did so but with the provision that Congress lacked authority to regulate the state or its policies regarding previous slaves. The state's law concerning "Domestic Relations of Persons of Color" set out rules defining vagrancy and establishing a special tax on blacks. Non-payment of the tax fell under the definition of vagrancy. It also set down terms for forced apprenticeship of black children whose parents failed to meet "habits of industry and honesty."[16]

Similar vagrancy and apprenticeship provisions were passed in Louisiana, North Carolina, and Florida in 1866. More controversy over apprenticeship occurred in Maryland. In that state, nearly half of all black citizens had been free before the Civil War, and, by 1866, former slave-owners pushed for laws allowing apprentice provisions even for freedmen and their children. The Maryland apprenticeship law was overturned by the Supreme Court.

In Texas, apprenticeship laws similar to those in South Carolina were passed. Negroes were barred from voting, holding public office, serving on juries or in militias, owning guns, or attending public schools. Negroes convicted of rape were given harsher sentences than whites, up to life in prison or a death sentence.[17]

In Tennessee, no specific black codes were passed. However, the state had already established vagrancy and apprenticeship laws which, although not distinguished on racial grounds, were enforced with a clear bias toward former slaves. Similarly, Kentucky laws did not mention blacks but specified penalties for loitering and vagrancy.

The Civil Rights Act of 1866

In the environment of black codes and continuation of slavery by other names, Congress enacted the first law meant to provide equal rights to all citizens. The legislation was passed in April 1866, but Johnson vetoed it. Congress overrode the president's veto with a two-thirds vote.

The law was expressed as enforcement of the Thirteenth Amendment, which ended slavery and effectively granted rights of citizenship on former slaves. Johnson's override was rationalized on the basis that several states had not yet seated representatives in Congress, but that reasoning painted Johnson as anti-emancipation and anti-suffrage. It tainted him as a president not willing to see equal rights granted to former slaves. The law provided for "full and equal benefit of all laws and proceedings for the security of person and property, as is enjoyed by white citizens...."[18]

Johnson's veto, based largely on a technicality, was called "the most disastrous miscalculation of his political career."[19] In Johnson's veto message, he questioned Congress's constitutional authority to enact the law, given that 11 of the 36 states were not yet represented in Congress. He further stated his objection to the act that proposed

the security of the colored race safeguards which go infinitely beyond any that the general government has ever provided to the white race. In fact, the distinction of race and color is by the bill made to operate in favor of the colored and against the white race.[20]

The racial tone of this message revealed Johnson's sentiments and set a tone for his presidency, which was in constant conflict with Congress and his own cabinet, and made the process of Reconstruction more painful and extended. In his veto message, Johnson said that the bill

> would discriminate in the Negros' favor against worthy foreigners, who had to wait five years before themselves becoming citizens; it might be better for the ex-slave "unfamiliar with our institutions and our lows," to "pass through a certain probation."[21]

This position revealed Johnson's insensitivity toward former slaves. Even those born in the United States and descended from generations of slaves also born in the country were, in his opinion, not worthy of being granted full rights of citizenship that would be granted under the Civil Rights bill. It further aligned Johnson with Democrats in Congress, who resisted any legal measures to provide protection to former slaves as promised in the Thirteenth Amendment:

> For many, Johnson's veto of the Civil Rights bill of 1866 would stand as his defining political blunder, setting a tone of perpetual confrontation with Congress that prevailed for the balance of his presidency. That veto ... fundamentally eroded his support among congressional Republicans. For Andrew Johnson, there would be no compromises and no negotiations with his congressional adversaries. The political life of the nation would be reduced to a single contest of will and power.[22]

One of the issues that continued the conflict between executive and legislative branches was the drafting of the Fourteenth Amendment. Johnson did not play a role in ratification, but he was opposed to this amendment. It was ratified and adopted by 1868 after a lengthy review by the states. The amendment defined all persons born or naturalized in the U.S. as citizens, and forbade any state passing laws to remove the privileges of citizenship.[23]

Johnson's opposition to the new amendment continued to feed the antagonism with Congress and confirmed for many that the president was not interested in civil rights for everyone, even when his home state of Tennessee ratified the new amendment. This was the only Southern or border state that voted for ratification. As debate over the new amendment moved forward among the states and in Congress, Johnson was allied with Democrats, who opposed ratification. Republicans were largely in favor of the amendment, and Johnson, desperate to win election in 1866, made one blunder after another. He proved to be a tone-deaf politician for the next two years.

During a campaign tour dubbed "Swing Around the Circle," Johnson visited Chicago, St. Louis, Indianapolis, Columbus, and other cities. In his stump speech, Johnson compared himself to Christ and had to contend with growing numbers of hecklers in the crowds. For example, in a speech in St. Louis, Johnson said, "Yes, yes; they are ready to impeach," to which a voice in the crowd shouted, "Let them try it." In a self-pitying manner, Johnson continued, finally asking, "So far as offenses are concerned—upon this question of offenses, let me ask you what offenses I have committed?" The response from one heckler was, "Plenty, here tonight."[24]

The tone-deaf approach Johnson employed in St. Louis (and elsewhere) demonstrated that he no longer had popular support. He

> had not lost his "reason"; he had simply lost touch with his audience, and the demons of unreality that are in the air when a man no longer knows what he is saying were all round about Andrew Johnson that night. It was not necessarily his method; it was rather the issue which overwhelming numbers of his hearers had already decided for themselves.[25]

This campaign effort foreshadowed an electoral disaster, and Johnson failed to win nomination as the party's candidate that year. The party selected New York Democrat Horatio Seymour as their candidate. Even without Johnson on the ticket, Republican candidate Ulysses S. Grant won 214 electoral votes versus only 80 for the Democratic ticket, and 52.7 percent of the popular vote. The major issue was on the question of how Reconstruction should be managed.

Johnson's Loyalty to the Democrats

With Johnson resisting efforts by Republicans in Congress to enforce the Thirteenth Amendment (for example, through the Civil Rights law), the South saw an ally in the president. The black codes passed by several Southern states perpetuated the conditions of slavery prior to the passage of the amendment, but Johnson aligned himself with Democrats opposed to equal rights for former slaves.

Johnson's positions led to civil unrest throughout 1866, including riots in Memphis in May and New Orleans in July:

> In May and July of 1866, Congress witnessed murderous anti-black riots in Memphis and New Orleans that were abetted by the police and civic officials. This violence convinced Congress that the political authorities in the South would not only deny blacks their right of citizenship, but also would willingly participate in their violent victimization.[26]

The Memphis Riot of 1866 took place between May 1 and 3, sparked by a conflict between a white police officer and black soldiers recently discharged from the Union Army. Federal troops were used to put down the violence, mostly civilians and policemen attacking black citizens. The outcome was 46 black and two white deaths; 75 black injuries; and over 100 robberies, as well as widespread property damage in black neighborhoods.[27]

In New Orleans that July, a group of blacks attending the Louisiana State Convention were confronted by a group of armed white men composed of Democrats, many of whom were ex–Confederates opposed to the expansion of black rights in the state. Many black citizens were beaten and federal troops were called in to control the situation.

Despite Johnson's efforts to align his policies with Democrats, the 1866 elections were an overwhelming rejection not only of Democratic Party positions, but also of the president. The public largely supported Republican efforts concerning civil rights and rejected the Democratic opposition. The party faced a choice: modify positions to gain more votes in future elections, or continue resisting Reconstruction efforts and face more losses. For many Democrats, losses were viewed only in geographic terms, as a defeat in the North but with continued support in the South. This continued reliance on ex–Confederate sympathies ignored the larger desire by the country to move forward with Reconstruction and put the

SCENES IN MEMPHIS, TENNESSEE, DURING THE RIOT—SHOOTING DOWN NEGROES ON THE MORNING OF MAY 2, 1866.—[SKETCHED BY A. R. W.]

The massive postwar Memphis Riot of 1866 resulted in many black deaths as well as widespread property damage in black neighborhoods.

past—including slavery—behind it. Typical of the stubborn opinion held by many Democrats was a statement by ex-president James Buchanan, "I have never known any good come to the Democratic party from hiding or suppressing their principles for the sake of expediency.... We should then hold up the principles of Jefferson and Jackson on our banners, and maintain them to the last."[28]

Other Democrats similarly held to their policies and refused to consider modifying them. Many blamed Johnson for the 1866 defeat, citing his weak policies and conflicts with Congress, including the inability to prevent Republican legislation from becoming law. Johnson's campaign style and offensive language also were cited as causes for 1866 losses, more so than any problems with Democratic policies. One editorial encouraged Democrats to

> cut loose from the Administration of Andrew Johnson, and leave that hybrid concern to float on the sea of public contempt into which it has some time entered, and from which no party power can rescue it.[29]

The election results led to increased mention of possible impeachment of the president. For many Democratic Party faithful, the idea was dreaded as potentially disastrous for the party. This was ironic given that Johnson was a Republican president, even though his policies and positions, as well as his opposition among Republicans, cast him as the Democrats' leader. Many editorials disagreed with the sentiments opposed to Johnson, encouraging fellow party members and the public to trust the administration, claiming that "it is entitled due credit and an equivalent degree of encouragement and support."[30]

Soon after the election, discussion resumed about the fate of the proposed Fourteenth Amendment. This would have granted citizenship on anyone born in the United States or naturalized, and banned any state laws limiting citizens' rights. Democrats, having not learned the lessons of the 1866 election, were opposed to this amendment. The hope was that by combining Johnson's opposition to it with the refusal of Southern states to ratify it, Republicans would be unable to achieve state approval for ultimate ratification. One Democrat stated that the strategy was to "give the radicals all the rope they want, hoping that they may hang themselves."[31]

By January 1867, the political mood was more polarized than ever. Republicans in the House introduced a resolution to begin investigating grounds of impeachment of President Johnson. The resolution passed with a strong majority. Within two months, Congress began debate on the Tenure of Office Act. This would have restricted the president's rights to appoint or later to remove federal officials outside of cabinet level. With the recent passage of the impeachment resolution, Republicans in the Senate

Andrew Johnson's impeachment trial, February 24, 1868. Johnson was the first president to be impeached, avoiding removal from office by a single vote.

added a provision to the draft of the Tenure Act declaring any presidential violation a "high misdemeanor" and creating grounds for impeachment.

The Tenure of Office Act was enacted on March 3, 1867, after yet another veto by the president and override by Congress. Johnson's Secretary of War, Edwin Stanton, was a Radical Republican and Johnson wanted to remove him from office. With the new law in place, this set the grounds for the impeachment battle to follow. In August, Johnson suspended Stanton while Congress was in recess. When the Senate reconvened in January 1868, it did not ratify the decision. Even so, Johnson proceeded with plans to appoint a new Secretary of War. This led to a three-month impeachment trial, resulting in a failure by one vote to remove Johnson from office. Ironically, Stanton resigned from his cabinet position a few months later.[32]

Concerns Among Democrats

Countering Johnson's resistance to civil rights for former slaves, both houses of Congress guaranteed black suffrage in newly added territories, making it a requirement. Unless a territory agreed to enfranchise black citizens, they would not be allowed to acquire statehood. Johnson worked with governors of several Southern states to develop a "Southern Plan" as an alternative to the Fourteenth Amendment. Unlike the existing draft, Johnson's Southern Plan required literacy and property ownership tests as qualification for suffrage (but exempted all who had been qualified to vote previously, meaning white citizens). The plan was sent to Southern state legislatures with a cover letter citing President Johnson's approval of the idea. The plan failed to win approval in Congress, however.[33]

Inevitably, the black vote became a reality even in Southern states. The 1867 election in Tennessee saw Radical Republican William G. Brownlow win reelection by a huge margin, based on the vote being granted to black citizens earlier the same year. Democrats saw this as the beginning of a trend in which black voters would favor Republicans by large margins in other states as well. At the same time, Johnson began plans to replace several cabinet officers (in particular, Republicans appointed by Lincoln and held over) with others more loyal to him and his anticivil rights policies. Changes were considered not only in the War Department, but also in the Treasury, State, and other cabinet positions.

As Johnson continued efforts to transform his largely Republican cabinet into a more Democratic-sympathizing one, the 1867 election made matters worse for the party. In Ohio that year, a racist campaign by Democratic candidates included appeals to white voters to fear black voting and other rights:

> Conspicuous in the Democratic processions were wagons filled with young girls, dressed in white, carrying banners inscribed with the appeal: "Fathers, save us from negro equality."[34]

Some regions of Ohio and Pennsylvania went for Democratic candidates, but by and large, voters favored Republicans. In New York, a desperate campaign focused almost solely on the racial question. The New York Democratic Convention formally condemned "Negro supremacy" and cited it as an inevitable trend that would destroy the Republic.[35]

This sentiment was also voiced in the press, with one New York-based editorial predicting that a danger existed with granting of suffrage upon "millions of stupid and ignorant people of an inferior race."[36] Similar criticism was expressed in other states as well. These arguments worked in some regions. Democrats prevailed in New York, New Jersey, and Maryland. However, the Democratic Party continued to hope for electoral victories and political power while gaining virtually no black votes. The obvious solution in their minds was to continue working to prevent widespread legalization of black suffrage.

Some Democrats, recognizing that this effort would fail, proposed gradual suffrage for former slaves, banning black voting until after 1868; and after, permitting voting only to black citizens who also were property owners. This plan, while acceptable to some Democrats, was for the most part unacceptable. Many accused fellow Democrats favoring even gradual emancipation as traitors, and called for their expulsion from the Democratic Party.[37]

The racist tone of Democratic candidates continued during 1867. Late in the year, Democratic spokesmen at the Alabama Constitutional Convention expressed confidence that eventually, emerging political power for blacks would alarm Northern voters and would prove the folly of that effort. One editorial described the move toward black voting rights:

> It is nothing more or less than trying to make water run up the hill, to make a pyramid stand on its apex, to make ignorance serve the tune of intelligence, and, in fine, to make black white.[38]

The Election of 1868

The dismal history of the Andrew Johnson presidency, coupled with growing numbers of black voters, brought Democratic politicians to a realization: The party was in trouble as long as black votes were cast primarily to Republican candidates. The elections in 1867 had been mixed, with some victories but many losses. As the party prepared for the presidential election, they also had to contend with the distraction of impeachment proceedings against Johnson.

Although the president had come to the office as a Republican vice president in Lincoln's administration, no one considered him a Republican in philosophy or spirit. Johnson intended to seek nomination in 1868 as a Democrat, which made sense to politicians on both sides. He had been at odds with Republicans for his entire term and had sided with Democrats at every opportunity. He opposed the Thirteenth and Fourteenth Amendments, the Civil Rights Act, and the Freedman's Bureau Bill.

Despite Johnson's political ambitions, the Democratic Party did not nominate him as their candidate. Instead, they selected Horatio Seymour, former governor of New York and a long-term Democrat faithful who had aligned with Copperhead sentiments during the war. His election prospects were dismal considering that he was running against a Republican candidate considered a hero of the war throughout the North, Ulysses S. Grant. Seymour was aligned against the victories of recent history:

> For many Americans the name of Horatio Seymour represents a politician who tried vainly to ignore the momentous issues which caused the Civil War, who quarreled openly with the Lincoln administration over the proper way to save the

Union, who condoned the draft riots in New York, who led a hopeless campaign to defeat General Grant for the presidency in 1868 and then passed into deserved oblivion.[39]

Seymour had entered the race reluctantly and had attended the Democratic Convention as a delegate. When his name was offered as a potential candidate, Seymour declined:

I must not be nominated by this Convention, as I could not accept the nomination if tendered. My own inclination prompted me to decline at the outset; my honor compels me to do so now. It is impossible, consistently with my position, to allow my name to be mentioned in this Convention against my protest.[40]

Unlike Seymour, Johnson wanted and even expected to be the Democratic nominee. However, he was not considered seriously as the party's candidate. He not only had shown himself to be a weak president and the source of great controversy, but also was the first president to be impeached. Even though he prevailed in the impeachment trial (by only one vote), his political reputation was damaged and could not recover. However, the selection of an alternate candidate was far from settled. It was not until the 18th ballot that Seymour was finally selected as the party's candidate.

Seymour—and the entire Democratic Party—remained controversial based on support for the Confederacy, slavery, and secession. A cartoon by Thomas Nast entitled "The Modern Sampson" was published the month before the 1868 election. In this drawing, Delilah is "Southern Democracy" and is cutting the hair of "Suffrage" while Sampson (a black man) awakens. In the background are several Democrats, including Nathan Bedford Forrest, Robert E. Lee, candidate Horatio Seymour wearing a Ku Klux Klan breastplate, vice presidential nominee Frank Blair, and others. To the right is a statue of Andrew Johnson holding a tablet labeled "veto."

The election took place on November 3, 1868. Three states were not allowed to vote, as they had not yet been accepted back into the Union. The election excluded Texas, Virginia, and Mississippi. The key issues in the election were sharply polarized. Republican candidate Grant agreed with the Radical Republicans favoring full rights of citizenship for ex-slaves, enforcement of the Thirteenth and Fourteenth Amendments, and suffrage for all freedmen. The Democratic platform criticized Negro supremacy and favored restoration of states' rights, a position that predated the Civil War, when that was a reference to states' rights for people to own slaves as property. In contrast to the Democratic candidate, Grant and his running mate, Schuler Colfax, were nominated on the first ballot during the Republican Convention, held May 20–21.

THE MODERN SAMSON.

"The Modern Sampson" (1867) featured prominent Democrats and leaders of the Ku Klux Klan.

The election was closer than many thought it would be. Grant won 52.7 percent of the popular vote and 214 Electoral College votes (versus 80 for Seymour).

A core issue in the election, not surprisingly, was black suffrage. Republicans favored universal suffrage everywhere, whereas Democrats were opposed to its realization anywhere. The evolution of the idea was inevitable, but many Democrats continued wishing for conditions prior to the Civil War. Many Democrats saw the 1868 presidential contest based primarily on the issue of race relations, the "Alpha and Omega of the Democratic faith."[41]

The election convinced Republicans that their mandate for support of suffrage was strong and that Reconstruction should be refocused on moving beyond the antagonisms of the war and racial strife. The Democrats, in pursuing policies contrary to the outcome of the war, subsequent amendments and laws, and, more than anything else, the choices made by voters, clung stubbornly to their outdated and unpopular strategies.

Upon losing the election and seeing a strong Republican take over as president, the Copperhead sentiment next turned to an even more extreme method for promoting their cause, expressed in the evolution of the Ku Klux Klan.

9

Presidents Grant and Hayes and the Ku Klux Klan

The Copperheads had lost the war and Confederate goals—secession, maintaining slavery, and the notion of states' rights—had all been overcome. Politically, the Democratic Party was in disarray and would not recover for decades.

In this dark time, an underground movement began, accelerated after the dismal Johnson administration, and became a fixture in American life for the next century. This movement was expressed through a number of secret organizations, and the best known of these groups was the Ku Klux Klan.

The image of the Ku Klux Klan has become a part of the American identity, a reaction to losing political power and seeing black rights of citizenship on the rise. The image is a strong one: dozens of men on horseback in the middle of the night, dressed in white sheets and hoods, pulling people out of their homes to be brutalized and murdered, all lit by torches, ending with burning churches and other buildings, in retribution for real or imagined wrongs committed against white America and pro–Southern ideals.[1]

The costumes worn by Klan members often were elaborate and imaginative. The association with white sheets and hoods originated from the fact that many Klan members were ex–Confederate soldiers. "It is well known that Ku-Klux frequently claimed to be ghosts of the Confederate dead."[2]

An irony of the Klan and its activities in Southern states is the contrast between nightly activities of terror and violence and the members' daily lives. Many Klan members were respected members of society, including law enforcement officers, judges, lawyers, and even members of the clergy. In fact, the Klan courted clergy actively and openly:

> Klan recruiters offered clergymen free membership, subscriptions to Klan publications, and a promise to actively promote the supremacy of Protestant Christianity.

TWO MEMBERS OF THE KU-KLUX KLAN IN THEIR DISGUISES.

Ku Klux Klan costumes often were bizarre in the early days. Some Klan members claimed to be the ghosts of dead Confederate soldiers.

Beyond that, the Klan promised to increase church attendance and even increase cash donations in the collection plate.... The Klan also made a practice of publicly rewarding ministers who were deemed to be friendly to the movement.... Frequently, such praise would be delivered in person as the Klansman, dressed in full regalia, would unexpectedly appear at a church service.[3]

A direct correlation can be drawn between Andrew Johnson's presidency and the ascendency of the Ku Klux Klan. Johnson was aligned with Democratic opinions and opposed amendments, laws, and other measures aimed at Reconstruction. This situation delayed Reconstruction through his administration, which ended in 1868. During that period, Congress passed several laws and two amendments (the Thirteenth and Fourteenth) despite opposition from the president. The laws that Johnson vetoed resulted in overrides. This conflict between what had been Lincoln's idea for healing the country and Johnson's opposition to that effort created a void.

President Grant's Election

The change of presidents from Johnson to Grant was a sharp contrast of policy and leadership. Johnson, sympathetic to the Democratic Party and opposed to suffrage for former slaves, was ineffective and tone-deaf to the mood of the country; Grant, war hero and commanding general of the army during the Civil War, was a strong leader in touch with prevailing sentiments and intent on moving Reconstruction forward to heal the wounds of the Civil War.

Grant's legacy as a two-term president is the successful execution of Reconstruction plans, removal of barriers to black suffrage, and introduction of a period of prosperity in the United States. Before winning election to the presidency, Grant had supervised army efforts in former Confederate areas during a time when army occupation was required to return the South to the Union.

Grant's impression of Johnson was negative from the moment of Lincoln's assassination. The swearing-in of Johnson on April 15, 1865, was recalled by the future president: "General Grant later said of that day that 'reconstruction had been set back, no telling how far.'"[4] As the year progressed, Grant's con-

As president, Ulysses S. Grant (photographed ca. 1875) attempted to make Reconstruction a reality.

"This is a white man's government!" was the Democrats' political slogan during the 1868 elections.

cern grew. He "looked with alarm during the last half of 1865 as Southern states began to craft constitutions denying the hard-won fruits of emancipation."[5]

In November of that first year of the new presidency, Johnson sent Grant to the South on a fact-finding mission. Grant recommended continuation of the Freedman's Bureau, which Johnson opposed strongly. Grant warned the president of threats to poor ex-slaves from disaffected ex–Confederates, foreshadowing the possibility of terrorist groups in a vacuum left after the end of the war. However, Johnson favored readmitting Confederate states without any guarantee of civil rights to ex-slaves.

In the election of 1868, Grant was nominated on the first ballot. No other candidates were even put forth in nomination. In his acceptance speech, Grant spoke four words that became his campaign slogan: "Let us have peace."[6]

Grant had not wanted the presidency but accepted the nomination with a sense of duty and devotion to the country. A month after his nomination, Grant wrote in a letter to General Sherman:

> I have been forced into this in spite of myself. I could not back down without, as it seems to me, leaving the contest for power for the next four years between mere trading politicians, the elevation of whom, no matter which party won, would lose to us, largely, the results of the costly war which we have gone through.[7]

In sharp contrast, the Democratic Party nominated Horatio Seymour, previous governor of New York. The Democratic platform focused on ending the effort of Reconstruction and returning power to the Southern states. The 1868 election was sharply drawn along lines of continuing Reconstruction, supported by Republicans, and opposing black suffrage, the platform of Democrats. A campaign slogan of the Democrats in 1868 was "This Is a White Man's Government! This Is a White Man's Country! Let the White Man Rule!"[8] This slogan was captured in a political cartoon of the election season.

The racist message did not work. Grant became at that time the youngest man elected to the presidency at age 46. This occurred even without Grant's actively campaigning. He promised at his inauguration to fight for ratification of the Fifteenth Amendment, granting the vote to all American adults without special poll taxes, property ownership requirements, or literacy tests. During his term in office, Grant appointed four new members of the Supreme Court, ending the Democrat-controlled court with majorities since 1805. Two of his appointees, Ward Hunt and Morrison Waite, had been among the founders of the Republican Party more than a decade earlier. The new appointments changed the nature of the Supreme Court just as elections were changing the mix of Congress.

Grant also had to contend with the difficulty of dismantling the terrorist Ku Klux Klan, which was focused on preventing Reconstruction and on preventing black suffrage. The history of the Klan from 1866 to its demise during Grant's term involved passage of new amendments and several laws, along with strict enforcement by Grant's Justice Department. The Klan thrived during the Johnson administration, when the president's policies were in agreement with Democrats and anti-black suffrage. Once Grant came into office, policies and enforcement changed.

The Klan was the latest in a series of secret societies on the American scene that can be traced back to the Revolutionary War. During times of conflict, such societies are expected to arise. The difference with the Klan is that it came into being not during the Civil War, but after. Its purpose was to subvert the Union victory and prevent realization of equal rights for former slaves. For a few years, this reign of terror by the "invisible empire" succeeded.

Origins of Secret Societies in the U.S.

Secret societies have fascinated historians and politicians since the founding of the United States. One of the more prominent of these was the Sons of Liberty, whose membership included Paul Revere, Samuel Adams, John Hancock, Patrick Henry, and Benjamin Rush, among other Founding Fathers. This anti-taxation group is best remembered for organizing and executing the protest of the Stamp Act on December 16, 1773, the famous Boston Tea Party. The Sons of Liberty introduced the motto, "No taxation without representation."

The Sons of Liberty was hatched among a group of colonists led by Samuel Adams. Meeting in pubs to discuss how to protest British taxation policies, the name Loyal Nine was first used by the group:

> It may have been in the back room of one of these smoke-filled pubs that Adams and his associates paid out plans for the organization of a new, secret society known as the Loyal Nine. Named for the number of its members, the Loyal Nine was formed for the specific purpose of thwarting the Stamp Act.[9]

The Loyal Nine became a core group within the Sons of Liberty. The power and influence of the organization sparked support for revolution, demonstrating that secret societies can be effective in bringing about change.

Although the Sons of Liberty ceased to exist once independence had been won, a new organization with the same name appeared as a secret society during the Civil War. It was an arm of the Knights of the Golden Circle, formed before the war began with the goal of annexing Mexico, Central America, the Caribbean, and the Northern areas of South America as new slave states to strengthen Southern political influence and power. This "golden circle" of territory was to be acquired through purchase or force of arms.

This organization, with its many name changes, was never able to gain traction for its ideas. Even so, it was monitored closely during the Civil War by the government, which was concerned with treasonous activities in the North:

> While the Government knew of the existence of this treasonable organization, and had kept track of the changes of names from its organization of the "Circle of Honor," going to the "Knights of the Golden Circle," later to the "Order of American Knights," and finally on the 22nd of February 1864 to the "Order of Sons of Liberty," it had never been about to get the manner in which it would ultimately carry out the intentions....[10]

The many secret societies in existence during the Civil War included the St. Louis-based Corps de Belgique and, in Chicago, the Democratic Invincible Club. The Louisville version was named the Democratic Reading Room and, as far away as California, Knights of the Columbian Star. In other regions, secret societies were named Knights of the Mighty Host, Knights of the Circle of Honor, and Mutual Protection Society (the MPS). All were offshoots of the Knights of the Golden Circle based in Ohio.[11]

By the end of the Civil War, these secret societies disbanded. However, before that, the government brought charges against several members of these organizations, charging them with conspiracy, affording aid and comfort to rebels, inciting insurrection, disloyal practices, and violation of the laws of war.[12]

The secret societies common during wartime tend to disband. Some, however, arise in response to the loss of war and, specifically, to the perceived loss of power and control. Among these were the *Knights of the White Camellia*, the *White Brotherhood*, and the *Ku Klux Klan*. Founded in 1866, it originally was formed for the purpose of protecting citizens against large numbers of ex-slaves, now called freedmen, and the perceived threat they posed to local white citizens.

The Klan was founded in Pulaski, Tennessee, in Giles County, where, during and before the Civil War, a large slave population had existed. The romanticized version of the Klan and its formation, as well as the underlying attitude toward black superstition, is explained in the following history of the "invisible empire" and its purpose:

> It is well to note that the very conception of the Ku Klux Klan was amid influences elevating and refining, and its charter members were gentlemen of education and refined tastes, and could not have conceived the organization of an order that had for its objects low purposes or brutal usages; Pulaski always, in a way, remained headquarters for the Klan, as many of the officers lived there, and the town was

proud of being the birthplace of this great organization, which was destined to play such an important part in the history of the Reconstruction period, 1865 to 1870.

The superstition of the negro is well known, and through this element in his makeup, the Ku Klux gained control. They made the negroes believe that they were the ghosts of their dead masters, and under the conviction that if they did wrong, spirits from the other world would visit them; the negroes became very quiet and subdued.[13]

The Klan founders, known as the "Pulaski Six," were ex–Confederate soldiers named Frank McCord, John Kennedy, James Crowe, John Lester, Calvin Jones, and Richard Reed. They were well-educated, church-going young men who had served the Confederacy with honor. When they met to form a club, bringing along additional potential members, their first task was to pick out a name. One suggestion was to use the word *Kukloi*, derived from the Greek *kuklos*, meaning a "band of brothers." From this, the term "Ku Klux" was next suggested, and "Klan" was added to it. The name had no specific meaning, but its members enjoyed the ominous sound of the name itself. Many versions of the name's source have been floated, including calling it an old Hebrew name; crediting prisoners at the Johnson Island Union Prison; a social fraternity called Kuklos Adelphion (Old Kappa Alpha); and an Asian-derived term associated with the opium trade.

Another cited source for the name was Cukucan, the god of light in Mexican culture. This god fought the forces of darkness and always won, and future Klansmen called themselves the "sons of light." With this title, they claimed to champion family values and chivalry, and especially protection of Southern white women against freedmen intent on rape.[14]

The initial boredom that inspired formation of a club was expanded as the initial core group began dressing up in elaborate ways. They introduced white sheets with the idea of pretending to be ghosts, later adding pointed hats and masks, and sewing meaningless symbols and insignia onto their robes. Next came assignment of ranks and titles, as meaningless as the costumes. The six originators held top posts in the group, which at first consisted of only themselves:

Developments in the Klan's formal garb influenced the Rules Committee, which came up with a hierarchy of six mystical offices, one for each of the members. The Grand Cyclops (McCord) functioned as president, the Grand Magi (Kennedy) as vice-president. Crowe became the first Grand Turk, an adjutant to the Grand Cyclops. Lester and Jones served as Night Hawks whose duty was to protect meetings of the group from outside interference, while Reed served as Lictor, charged with maintaining order within the meetings.[15]

The initial activities of the Klan, limited at the time to Pulaski, Tennessee, were immature and lacked purpose beyond amusement and harmless rituals. Eventually, word of Klan activities spread to other counties of

Tennessee as well as Alabama. Local Klan groups were established and quickly spread throughout many areas of the South.

The Klan's Purpose Evolves

The original six Pulaski founders of the Klan quickly lost control of the organization, which was not centralized but was more likely to be operated on a local level. At some point in 1867, nighttime visits to homes of black citizens began, employing intimidation to frighten them into compliance with white rule. The appeal of spreading terrorism among the black population after the loss of the Civil War clearly was widespread and groups embraced the idea openly. The Klan was not the only group that began using such tactics, but they emerged as the primary group, perhaps due to their memorable costumes:

> Other groups collaborating with the Klan or mimicking its tactics during Reconstruction were the Red Caps, Red Jackets and Yellow Jackets of Tennessee; the Native Sons of the South, Society of the White Rose, Knights of the Black Cross and the Robertson Family in Mississippi; Alabama's Knights of the White Carnation; South Carolina's Red Strings and Heroes of America; and Louisiana's Seymour Knights. Throughout the late Confederacy, Democratic Clubs and Rifle Clubs also committed wholesale acts of terrorism, frequently without disguises.[16]

The use of threats and even murder had limited success at first and its goal of relinquishing Republican politicians as a governing power did not succeed. The romanticized notion that the Klan somehow was the savior of Southern ideals expressed before and during the Civil War fell quickly as Klan activities became increasingly violent:

> The Ku Klux Klan was not the instrument of "redemption" for the southern states. The organization's career, though occasionally spectacular, was brief. The Klan declined in strength in part because of internal weaknesses; its lack of central organization and the failure of its leaders to control criminal elements and sadists. More fundamentally, it declined because it failed to achieve its central objective— the overthrow of Republican state governments in the South.[17]

The Klan's influence never achieved the level it envisioned. Even so, the organization continued spreading, to the point that the originators decided to formalize its rules and regulations. An organizational meeting called by the Pulaski Grand Cyclops for Klan leaders was held in Nashville in 1867, and intended to impose a constitution of sorts, which was called the Prescript, to be adhered to by all of the dens of the Klan throughout the South. The Prescript had been drafted by two important Klan members, both former Confederate generals residing in Pulaski: John C. Brown and George W. Gordon. The document was complex and included a confusing and overlapping set of officers and their duties. New officer titles beyond the original six included a Grand Monk, Grand Sentinel, Grand Ensign, Grand Scribe, and Grand Exchequer. A county-level leader, operating above the local Grand Cyclops, was the Grand Giant of the Province, aided by a series of Goblins. An even higher-level Grand Titan of the Dominion was assisted by Furies. At the state level was the Grand Dragon of the Realm and his assistants, the Hydras. At the very top was the Grand Wizard of the Empire and his ten Genii.[18]

At about the same time in 1867, a new leader of the Klan emerged. Nathan Bedford Forrest, as newly appointed Grand Wizard of the Nashville Klan, had served in the Confederate Army and was well known as a Confederate hero. His views agreed with those of the Klan. He saw the development of the black group, the Union League, as part of a broader conspiracy among blacks, Republicans, and Northern carpetbaggers and scalawags to destroy the white Southern code of honor. Under Forrest's leadership, the Klan rose to new visibility and prominence. His association with the Klan lasted only two years. His influence defined the Klan during that time and later, but Forrest saw the group moving away from what he perceived as Southern honor and tradition, overtaken by vigilantes:

> As the Klan grew in membership, it also grew more violent. Some of its members engaged in beatings, mutilations, and murder. In 1869, Forrest ordered the Klan to disband, but it persisted.[19]

Although Forrest was instrumental in growing influence of the Klan, he ultimately lost control over its activities and left the organization. Even without Forrest's leadership, however, the Klan continued operating as a force to suppress Republican

Nathan Bedford Forrest (photographed in 1877). As the Klan started to become an influential political organization, Forrest was appointed Grand Wizard of the Nashville Ku Klux Klan.

government, black rights, and any dissent from what was perceived as white supremacy. The Klan evolved into a group active in politics as well as in terrorism, intent on promoting the Democratic Party despite Republican dominance in most of the former Confederate states. Assassination was part of this evolution:

> In wide areas of the South, Reconstruction's opponents resorted to terror to secure their aim of restoring Democratic rule and white supremacy. Secret societies sprang up whose purpose was to prevent blacks from voting, and to destroy the infrastructure of the Republican party by assassinating local leaders and public officials.
>
> The most notorious such organization was the Ku Klux Klan, which in effect served as a military arm of the Democratic party.... During the 1868 presidential election, Klansmen assassinated Arkansas congressman James M. Hinds, three members of the South Carolina legislature, and other Republican leaders. In Georgia and Louisiana, the Klan established a reign of terror so complete that blacks were unable to go to the polls to vote, and Democrats carried both states for Horatio Seymour.[20]

The Klan as an Underground Terrorist Organization

The arrival of the Ku Klux Klan on the scene of Reconstruction was by no means spontaneous. As it evolved into a terrorist group, it was an expression of Southern resistance to the Union in the post–Civil War era. The goal expressed by Lincoln toward the end of the war was not to restore the old South, but to build a new unified nation, to change the future by doing away with the attitudes that promoted slavery and, after the war, racial hatred. In the minds of the extreme elements of the South, Reconstruction would destroy the aristocracy that had dominated Southern culture and politics for decades.

Political activism by Northerners, often intended as part of the effort to participate in state government or to teach in schools, was derided as interference by many Southerners, referring collectively to those coming to the South as carpetbaggers. With little doubt, many Northerners went to the South during Reconstruction for their own financial gain, but the term was applied broadly to any and all Northerners relocating into previously Confederate states. A related term, "scalawags," referred to white Southerners who cooperated with Republican governments and helped black freedmen.

During the 1868 election season, a cartoon appeared promising that the Klan would lynch scalawags and carpetbaggers on the day the new president took office, assuming the Democrat Horatio Seymour would prevail.

A PROSPECTIVE SCENE IN THE CITY OF OAKS, 4TH OF MARCH, 1869.

An 1868 cartoon promised that scalawags and carpetbaggers would be lynched by the Klan upon a Democratic victory.

The use of such terms defined everyone who disagreed with the Southern traditions as an enemy of what Southerners believed should have been the ruling class. For decades, a Southern aristocracy had ruled the region and controlled the slave trade, and the Civil War destroyed that power structure. In response, the Klan became not only an activist group but a political group as well.

That translated to escalating levels of violence, from beatings and murders of black voters to assassination of Republican officials. However, these extreme measures did not stop the flow of progress made politically and legally. By 1869, in the last month of Johnson's administration, Congress voted in favor of the Fifteenth Amendment, which legalized the vote for all citizens of legal age, without exclusion of freedmen. The amendment read: "The right of citizens to vote shall not be denied or abridged by the United States or by any State on account of race, color, or previous condition of servitude."[21]

The ramifications of this new amendment were viewed politically:

For Democrats, the amendment was yet another example of the autocratic, Republican-dominated federal government imposing its will on the vanquished Southland. They viewed this development as the "most revolutionary measure" ever devised by Congress, loathsome because it specifically adopted "the colored race as its special wards and favorites."[22]

The amendment did not prevent states from imposing literacy tests on would-be voters, assessing special poll taxes, or passing laws requiring voters to also be property owners. Consequently, the amendment lacked mechanisms to enforce its underlying intention. The Klan, in response to the amendment, was determined to prevent it from being applied to allow blacks to vote. The invisibility of the Klan and its membership aggravated this problem. The federal Justice Department had to contend with reality, seeing that

> the American Civil War had not really ended in 1865, but that it had resumed as a guerilla war. During the presidential campaign, the Ku Klux Klan emerged as a paramilitary wing of the Democratic Party and embarked on a campaign of terror for the purpose of destroying the Republican Party in the Southern states and reducing Southern blacks to the control of white supremacists…. Victims of Klan violence were the most defenseless members of society, lacking resources and often not equipped to testify, primarily out of fear of retribution. These same victims could not rely on local law enforcement officers because local officers often were Klansmen who participated in the terrorism. Even when local officials wanted to bring the criminals to justice, fear or weakness prevented them from doing so. Often, the enormous number of Klansmen who engaged in a single incident of terrorism overwhelmed the meager resources of local governments, making it difficult to bring a case given limited resources.[23]

Congress attempted to remedy the problems of enforcing the Fifteenth Amendment by passing three new laws. First was the Enforcement Act of 1870 (also known as the Civil Rights Act of 1870 or the First Ku Klux Klan Act). This new law gave the president the power to enforce the new amendment and to prosecute attacks by the Ku Klux Klan on black citizens or state officials. This new act did not change matters, for the same reasons that had led to its passage. It "was inadequate, and victims often failed to testify because of the intimidation they faced."[24]

A second law, the Second Enforcement Act (also called the Civil Rights Act of 1871 or the Second Ku Klux Klan Act), was intended to strengthen provisions of the 1870 bill, but had little effect. The third law, the Third Enforcement Act (also known as the Third Ku Klux Klan Act), allowed the president to suspend the writ of *habeas corpus* as a measure to combat the Klan and other terrorist groups. Using this new power, newly elected President Grant was able to shut down the Klan, which did not reemerge until the following century.

The success of the Third Enforcement Act in disbanding the Klan in the South was a convincing argument, even though several Democrats in the House of Representatives had argued against the bill. For example, Representative Samuel S. Cox (D–NY) argued while the bill was under consideration that the Klan's activities had been exaggerated by Republican lawmakers, but that to the extent that vigilante actions took place, it was the result of forcing white Southerners to be ruled by inexperienced and incompetent blacks. He stated on the record that Congress had placed those state governments in the hands of "the inferior race." He also claimed that the Klan had been formed "only to 'scare' the superstitious blacks." Justifying the Klan's activities, Cox asked, "Can we not understand why men, born free ... are compelled to hide in Ku Klux Klan or other secret clans, and strike against this ruin and desolation?"[25]

The apologetic tone set by Cox and other Democrats did not stop the vote from gaining approval. Support for the bill was primarily Republican and opposition primarily Democratic. However, the results were impressive in terms of shutting down the terrorism. As a result of passing the new law, Congress began a series of effective actions to correct the situation. The use of federal troops in place of state militias to enforce the new law and prosecution in federal courts was effective because it removed the local intimidation that had previously prevented enforcement. Hundreds of Klan members were imprisoned in South Carolina alone, where the Klan had been particularly active. The impact of bringing in federal courts and juries spread rapidly throughout the rest of the South, shutting down the Klan.

Even with many Democrats in Congress voting against the Third Enforcement Act, it proved effective when used to imprison Klan members on conspiracy charges. This destroyed the power and influence of the Klan in the South, even though it was not effective in netting the biggest offenders:

> Despite their success in winning convictions time after time on conspiracy charges, the government attorneys were unable to prosecute the most wanted Klansmen, most of whom had fled. Those who stood trial were generally not the influential members of the community responsible for spearheading the Klan's activities....[26]

Grant's Second Administration

Among the most important and noteworthy successes of Grant's first administration was the dismantling of the Ku Klux Klan. However, even with the Klan discredited and removed from influence, other groups continued subverting Southern state governments. These included so-called "Redeemers," who represented a segment of the Democratic Party pursuing policies of redemption (meaning getting Republicans out of office in the South) and replacing them with anti–Reconstruction and anti-black suffrage candidates.

Redeemers tended to lump together the forces of Republicanism with freedmen, carpetbaggers (Northerners interfering in Southern affairs), and scalawags (Southerners sympathetic with Republican policies). Redeemers wished for a return to power among the wealthy landowners and plantation class that had dominated in the South before the Civil War. The reality in the period after the Civil War was that Republicans were firmly in control of state governments in most of the previously Confederate states. With the Confederate desire for secession discredited, and with the new federally enforced black vote, the Democratic Party was out of touch with the new political direction.

The three amendments passed since the end of the war (the 13th, 14th, and 15th) were largely a part of the new landscape, even as many white Southern citizens did not approve of the massive cultural changes brought about after the war, including black suffrage and other civil rights. Denying the ramifications of defeat by the Union, this segment of Southern society had difficulty adjusting to the new realities of life in the former Confederacy. This is what had given rise to the Ku Klux Klan, notably during the Johnson administration, when the executive branch of the federal government had no direct interest in enforcing newly won rights for ex-slaves. Under Grant's first administration that had all changed, with enforcement of amendments to the Constitution, anti–Klan laws, and direct legal action ending the Klan's activities during Reconstruction.

Redeemers supported paramilitary organizations that rose up after the disappearance of the Klan. The names were different but tactics and sentiment were the same. The secret societies appearing in Grant's second administration continued using violence and intimidation to suppress the black vote and discourage or threaten Republican candidates.

The Red Shirts was a group supporting white supremacy and opposed to black suffrage and government policies during Reconstruction. The group first appeared in Mississippi near the end of Grant's second term in 1875. It gained the name when members of the Democratic Party wore red shirts as part of a campaign of threats to Republican candidates and freedmen during election campaigns.

The Red Shirt movement, as part of the Democratic Party, was massive and effective, not only in voter suppression but also in bringing Reconstruction to an end. Grant and his administration had dismantled the Klan, but that led to replacement by a more visible and more organized movement. The Red Shirts were able to recruit large numbers of Democratic Party members and to intimidate Republican voters and candidates as well as black voters:

> In South Carolina, the end of Reconstruction was brought about by the massive mobilization of white Democratic men in Red Shirt units. Historians estimate that at the height of the 1876 campaign nearly three hundred of these units existed, with as many as fifteen thousand men.[27]

The basis of white supremacy for the Red Shirts, coupled with its direct association with the Democratic Party, defined the Southern political swing away from Republican control and toward Democratic control of Southern state governments. This occurred as Grant's administration wound up, and as Reconstruction ended. After Grant, the new president, Rutherford B. Hayes, was ineffective and unable to continue protecting the civil rights of blacks in the South. In fact, Hayes undid much of the progress Grant had made previously in protecting civil rights.

Hayes enacted what has been called his "Southern Policy." It was based on compromise rather than enforcement of law. He believed a new Republican South would combine Republicans and black voters and that Southern white citizens would welcome this policy in which moderation replaced the enforcement of law practiced in the previous administration. This policy consisted of four articulated principles: elimination of violence against black Southerners based on politics, agreement among white Southerners with the three new constitutional amendments, education and federal aid to help the economy of the South, and strong local government throughout the region. The Southern Policy was doomed to fail because it relied on the cooperation of Democrats, which could not occur just due to declaring a new Southern Policy. To many Republicans, all of the progress made by Grant was undone by Hayes:

> To Southern Radicals as well as to many Northern ones, Hayes had made a blunder in his Southern policy. He had deserted his party in the South and was, therefore, not a good Republican.[28]

The White League (also called the White Man's League) appeared in Louisiana. This group operated

Rutherford B. Hayes (photographed ca. 1875) followed Grant as president, but was ineffective in continuing Reconstruction policies. He believed the Southern states would solve racial problems if left alone.

out in the open, unlike the secretive and "invisible" Ku Klux Klan, but held closely to the same values: anti-black and anti–Republican, as well as anyone else perceived as traitors. Their stated purpose was to overthrow Reconstruction-era Republican state governments. The White League was represented in a cartoon of the times, showing the old Copperhead slogan during the Civil War, "the Union as it was, the Constitution as it is." A black family cowers between a lynched black body on the left and a burned schoolhouse on the right, with the label, "Worse than slavery." Shaking hands are representatives of the White League and the Ku Klux Klan.

"The Union as It Was" (1874). The White League continued the efforts of the Ku Klux Klan to promote white supremacy as a core purpose of the Democratic Party.

A change in policy in the Hayes administration encouraged this theme as well as the ability to operate out in the open, and by 1874, the goal and purpose of the White League—to promote white supremacy—were endorsed by the Democratic Party, which was affiliated with the White League directly:

> The White Leaguers shared a singular animus against the traitors to their race, both scalawags and carpetbaggers, who had aliened the black masses from them. They favored the social and economic ostracism of these white Judases and Benedict Arnolds, and many of their rasher statements contained faintly concealed threats against the lives of white Republicans.... The White League operated openly with extensive press coverage of its activities. Few persons tried to conceal their membership in the organization, perhaps because there was decreasing danger that the federal government would move against them.... The relationship between the White League and the Democratic party was simple: the party convention, which met in Baton Rouge in August, adopted a platform calling for ... the preservation of white civilization.[29]

When the Democratic Party regained political control in Louisiana's government in 1876, the White League was absorbed by the state militias and the National Guard. By the same year, Democrats (with support of the "Redeemer" groups) had retaken control of all except three of the Southern state governments. Violence against black voters and Republican politicians began escalating once again. A new law, the Civil Rights Act of 1875, had passed in Congress but it was not strongly enforced. (This law was declared unconstitutional by the Supreme Court in 1883.) This last piece of legislation marked the end of Reconstruction, as President Hayes enacted a policy of non-intervention in the affairs of Southern states; he showed little interest in enforcement of amendments and laws protecting civil rights for ex-slaves.

President Hayes ended sending federal troops to the South despite widespread violence against blacks while trying to vote. This was based on assurances by Southern state leaders that they would protect blacks and ensure their rights, a promise that was not kept. Hayes was responding to frustrations with the slow pace of Reconstruction and a desire for the period to come to an end. Thus it was that politicians in both parties abandoned the ideals expressed by Lincoln. Emancipation was delayed, and Reconstruction ended not with a true victory, but with a whimper.[30]

Chapter Notes

Chapter 1

1. "A Pill Too Bitter to Swallow." *The Observer* (November 11, 2000). Comparing the election of 2000 to that of 1876 and the polarizing consequences of uncertain electoral outcomes.

2. http://us-presidents.insidegov. com/.

3. Civil War Trust. www.civilwar.org.

4. Oxford English Dictionary. oed. com. 2013.

5. Potter, D. M. (1976). *The Impending Crisis, 1848–1861*. New York: Harper Collins, 450.

6. "Race, Voting Rights and Segregation." *University of Michigan*. http://umich. edu/~lawrace/votetour2.htm. Retrieved March 23, 2017.

7. Woodson, C. G. (1925). *Negro Orators and Their Orations*. Washington, D.C.: The Associated Publishers, Inc., 375.

8. Strausbaugh, J. (2006). *Black Like You: Blackface, Whiteface, Insult and Imitation in American Popular Culture*. New York: Jeremy P. Tarcher, Penguin, 92–93.

9. Woodward, C. V. & McFeely, W. S. (2001). *The Strange Career of Jim Crow*. New York: Oxford University Press, 7.

10. Rable, G. C. (1984). *But There Was No Peace: The Role of Violence in the Politics of Reconstruction*. Athens: University of Georgia Press, 132.

11. www.history.com/topics/ku-klux-klan. Retrieved March 28, 2017.

12. McClennan, G. B. 1864 Election Broadside. *Civil War Trust*. www. civilwar.org/education. Retrieved March 28, 2017.

Chapter 2

1. "The most oppressive dominion ever exercised by man over man." James Madison quote referring to the institution of slavery, in Cheney, L. (2014). *James Madison: A Life Reconsidered*. New York: Viking, 214.

2. United States Constitution (1776). *Preamble*.

3. The phrase "peculiar institution" is a reference to the practice of slavery.

4. http://www.civil-war.net/pages/ 1860_census.html.

5. http://www.civilwarhome.com/ casualties.html.

6. Detweiler, F. (April 1958). "Congressional Debate on Slavery and the Declaration of Independence, 1819–1821." *American Historical Review* 63: 605.

7. Singh, M. "Traditional or Chattel Slavery." *The Feminist Sexual Ethics Project*. http://www.brandeis.edu/projects/ fse/slavery/contemporary/essay-chattel-slavery.html. Retrieved April 12, 2016.

8. Donoghue, J. (October 2010). "Out of the Land of Bondage: The English Revolution and the Atlantic Origins of Abolition." *The American Historical Review*.

9. Higginbotham, A. L. (1975). *In the Matter of Color: Race and the American Legal Process: The Colonial Period*. Westport, CT: Greenwood Press, 62, 126.

10. Wood, W. J. (January 1970). "The Illegal Beginning of American Negro Slavery." *American Bar Association Journal* 56: 45–49.

11. Banks, T. L. (2008). "Dangerous Women: Elizabeth Key's Freedom Suit— Subjecthood and Racialized Identity in Seventeenth Century Colonial Virginia." *Akron Law Review*: 799–837.

12. Virginia Slave Codes (1705).

13. Wills, G. (2003). *Negro President: Jefferson and the Slave Power.* Boston: Houghton Mifflin, 51–52.

14. Morton, J. C. (2005). *Shapers of the Great Debate at the Constitutional Convention of 1787: A Biographical Dictionary.* Westport, CT: Greenwood Publishing Group, 306.

15. Maltz, E. M. (Spring 1997). "The Idea of a Proslavery Constitution." *Journal of the Early Republic* 17: 48–9.

16. Ferrand, M., ed. (1967). *Records of the Federal Convention of 1787.* New Haven, CT: Yale University Press, 221–3.

17. Beeman, R. (2009). *Plain Honest Men: The Making of the American Constitution.* New York: Random House, 154–155.

18. Griffith, E. (1907). *The Rise and Development of the Gerrymander.* Chicago: Scott, Foresman and Co., 72–73. The term "gerrymander" was first used in the *Boston Gazette* on March 26, 1812.

19. Maloney, C. (March 23, 1999). In *Congressional Record—House,* 5344.

20. United States Constitution. Article 1. Section 2. Clause 3.

21. *Ibid.,* as revised.

22. Wills, 5–6.

23. Hamilton, A., cited in Elliot, J., ed. (1866). *The Debates in The Several State Conventions On The Adoption Of The Federal Constitution, As Recommended By The General Convention At Philadelphia, In 1787.* Philadelphia, PA: J.B. Lippincott & Co., 237.

24. Richards, L. L. (2000). *The Slave Power: The Free North and Southern Domination, 1780–1860.* Baton Rouge: Louisiana State University Press, 3.

25. Peace Democrats, also called Copperheads, were Northern Democrats who favored making peace with the South to end the Civil War and allowing the institution of slavery to continue.

26. Divine, R. A.; Breen, T. H.; Williams, R. H.; Gross, A. J.; & Brands, H. W. (2007). *The American Story,* 5th ed. New York: Pearson, 147.

27. Nevins, A. (1947). *Ordeal of the Union: Fruits of Manifest Destiny, 1847–1852.* New York: Scribner, 111–112.

28. Story, J. (1873). *Commentaries on the Constitution of the United States.* New York: Little, Brown, 228.

29. *Strader v. Graham* (1851). 51 U.S. 82, 96, 97.

30. Finkelman, (Winter 1986). "Slavery and the Northwest Ordinance: A Study in Ambiguity." *Journal of the Early Republic* 6(4): 345.

31. United States Constitution. Article 4. Section 2. Clause 3.

32. Gutzman, K. R. (Winter 1995). "A Troublesome Legacy: James Madison and 'The Principles of '98,'" *Journal of the Early Republic* 15(4): 569–90.

33. Pohlmann, M. & Whisenhunt, L. (2002). *Student's Guide to Landmark Congressional Laws on Civil Rights.* Westport, CT: Greenwood Publishing Group, 22.

34. Baker, R. (2014). "A Better Story in Prigg v. Pennsylvania?" *Journal of Supreme Court History* 39: 171.

35. Chernow, R. (2004). *Alexander Hamilton.* New York: Penguin, 587.

36. Slave Trade Act of 1794, Section 1.

37. Williams, E. (1994). *Capitalism and Slavery.* Chapel Hill: University of North Carolina Press, 7.

38. Stewart, D. O. (2007). *The Summer of 1787.* New York: Simon & Schuster, 71.

39. *Ibid.,* 68–70.

40. "United States Department of Labor and Commerce Bureau of the Census" (1909). *A Century of Population Growth From the First Census of the United States to the Twelfth, 1790–1900.* Washington, D.C.: Government Printing Office, 132–139.

41. Beeman, 318–329.

42. Burgan, M. (2002). *The Louisiana Purchase.* Minneapolis, MN: Compass Point Books, 36.

43. United States Constitution. Article 1. Section 9.

44. Jefferson, T. (December 2, 1806). "Annual Message to Congress," in *The Avalon Project.* Yale Law School. http://avalon.law.yale.edu.

45. Cutler, C. C. (1984). *Greyhounds of the Sea,* 3rd Ed. Annapolis, MD: Naval Institute Press, 39.

46. Moore, G. (1966). *The Missouri Compromise, 1819–1821.* Lexington: University of Kentucky Press, 114.

47. Bailyn, B. (1992). *The Ideological Origins of the American Revolution.* Cambridge, MA: Belknap Press, 246.

48. Both men belonged to the Demo-

cratic Republican Party, which was later renamed the Democratic Party.

49. Muzzey, D. & Link, A. (1968). *Our Country's History*, 21st ed. Boston: Ginn and Co., 208.

50. Peterson, M. D. (1960). *The Jefferson Image in the American Mind*. Charlottesville: University of Virginia Press, 548.

51. Tocqueville, A. de (1835). *Democracy in America*, Chapter XVIII, "The Present and Probable Future Condition of the Three Races that Inherit the Territory of the United States."

52. Smith, W. H. (1903). *A Political History of Slavery*. Ann Arbor: University of Michigan Press, 83, 102.

53. Weisenberger, F. P. (1941). *The Passing of the Frontier: 1825–1850*. Columbus: Ohio State Archaeological Society, 450.

54. Going, C. B. (1924). *David Wilmot: Free-Soiler*. New York: Appleton, 134–135.

55. Wilmot, D. (October 29, 1847). Speech in Albany, NY.

56. *New York Herald*. August 11, 1946.

57. Foner, E. (September 1969). "The Wilmot Proviso Revisited." *The Journal of American History* 56(2): 262–279.

58. Richards, 152.

59. The term "doughface" was devised by John Randolph of Virginia to describe Northern politicians who voted with the South.

60. *Ibid.*, 159.

61. Cooper, W. J., Jr. (1980). *The South and the Politics of Slavery, 1828–1856*. Baton Rouge: Louisiana State University Press, 233–234.

62. Nevins, 12–13.

63. Schlesinger, A. M., Jr. (October 1949). "The Causes of the Civil War: A Note on Historical Sentimentalism." *Partisan Review* 16: 969–981.

64. Potter, D. M. (1976). *The Impending Crisis, 1848–1861*. New York: Harper Collins, 51–52.

65. Berwanger, E. H. (1967). *The Frontier Against Slavery: Western Anti-Negro Prejudice and the Slavery Extension Controversy*. Urbana: University of Illinois Press, 123–137.

66. Potter, 159.

67. *Ibid.*, 97.

68. Morris, T. D. (1974). *Free Men All*. Baltimore, MD: Johns Hopkins University Press, 49

69. Gates, W. (1954). *Fifty Million Acres: Conflicts Over Kansas Land Policy*. Ithaca, NY: Cornell University Press, 19–22, 48–70.

70. Chase S. P. & Giddings, J. (January 24, 1854). "The Appeal of the Independent Democrats in Congress to the People of the United States." *Washington National Era*.

71. Cutler, W. G. (1883). *History of the State of Kansas*. Davenport, IA: A. T. Andreas, 1586.

72. Martis, K. C. (1989). *The Historical Atlas of Political Parties in the United States Congress, 1789–1989*. New York: Prentice Hall College Division, 380–390.

73. Maier, (1998). *American Scripture: Making the Declaration of Independence*. New York: Vintage Press, 200.

74. Potter, 154–155.

75. Woodward, C. (2011). *American Nations: A History of the Eleven Rival Regional Cultures of North America*. New York: Penguin, 207.

76. Potter, 190.

77. Brown, C. H. (1980). *Agents of Manifest Destiny: The Lives and Times of the Filibusters*. Chapel Hill: University of North Carolina Press, 141.

Chapter 3

1. Adams, J. (October 2, 1780). Letter to Jonathan Jackson: "There is nothing which I dread so much as a division of the republic into two great parties, each arranged under its leader, and concerting measures in opposition to each other. This, in my humble apprehension, is to be dreaded as the greatest political evil under our Constitution."

2. Jefferson, T. (April 1898). Letter to John Wise, in Thorpe, F. N., ed. *American Historical Review* 3(3): 488–89.

3. Chambers, W. N., ed. (1972). *The First Party System: Federalists and Republicans*. Hoboken, NJ: John Wiley & Sons, 124.

4. Lampi, J. (2013). "The Federalist Party Resurgence, 1808–1816." *Journal of the Early Republic* 33(2): 255–281, citing Elkins, S. & McKitrick, E. (1995). *The Age of Federalism*. New York: Oxford University Press, 83.

5. King-Owen, S. (2012). "To 'Write Down the Republican Administration':

William Boylan and the Federalist Party in North Carolina, 1800–1805." *North Carolina Historical Review* 89(2): 155–183.

6. Richards, L. L. (2000). *The Slave Power: The Free North and Southern Domination, 1780–1860.* Baton Rouge: Louisiana State University Press, 112.

7. Wilentz, S. (September 2010). "Book Reviews." *Journal of American History* 97(2): 476.

8. Formisano, R. P. "State Development in the Early Republic," in Shafer, B. & Badger, A., eds. (2001). *Contesting Democracy: Substance and Structure in American Political History, 1775–2000.* Lawrence: University Press of Kansas, 7–35.

9. Diggins, J. P. (1994). *Up from Communism.* New York: Columbia University Press, 390.

10. Parsons, L. (2009). *The Birth of Modern Politics: Andrew Jackson, John Quincy Adams, and the Election of 1828.* New York: Oxford University Press, 164.

11. Shalhope, R. E. (2009). *The Baltimore Bank Riot: Political Upheaval in Antebellum Maryland.* Champaign: University of Illinois Press, 147.

12. Potter, D. M. (1976). *The Impending Crisis, 1848–1861.* New York: Harper Collins, 118.

13. Holt, M. F. (1999). *The Rise and Fall of the American Whig Party.* New York: Oxford University Press, 83.

14. Potter, 226.

15. Sewell, R. H. (1965). *John P. Hale and the Politics of Abolition.* Cambridge, MA: Harvard University Press, 87.

16. Foner, E. (October 1965). "Politics and Prejudice: The Free Soil Party and the Negro, 1849–1852." *The Journal of Negro History* 50(4): 239–256.

17. Rawley, J. A. (1969). *Race and Politics.* Philadelphia: J. B. Lippincott, 13–14.

18. Richards, 156–157.

19. The original Republican Party (later named the Democratic Party) was also referred to during this time as the Democratic Republican Party.

20. Wilentz, S. (2008). *The Rise of American Democracy: Jefferson to Lincoln.* New York: Horton, 42.

21. Russell, B., in the Boston *Columbian Centinel* (July 12, 1817).

22. Remini, R. V. (1959). *Martin Van Buren and the Making of the Democratic Party.* New York: Columbia University Press, 24.

23. Engerman, S. L. & Sokoloff, K. L. (2005). *The Evolution of Suffrage Institutions in the New World.* Cambridge, MA: National Bureau of Economics, 14; and Keyssar, A. (2009). *The Right to Vote: The Contested History of Democracy in the United States.* New York: Basic Books, 54.

24. Norton, M. B.; Sheriff, C.; Katzman, D. M.; Blight, D. W.; & Chudacoff, H. (2007). *A People and a Nation: A History of the United States, Vol. 1: To 1877.* Boston: Houghton Mifflin Harcourt, 327.

25. The term was first used regarding the Adams and Clay deal in 1824. Two additional political events were also called corrupt bargains. These were the election of 1876, in which Rutherford B. Hayes won the election amidst accusations of a corrupt deal, and, more recently, the 1974 pardon of Richard Nixon by Gerald Ford, in which a deal exchanging the pardon for the presidency took place.

26. Norton, *et al.*, 287.

27. Van Buren, M. First Inaugural Address (March 4, 1837). www.gutenberg.org.

28. Brown, R. H. (Winter 1966). "The Missouri Crisis, Slavery, and the Politics of Jacksonianism." *South Atlantic Quarterly* 61: 55–72.

29. Ellis, R. E. (1987). *The Union at Risk: Jacksonian Democracy, States' Rights, and the Nullification Crisis.* New York: Oxford University Press, 4.

30. Korsi, M. J. (2004). *A Seat of Popular Leadership: The Presidency, Political Parties, and Democratic Government.* Amherst: University of Massachusetts Press, 132.

31. Decredico, M. A. "Sectionalism and the Secession Crisis," in Boles, John B., ed. (2004). *A Companion to the American South.* Hoboken, NJ: Wiley-Blackwell, 240.

32. Burnham, W. B. (1955). *Presidential Ballots.* Baltimore: Johns Hopkins University Press, 77.

33. Chicago: University of Chicago Press, 42.

34. Potter, 445.

35. *Ibid.*, 423.

36. Trefousse, H. (1991). *Historical Dictionary of Reconstruction.* Westport, CT: Greenwood Publishing, 175–176.

37. Benson, G. (1938). *Abraham Lincoln*. Garden City, NY: Garden City Publishing, 117.

38. Johnson, C. W., ed. (1893). *Proceedings of the First Three Republican National Conventions of 1856, 1860 and 1864*. Minneapolis, MN: Harrison and Smith Printers, 4.

39. Schlesinger, A. M., Jr.; Troy, G.; & Israel, F. L. (2011). *History of American Presidential Elections*. New York: Facts on File, 1020.

40. Gienapp, W. E. (1985). "Nativism and the Creation of a Republican Majority in the North Before the Civil War." *Journal of American History* 72(3): 529–559.

41. Leonard, I. M. (1966). "The Rise and Fall of the American Republican Party in New York City, 1843–1845." *New York Historical Society Quarterly* 50: 151–92.

42. Jaffa, H. V. (2000). *A New Birth of Freedom: Abraham Lincoln and the Coming of the Civil War*. Lanham, MD: Rowman & Littlefield, 299–300.

43. White, R. C., Jr. (2009). *A. Lincoln: A Biography*. New York: Random House, 251.

44. Wender, H. (1930). *Southern Commercial Conventions*. Baltimore, MD: Johns Hopkins University Press, 234.

45. Freehling, W. W. (2007). *The Road to Disunion*, Vol II. New York: Oxford University Press, 267.

46. Luthin, R. H. (1944). *The First Lincoln Campaign*. Cambridge, MA: Harvard University Press, 227.

47. Wentworth, J. (August 1, 1860), in *New York Herald*.

Chapter 4

1. From the decision in *Dred Scott v. Sandford* (1857). 60 U.S. 393: "Scott and his family upon their return were not free, but were, by the laws of Missouri, the property of the defendant; and that the Circuit Court of the United States had no jurisdiction, when, by the laws of the State, the plaintiff was a slave, and not a citizen."

2. Card, R. (2010). "Can States 'Just Say No' to Federal Health Care Reform? The Constitutional and Political Implications of State Attempts to Nullify Federal Law." *B.Y.U. Law Review*, 1795, 1808.

3. United States Constitution (1776). Article 6. Clause 2.

4. Madison, J. (January 25, 1788). *Federalist* No. 44.

5. Tocqueville, A. de (1835). *Democracy in America*, Chapter VI, "Judicial Power in the United States, and Its Influence on Political Society."

6. Hamilton, A. (May 28, 1788). *Federalist* No. 78.

7. *McCulloch v. Maryland* (1819). 17 U.S. 316.

8. United States Constitution. Article 1. Section 8. Clause 18.

9. Newmyer, R. K. (2000). "John Marshall, McCulloch v. Maryland, and the Southern States' Rights Tradition." *Faculty Articles and Papers*, 182.

10. *Gibbons v. Ogden* (1824). 22 U.S. (9 Wheaton) 1, 33–159.

11. Lightner, D. L. (November 2004). "The Supreme Court and the Interstate Slave Trade: A Study in Evasion, Anarchy, and Extremism." *Journal of Supreme Court History* 29(3): 229–253.

12. *The Antelope*, 23 U.S. 66 (1825).

13. Noonan, J. T. (1977). *The Antelope: The Ordeal of the Recaptured Africans in the Administrations of James Monroe and John Quincy Adams*. Oakland: University of California Press, 17–19.

14. *Statutes at Large of the United States of America, 1789–1873* (1845). Vol. 3. pp. 532–34.

15. *Ibid.*, 31–32.

16. *Ibid.*, 32–33, 43, 44.

17. Newmyer, R. K. (1968). *The Supreme Court Under Marshall and Taney*. Storrs: University of Connecticut, 93.

18. Huebner, T. S. (2010). "Roger B. Taney and the Slavery Issue: Looking Beyond—and Before—Dred Scott." *Journal of American History* 97(1): 17–38.

19. Konig, D. T.; Finkelman, P.; & Bracey, C. A. (2014). *The Dred Scott Case: Historical and Contemporary Perspectives on Race and Law*. Athens: Ohio University Press, 228.

20. Horne, G. (2012). *Negro Comrades of the Crown: African Americans and the British Empire Fight the U.S. Before Emancipation*. New York: New York University Press, 97–98.

21. Dunham, A. & Kurland, B., eds. (1964). *Mr. Justice*, quoting Carl Brent

Swisher: "Mr. Chief Justice Taney." Chicago: University of Chicago Press, 43.

22. *Mayor of New York v. Miln* (1837). 33 U.S. 120.

23. *United States v. Libellants and Claimants of the Schooner Amistad* (1841). 40 U.S. 518.

24. Davis, D. B. (2006). *Inhuman Bondage: The Rise and Fall of Slavery in the New World.* New York: Oxford University Press, 15.

25. Adams, J. Q. (2010). *Arguments of John Quincy Adams Before the Supreme Court of the U.S. In the Case of the U.S. vs. Cinque and Others, Africans Captured in the Schooner Amistad (1841).*Whitefish, MT: Kessinger Publishing, 10.

26. The Adams–Onís Treaty between the U.S. and Spain in 1819 ceded Florida to the U.S. and established the border between the U.S. and New Spain (Mexico).

27. Jones, H. (1997). *Mutiny on the Amistad: The Saga of a Slave Revolt and Its Impact on American Abolition, Law, and Diplomacy,* Chapter 5. New York: Oxford University Press.

28. *Prigg v. Pennsylvania* (1842). 41 U.S. 539.

29. *Ibid.*

30. United States Constitution. Article 4. Section 2. Clause 2.

31. State of Pennsylvania (March 1, 1780). "An Act for the Gradual Abolition of Slavery, amendment."

32. Amar, A. R. (2005). *America's Constitution: A Biography.* New York: Random House, 262.

33. *Prigg.* Opinion of Justice Joseph Story.

34. United States Constitution. Article 6. Clause 2.

35. *Prigg.*

36. Gara, L. (September 1964). "The Fugitive Slave Law: A Double Paradox." *Civil War History* 10(3): 229–240.

37. *Strader v. Graham* (1851). 51 U.S. 82.

38. *Ibid.*

39. *Jones v. Van Zandt* (1847). 46 U.S. 215.

40. *Kentucky Law Journal* 97(3): 353–438.

41. *Dred Scott v. Sandford* (1857). 60 U.S. 393.

42. Huebner, T. S. (2015). "'The Unjust Judge': Roger B. Taney, the Slave Power, and the Meaning of Emancipation." *Journal of Supreme Court History* 40(3): 249–262.

43. Konig, *et al.,* 213.

44. Vincent C. H. (1967). *Dred Scott's Case.* New York: Russell & Russell, 2.

45. *Somerset v. Stewart* (1772). 98 Eng. Rep. 499 (K.B.).

46. *Winny v. Whitesides* (November 1824). Supreme Court of Missouri, St. Louis District, 1 Mo. 472.

47. *Ibid.*

48. Ehrlich, W. (1979). *They Have No Rights: Dred Scott's Struggle for Freedom.* Westport, CT: Greenwood Press.

49. *Rachel v. Walker* (1834). 4, Mo. 350.

50. Maltz, E. M. (2007). *Dred Scott and the Politics of Slavery.* Lawrence: University Press of Kansas, 115.

51. *Dred Scott.*

52. Paterson, I. (Summer, 1949). "The Riddle of Chief Justice Taney in the Dred Scott Decision." *The Georgia Review* 3(2): 192–203.

53. *Ibid.*

54. Ross, M. A. (2003). *Justice of Shattered Dreams: Samuel Freeman Miller and the Supreme Court During the Civil War Era.* Baton Rouge: Louisiana State University Press, 41.

55. Huston, J. L. (1987). *The Panic of 1857 and the Coming of the Civil War.* Baton Rouge: Louisiana State University Press, 262.

56. The term "cuffee" was used in this period as a name for a black person.

57. Davis, J. (D–MS) (May 7, 1860). Speech to the U.S. Senate.

58. *Daily Morning News* (March 19, 1857). "The Decision of the Supreme Court in the Dred Scott Case, and Its Tremendous Consequences."

59. *Chicago Daily Tribune* (March 13, 1857). "The Political Decision."

60. *Ableman v. Booth* (1859). 62 U.S. 506.

61. Taylor, M. J. C. (2003). "'A More Perfect Union': Ableman v. Booth and the Culmination of Federal Sovereignty." *Journal of Supreme Court History* 28(2): 101–115.

62. *United States v. Amy* (1859). 24 F Cas 792 (CCD VA).

63. *Ibid.*

64. *Liberator* (June 24, 1859). "Another Dred Scott Decision."

65. Oswald, A. (2012). "The Reaction to the Dred Scott Decision." *Voces Novae: Chapman University Historical Review* 4(1).

66. McPherson, E. (1882). *The Political History of the United States of America, During the Great Rebellion*. La Jolla: University of California Libraries, p. 50.

67. Williams, E. (2014). *Capitalism and Slavery*. Chapel Hill: University of North Carolina Press, p. 7.

68. Eltis, D. (1999). *The Rise of African Slavery in the Americas*. Cambridge, UK: Cambridge University Press, p. 64.

69. Tocqueville, A. de (1835). *Democracy in America* (2000 ed.). Indianapolis, IN: Hackett Publishing, p. 378.

Chapter 5

1. Thomas "Stonewall" Jackson's last words: "Let us cross over the river, and rest under the shade of the trees."

2. Rhea, G. (January 25, 2011). "Why Non-Slaveholding Southerners Fought." Address to the Charleston Library Association, quoting Handy, H.

3. McPherson, J. M. (1988). *Battle Cry of Freedom: The Civil War Era*. New York: Oxford University Press, p. 233, quoting *New Orleans Delta* (November 3, 1860).

4. "The News of Lincoln's Election" (November 8, 1860). *Charleston Mercury*.

5. White, L. A. (1931). *Robert Barnwell Rhett, Father of Secession*. Washington, D.C.: American Historical Association, p. 172.

6. Cauthen, C. E. (1950). *South Carolina Goes to War, 1860–1865*. Chapel Hill: University of North Carolina Press, p. 84.

7. Potter, D. M. (1976). *The Impending Crisis, 1848–1861*. New York: Harper Collins, p. 493.

8. Dumond, D. L. (1931). *Secession Movement*. New York: Macmillan, pp. 121–124.

9. Potter, pp. 496–497.

10. Yearns, W. B. (2010). *The Confederate Congress*. Athens: University of Georgia Press, p. 24.

11. Lipset, S. M. (1960). *Political Man*. New York: Doubleday, pp. 344–354.

12. Botts, J. M. (2005, reprinted from original 1866 ed.). *The Great Rebellion: Its Secret History, Rise, Progress, and Disastrous Failure*. Carlisle, MA: Applewood Books, pp. 212–213.

13. Harkins, A. (2004). *Hillbilly: A Cultural History of an American Icon*. New York: Oxford University Press, p. 39.

14. Goad, J. (1998). *The Redneck Manifesto: How Hillbillies, Hicks, and White Trash Became America's Scapegoats*. New York: Simon & Schuster, pp. 17–19.

15. Morison, S. E. (1965). *The Oxford History of the American People*. New York: Oxford University Press, p. 609.

16. Waldstreicher, D. (2009). *Slavery's Constitution: From Revolution to Ratification*. New York: Hill & Wang, pp. 98–99.

17. Whitcomb, G. (February 1, 1861). Editorial. *Charleston Courier* (Charleston, MO). p. 2.

18. Crofts, D. W. (2014). *Reluctant Confederates: Upper South Unionists in the Secession Crisis*. Chapel Hill: University of North Carolina Press, pp. 201, 206.

19. United States Constitution (1776). *Preamble*.

20. Gunderson, R. G. (1961). *Old Gentlemen's Convention: The Washington Peace Conference of 1861*. Madison: University of Wisconsin Press, pp. 24–25.

21. Potter, p. 552.

22. Potter, D. M. (1995). *Lincoln and His Party in the Secession Crisis*. New Haven, CT: Yale University Press, p. 78.

23. Link, W. A. (2003). *Roots of Secession: Slavery and Politics in Antebellum Virginia*. Chapel Hill: University of North Carolina Press, p. 217.

24. Robertson, J. (1993). *Civil War Virginia: Battleground for a Nation*. Charlottesville: University of Virginia Press, pp. 3–4.

25. Benning, H. L. (February 18, 1861). Speech, in *Proceedings of the Virginia State Convention of 1861*, Vol. 1, pp. 62–75.

26. Davis, W. C. & Hoffman, J., eds. (1991). *The Confederate General*, Vol. 1. pp. 100–101.

27. Riggs, David F. (July 1978). "Robert Young Conrad and the Ordeal of Secession." *The Virginia Magazine of History and Biography* 86(3): 264.

28. Goodwin, D. K. (2005). *Team of Rivals: The Political Genius of Abraham Lincoln*. New York: Simon & Schuster, p. 350.

29. Freeman, D. S. (1934). *R. E. Lee: A Biography*. New York: Charles Scribner's Sons, p. 425.

30. Basler, R. P. (1953). *The Collected Works of Abraham Lincoln*, Vol. 4. New Brunswick, NJ: Rutgers University Press, p. 172.

31. Calore, P. (2008). *Causes of the Civil War*. Jefferson, NC: McFarland, p. 277.

32. Basler, p. 216.

33. *Ibid.*, p. 237.

34. Lincoln, A. (March 4, 1861). First Inaugural Address.

35. *Ibid.*

36. McPherson, J. M. (2001). *Ordeal by Fire: The Civil War and Reconstruction*, 3rd ed. Boston: McGraw-Hill, p. 164.

37. Thomas, B. P. (1952). *Abraham Lincoln: A Biography*. New York: Alfred A. Knopf, p. 377.

38. Tidwell, W. A. (1995). *April '65: Confederate Covert Action in the American Civil War*. Kent, OH: Kent State University Press, p. 158.

39. Snodgrass, M. E. (2011). *The Civil War Era and Reconstruction*. New York: Routledge, p. 185.

40. Summers, M. W. (2009). *A Dangerous Stir: Fear, Paranoia, and the Making of Reconstruction*. Chapel Hill: University of North Carolina Press, p. 38.

41. "The editor of the Metropolitan Record arrested for inciting Gov. Seymour to resist the draft" (August 20, 1864). *New York Times*.

42. Woodward, C. (2011). *American Nations: A History of the Eleven Rival Regional Cultures of North America*. New York: Penguin, p. 207.

43. Weber, J. L. (2006). *Copperheads: The Rise and Fall of Lincoln's Opponents in the North*. New York: Oxford University Press, p. 1.

44. *Cincinnati Commercial*, August 11, 1861.

45. *New York Herald*, August 13, 1861.

46. Silber, S. & Sievens, M. B., eds. (1996). *Yankee Correspondence: Civil War Letters Between New England Soldiers and the Home Front*. Charlottesville: University Press of Virginia, p. 56.

47. McPherson, p. 164.

48. *Dubuque Herald*, April 14, 1861.

49. Weber, p. 23.

50. Holcombe, J. P. (1860). "The Election of a Black Republican President: An Overt Act of Aggression on the Right of Property in Slaves: The South Urged to Adopt Concerted Action for Future Safety." Pamphlet.

51. Crenshaw, O. (October 1941). "The Knights of the Golden Circle: The Career of George Bickley." *American Historical Review* 47: 23–50.

52. United States Constitution. Article 1. Section 9. Clause 2.

53. *Ex Parte Merryman*, 17 F. Cas. 144 (C.C.D. Md. 1861).

54. Neely, M. E. (2011). *Lincoln and the Triumph of the Nation: Constitutional Conflict in the American Civil War*. Chapel Hill: University of North Carolina Press, p. 68.

55. Dunning, W. A. (1898). *Essays of the Civil War and Reconstruction*. New York: Macmillan, p. 38.

56. Whiting, W. (2002). *War Powers Under the Constitution of the United States*, 3rd ed. Union, NJ: Lawbook Exchange, p. 191.

57. National Archives. www.archives.gov. Retrieved April 20, 2017.

58. *Chicago Times*, November 26, 1861.

59. Kaplan, S. (1996). *American Studies in Black and White*. Amherst: University of Massachusetts Press, p. 71.

60. *New York Times*, March 19, 1864.

Chapter 6

1. *Canton Daily Ledger*, January 29, 2011.

2. Zorick, R. J. (1964). "Study of the Union and the Confederate Reactions to the Emancipation Proclamation." Master of Arts thesis, University of Montana, UMIEP36175, p. 32.

3. Olsen, C. J. (2002). *Political Culture and Secession in Mississippi: Masculinity, Honor, and the Antiparty Tradition*. New York: Oxford University Press, p. 237.

4. Hubbard, C. M. (2000). *The Burden of Confederate Diplomacy*. Knoxville: University of Tennessee Press, pp. 76–78.

5. O'Connor, T. H. (1997). *Civil War Boston: Home Front and Battlefield*. Boston, MA: Northeastern University Press, p. 117.

6. Beale, H. K., ed. (1960). *Diary of*

Gideon Welles, Vol. 1. New York: W. W. Norton, pp. 70–71.

7. Whiting, W. (1997). *War Powers Under the Constitution of the United States.* Delran, NJ: Legal Classics Library, p. 134.

8. Second Confiscation Act (1862). 37th Congress.

9. Nevins, A. (1959). *The War for the Union: The Improvised War, 1861–1862.* New York: Scribner, p. 163.

10. Blight, D. W. (1989). *Frederick Douglass' Civil War: Keeping Faith in Jubilee.* Baton Rouge: Louisiana State University Press, p. 148.

11. Klement, F. L. (1960). *The Copperheads in the Middle West.* Chicago: University of Chicago Press, p. 19.

12. Weber, J. L. (2006). *Copperheads: The Rise and Fall of Lincoln's Opponents in the North.* New York: Oxford University Press, p. 54.

13. Grimstead, D. (1998). *American Mobbing, 1828–1861: Toward Civil War.* New York: Oxford University Press, p. viii.

14. Welles, G. (December 1872). "The History of Emancipation." *Galaxy:* 538–42.

15. Foner, P. S. (1952). *The Life and Writings of Frederick Douglass.* New York: International Publishers, p. 25.

16. Nicolay, J. G. (1917). *A Short Life of Abraham Lincoln.* New York: The Century Co., p. 332.

17. Silber, N. & Sievens, M. B., eds. (1996). *Yankee Correspondence: Civil War Letters Between New England Soldiers and the Home Front.* Charlottesville: University of Virginia Press, pp. 145–146.

18. Cannan, J. (1994). *The Antietam Campaign: August–September 1862.* Mechanicsburg, PA: Stackpole, p. 201.

19. Whitman, T. S. (2012). *Antietam 1862: Gateway to Emancipation.* Santa Barbara, CA: Praeger, p. 154.

20. Basler, R. P. (1953). *The Collected Works of Abraham Lincoln*, Vol. 5. New Brunswick, NJ: Rutgers University Press, pp. 419–425.

21. Commager, H. S., ed. (1950). *The Blue and the Gray.* New York: Bobbs-Merrill, p. 1088.

22. Emancipation Proclamation (preliminary), September 22, 1862.

23. Nevins, pp. 239–240.

24. Hesseltine, W. B. (1955). *Lincoln and the War Governors.* New York: Alfred A. Knopf, p. 244.

25. *New York Times*, September 23, 1862.

26. *Chicago Tribune*, September 24, 1862.

27. *New York Tribune*, September 24, 1862.

28. Winters, J. D. (1963). *The Civil War in Louisiana.* Baton Rouge: Louisiana State University Press, p. 237.

29. *Chicago Times*, September 24, 1862.

30. Weber, pp. 63–64.

31. *New York Journal of Commerce*, September 24, 1862.

32. *Detroit Free Press*, September 28, 1862.

33. *New York Express*, October 20, 1862.

34. *Chicago Tribune*, October 21, 1862.

35. Nevins, p. 308.

36. *Richmond Examiner*, September 29, 1862.

37. *Ibid.*, September 30 and October 1, 1862.

38. Nevins, p. 320.

39. McPherson, J. M. (2001). *Ordeal by Fire: The Civil War and Reconstruction*, 3rd ed. Boston: McGraw-Hill, pp. 319–320.

40. Franklin, J. H. (1963). *The Emancipation Proclamation: The Dramatic Story of Abraham Lincoln's Greatest Document and Its Significance in American History.* New York: Doubleday, p. 84.

41. Throne, M., ed. (1960). "Iowa Doctor in Blue: Letters of Seneca B. Thrall, 1862–1864." *Iowa Journal of History* 58: 109–110.

42. Eicher, D. J. (2001). *The Longest Night: A Military History of the Civil War.* New York: Simon & Schuster, 2001, p. 405.

43. Goolrick, W. K. (1985). *Rebels Resurgent: Fredericksburg to Chancellorsville.* Alexandria, VA: Time-Life Books, p. 779.

44. *Boston Pilot*, December 27, 1862.

45. *Richmond Examiner*, December 15, 1862.

46. Patrick, R. W. (1944). *Jefferson Davis and His Cabinet.* Baton Rouge: Louisiana State University Press, p. 6.

47. Emancipation Proclamation (final), January 1, 1863.

48. *National Intelligencer*, January 3, 1863.

49. *New York Tribune*, January 10, 1863.

50. *Charleston Courier*, February 18, 1863.

51. Seiple, D. W. (1998). "The Presidential Election of 1864 in Northampton County, Pennsylvania: Continued Dominance of the Democratic Party Despite Fervent Union Nationalism and Support for the Civil War." Theses and Dissertations. Paper 544, p. 43.

52. Fuld, J. (2012). *The Book of World-Famous Music: Classical, Popular, and Folk*, 5th ed. Mineola, NY: Dover Publications, pp. 609–610.

53. *Easton Argus*, March 5, 1863.

54. Wood, F. G. (1970). *Black Scare: The Racist Response to Emancipation and Reconstruction*. Berkeley: University of California Press, p. 24.

55. Siegel, A. A. (2001). *Beneath the Starry Flag: New Jersey's Civil War Experience*. New Brunswick, NJ: Rutgers University Press, pp. 92–93.

56. Weber, J. L. (2006). *Copperheads: The Rise and Fall of Lincoln's Opponents in the North*. New York: Oxford University Press, p. 83.

57. Morse, S. (1863). "An Argument on the Ethical Position of Slavery in the Social System, and Its Relation to the Politics of the Day." *Papers from the Society for the Diffusion of Political Knowledge*. New York.

58. Dugdale, A.; Fueser, J. J.; & Alves, J. (2001). *Yale, Slavery and Abolition*. New Haven, CT: Yale University, p. 25.

59. Silber, S. & Sievens, M. B., eds. (1996). *Yankee Correspondence: Civil War Letters Between New England Soldiers and the Home Front*. Charlottesville: University Press of Virginia, p. 114.

60. "Who Fought?" Civil War Trust. www.civilwar.org/learn/articles/who-fought. Retrieved May 25, 2017.

61. Paludin, P. S. (October 1972). "The American Civil War Considered as a Crisis in Law and Order." *American Historical Review* 77(4): 1013–34.

62. Basler, R. P. (1953). *The Collected Works of Abraham Lincoln*, Vol. 6. New Brunswick, NJ: Rutgers University Press, pp. 149–150.

63. Wood, pp. 42–44.

64. Foner, E. (2014). *Reconstruction: America's Unfinished Revolution, 1863–1877*. New York: Harper & Row, pp. 32–33.

65. Harris, L. M. (2003). *In the Shadow of Slavery: African Americans in New York City, 1626–1863*. Chicago: University of Chicago Press, pp. 279–288.

66. McPherson, E. (1882). *The Political History of the United States of America, During the Great Rebellion*. La Jolla: University of California Libraries, p. 261.

67. Vallandigham, C. L. (1864). *Addresses and Letters of Clement L. Vallandigham*. New York: J. Walter, pp. 459–460.

68. Bayard, J. A. (1863). *Two Speeches of James A. Bayard of Delaware*. Baltimore, MD: W. M. Innis, p. 4.

69. Hallock, J. L. (1983). "The Role of the Community in Civil War Desertion." *Civil War History* 29: 125.

70. Levine, P. (1981). "Draft Evasion in the North During the Civil War, 1863–1865." *Journal of American History* 67: 817–821.

71. Gambill, E. L. (1981). *Conservative Ordeal: Northern Democrats and Reconstruction*. Ames: Iowa State University Press, p. 9.

72. Klement, F. L. (1965). "Clement L. Vallandigham's Exile in the Confederacy, May 25–June 17, 1863." *Journal of Southern History* 31: 150–152.

73. *Columbus Crisis*, May 13, 1863.

74. *Bergen Democrat*, May 15, 1863.

75. www.americancivilwar.com/cwstats.html. Retrieved May 28, 2017.

76. Curry, R. (1967). "The Union as It Was: A Critique of Recent Interpretations of the Copperheads." *Civil War History* 13: 25–39.

77. Wheeler, K. H. (1999). "Local Autonomy and Civil War Draft Resistance: Holmes County, Ohio." *Civil War History* 45: 153–154.

78. Klement, F. (1964). "Midwestern Opposition to Lincoln's Emancipation Proclamation." *Journal of Negro History* 49: 169–183.

79. Man, A. (1951). "Labor Competition and the New York Draft Riots of 1863." *The Journal of Negro History*, 36(4): 375–405.

80. Bernstein, I. (1990). *The New York City Draft Riots: Their Significance for American Society and Politics in the Age of the Civil War*. New York: Oxford University Press, p. 8.

81. Dupree, A. & Fishel, L. (1960). "An Eyewitness Account of the New York Draft Riots, July, 1863." *The Mississippi Valley*

Historical Review 47(3): 476; Ericson, C. & Austen, B. (2000). "On the 'Front Lines' of the Civil War Home Front." *Connecticut History* 39: 155–156.

Chapter 7

1. Wilson, C. R. (1936). "The Original Chase Organization Meeting and the Next Presidential Meeting." *Mississippi Valley Historical Review* 23: 62–65.
2. Goodwin, D. K. (2005). *Team of Rivals: The Political Genius of Abraham Lincoln*. New York: Simon & Schuster, pp. 605–07.
3. McPherson, J. M. (2001). *Ordeal by Fire: The Civil War and Reconstruction*, 3rd ed. Boston: McGraw-Hill.
4. *New York Herald*, February 22, 1864.
5. Malanson, J. J. (Summer 2015). "The Founding Fathers and the Election of 1864." *Journal of the Abraham Lincoln Association* 36(2): 1–25; and Zornow, W.F. (1954). *Lincoln and the Party Divided*. Norman: University of Oklahoma Press, pp. 72–86.
6. Williams, T. H. (1938). "Frémont and the Politicians." *Journal of the American Military History Foundation* 2: 191.
7. Long, D. E. (1994). *The Jewel of Liberty: Abraham Lincoln's Re-Election and the End of Slavery*. Mechanicsburg, PA: Stackpole, p. 23.
8. Long, A. (April 8, 1864). In Stellato, J., ed. (2012). *Not In Our Name: American Antiwar Speeches, 1846 to the Present*. University Park, PA: Penn State University Press, pp. 52–53.
9. *New York Times*, July 20, 1864.
10. Tregarthen, T. D. & Rittenberg, L. (1999). *Macroeconomics*. New York: Macmillan, p. 240.
11. Tarnoff, B. (2011). *Moneymakers: The Wicked Lives and Surprising Adventures of Three Notorious Counterfeiters*. New York: Penguin Press, p. 235.
12. Weidenmier, M. (1999). "Bogus Money Matters: Sam Upham and His Confederate Counterfeiting Business." *Business and Economic History* 28(2): 313–324.
13. Sears, S. W. (1988). *George B. McClellan: The Young Napoleon*. New York: Ticknor & Fields, p. 374.
14. *Ibid.*, pp. 375–376.
15. Sears, S. W. (1992). *The Civil War*

Papers of George B. McClellan: Selected Correspondence, 1860–1865. Boston, MA: De Capo Press, p. 381.
16. *Boston Pilot*, September 10, 1864.
17. Randall, J. G. & Current, R. (1955). *Lincoln the President: Last Full Measure*. Champaign: University of Illinois Press, p. 307.
18. Nelson, L. E. (1978). "Black Leaders and the Presidential Election of 1864." *Journal of Negro History* 63: 53–54.
19. Democratic Party platform (August 1864).
20. Vorenberg, M. (2001). *Final Freedom: The Civil War, the Abolition of Slavery, and the Thirteenth Amendment*. Cambridge, MA: Cambridge University Press, p. 238.
21. *New York Times*, October 18, 1864.
22. Republican Party platform (June 1864).
23. Burr, C. (January 1863). "Abolition Preachers Versus Christ and the Apostles." *Old Guard* 1(1): 7–13.
24. *Ibid.* (June 1864). "The Tricks of Tyrants": 132–133.
25. *Detroit Free Press*, September 1, 1864.
26. Cimbala, P. A. & Miller, R. M. (2002). *Union Soldiers and the Northern Home Front: Wartime Experiences, Postwar Adjustments (The North's Civil War)*. New York: Fordham University Press, p. 66.
27. Geary, J. W. (1991). *We Need Men: The Union Draft in the Civil War*. DeKalb: Northern Illinois University Press, p. 264.
28. Wubben, H. H. (1980). *Civil War Iowa and the Copperhead Movement*. Ames: Iowa State University Press, p. 173.
29. McKitrick, E. L., in Chambers, W. N. & Burnham, W. D., eds. (1967). *Party Politics and the Union and Confederate War Efforts*. New York: Oxford University Press, p. 141.
30. Klement, F. L. (1989). *Dark Lanterns: Secret Political Societies, Conspiracies and Treason Trials in the Civil War*. Baton Rouge: Louisiana State University Press, p. 173.
31. Stampp, K. M. (1944). "The Milligan Case and the Election of 1864 in Indiana." *Mississippi Valley Historical Review* 31: 41–58.
32. Davis, J., in Monroe, H. M. (author); Williams, K. H. (ed.); Dillard, P. L. (ed.);

& Crist, L. L. (ed.). (1999). *The Papers of Jefferson Davis*, Vol. 10. Baton Rouge: Louisiana State University Press, p. 609.

33. Gray, W. (1942). *The Hidden Civil War: The Story of the Copperheads*. New York: Viking Press, pp. 167–179.

34. Headley, J. W. (1984). *Confederate Operations in Canada and New York*. New York: Time-Life Books, p. 221.

35. Linden, F. van der (2007). *The Dark Intrigue: The True Story of a Civil War Conspiracy*. Golden, CO: Fulcrum Publishing, p. 182.

36. Basler, R. P., ed. (1953). *The Collected Works of Abraham Lincoln*, Vol. 7. New Brunswick, NJ: Rutgers University Press, pp. 517–518.

37. Simpson, B. D. & Grimsley, M., eds. (2002). *The Collapse of the Confederacy*. Lincoln: University of Nebraska Press, p. 21.

38. Tidwell, W. A. (1995). *April '65: Confederate Covert Action in the American Civil War*. Kent, OH: Kent State University Press, pp. 39–41.

39. Flood, C. B. (2009). *1864: Lincoln at the Gates of History*. New York: Simon & Schuster, p. 144.

40. Borchard, G. A. (2011). *Abraham Lincoln and Horace Greeley*. Carbondale: Southern Illinois University Press, p. 84.

41. Weber, J. L. (Winter 2011). "Lincoln's Critics: The Copperheads." *Journal of the Abraham Lincoln Association* 32(1): 33–47.

42. Garrett, F. (1987). *Atlanta and Environs: A Chronicle of Its People and Events*, Vol. 1. Athens: University of Georgia Press.

43. Cox, J. D. (1994). *Sherman's Battle for Atlanta*. Boston, MA: De Capo Press, p. xv.

44. Boyer, P.; Clark, C.; Kett, J.; Salisbury, N.; Sitkoff, H.; & Woloch, N. (2007). *The Enduring Vision* (6th ed.). Boston, MA: Houghton Mifflin, p. 457.

45. Weber, J. L. (2006). *Copperheads: The Rise and Fall of Lincoln's Opponents in the North*. New York: Oxford University Press, p. 202.

46. Witcover, J. (November 16, 2014). "Lincoln's Vice-Presidential Switch Changed History." *Chicago Tribune*.

47. Pomeroy, B. (August 23, 1864). *Wisconsin Democrat*.

48. Wisconsin Legislative Reference Library (1962). *State of Wisconsin Blue Book*. Madison: Wisconsin Legislative Reference Bureau, p. 172.

49. Hutter, J. H. & Abrams, R. A. (1935). "Copperhead Newspapers and the Negro." *Journal of Negro History* 20: 140–141.

50. Gienapp, W. E. (2002). *This Fiery Trial: The Speeches and Writings of Abraham Lincoln*. New York: Oxford University Press, p. 205.

51. United States Constitution. 13th Amendment.

52. Donald, D. H. (1996). *Lincoln*. New York: Simon & Schuster, p. 554.

53. Witcover, J.

54. Harris, W. C. (Winter 2011). "His Loyal Opposition: Lincoln's Border States' Critics." *Journal of the Abraham Lincoln Association* 32(1): 1–17; and Harrison, L. H. (2000). *Lincoln of Kentucky*. Lexington: University Press of Kentucky, pp. 10–11.

Chapter 8

1. Weber, J. L. (2006). *Copperheads: The Rise and Fall of Lincoln's Opponents in the North*. New York: Oxford University Press, p. 217.

2. *Detroit Free Press*, July 1, 1865.

3. *New York World*, March 7, 1876.

4. Trefousse, H. L. (1997). *Andrew Johnson: A Biography*. New York: W.W. Norton, p. 192.

5. *Hartford Daily Times*, May 6, 1865.

6. *New York World*, June 22, 1865.

7. *Columbus Crisis*, July 19, 1865.

8. *Chicago Times*, July 17, 1865.

9. Freedmen's Bureau Bill, 13 Stat. 507, March 3, 1865.

10. Gambill, E. L. (1981). *Conservative Ordeal: Southern Democrats and Reconstruction*. Ames: Iowa State University Press, p. 7.

11. Johnson, A. (July 16, 1866). Veto Message.

12. Gambill, p. 40.

13. Blackmon, D. A. (2008). *Slavery by Another Name: The Re-Enslavement of Black Americans from the Civil War to World War II*. New York: Random House, p. 4.

14. DeBois, W. E. B. (1935). *Black Reconstruction: An Essay Toward a History of the Part Which Black Folk Played*

in the Attempt to Reconstruct Democracy in America, 1860–1880. New York: Russell & Russell, p. 178.

15. Novak, D. A. (1978). *The Wheel of Servitude: Black Forced Labor After Slavery.* Lexington: University Press of Kentucky, p. 3.

16. *Ibid.*, p. 4.

17. Crouch, B. A. (July 1993). "'All the Vile Passions': The Texas Black Code of 1866." *Southwestern Historical Quarterly* 97(1).

18. Civil Rights Act of 1866.

19. Foner, E. (2002). *Reconstruction: America's Unfinished Revolution.* New York: Harper Collins, p. 251.

20. Johnson, A. (March 27, 1866). Veto Message.

21. McKitrick, E. L. (1988). *Andrew Johnson and Reconstruction.* New York: Oxford University Press, p. 314.

22. Stewart, D. O. (2009). *Impeached: The Trial of President Andrew Johnson and the Fight for Lincoln's Legacy.* New York: Simon & Schuster, pp. 53–54.

23. United States Constitution. 14th Amendment.

24. *New York Herald,* September 10, 1866.

25. McKitrick, p. 436.

26. Forte, D. F. (1998). "Spiritual Equality, the Black Codes, and the Americanization of the Freedmen." *Loyola Law Review* 43: 608.

27. Ryan, J. G. (1977). "The Memphis Riots of 1866: Terror in a Black Community During Reconstruction." *The Journal of Negro History* 62(3): 243–257.

28. Buchanan, J. (1910). *The Works of James Buchanan, Comprising His Speeches, State Papers, and Private Correspondence,* Vol. 11 (1860–68). In Moore, J. B., ed. Philadelphia: J. B. Lippincott, p. 429.

29. *Chicago Times,* November 12, 1866.

30. *Milwaukee News,* November 14, 1866.

31. *New York Times,* December 6, 1866.

32. Stewart, D. O. (2010). *Impeached: The Trial of President Andrew Johnson and the Fight for Lincoln's Legacy.* New York: Simon & Schuster, pp. 136–137.

33. Schroeder, G. R. & Zucaek, R. (2001). *Andrew Johnson: A Biographical Companion.* Santa Barbara, CA: ABC-CLIO, p. 60.

34. Porter, G. H. (2010). *Ohio Politics During the Civil War Period.* Charleston, SC: Nabu Press, p. 247.

35. Gellman, D. N. & Quigley, D. (2003). *Jim Crow New York: A Documentary History of Race and Citizenship.* New York: New York University Press, p. 279.

36. *New York World,* October 12, 1867.

37. *Cincinnati Daily Enquirer,* November 21, 1867.

38. *Boston Post,* November 20, 1867.

39. Krout, J. A. (December 1, 1938). "Horatio Seymour of New York (review)." *Journal of American History* 25(3): 430.

40. Stone, I. (1943). *They Also Ran.* Garden City, NY: Doubleday & Doran, 280.

41. Gambill, 140.

Chapter 9

1. Trelease, A. W. *White Terror: The Ku Klux Klan Conspiracy and Southern Reconstruction.* Baton Rouge: Louisiana State University Press, 367–368.

2. Parsons, E. F. (2015). *Ku-Klux: The Birth of the Klan During Reconstruction.* Chapel Hill: University of North Carolina Press, 81.

3. McVeigh, R. (2009). *The Rise of the Ku Klux Klan: Right-Wing Movements and National Politics.* Minneapolis: University of Minnesota Press, 146–147.

4. McFeely, W. S. (2002). *Grant.* New York: W. W. Norton, 227.

5. White, R. C. (2017). *American Ulysses: A Life of Ulysses S. Grant.* New York: Random House, 421.

6. Bennett, W. J. (2002). *America: The Last Best Hope (Volume I): From the Age of Discovery to a World at War.* Nashville, TN: Thomas Nelson, 411.

7. White, 421.

8. Ambrose, S. (2002). *To America: Personal Reflections of an Historian.* New York: Simon & Schuster, 63.

9. Irvin, B. H. (2002). *Samuel Adams: Son of Liberty, Father of Revolution.* New York: Oxford University Press, 54.

10. Stidger, F. G. (1997). *Knights of the Golden Circle Treason History, Sons of Liberty, 1864.* Brandon, MS: Dogwood Press, 119.

11. *Chicago Daily Tribune,* Feb. 11, 1862.

12. Marshall, J. A. (1881). *American*

Bastile: A History of the Illegal Arrests and Imprisonment of American Citizens in the Northern and Border States During the Late Civil War. Philadelphia, PA: T. W. Hartley & Co., 75.

13. Rose, S. E. F. (1914). *The Ku Klux Klan: Or Invisible Empire*. New Orleans: L. Graham Co., 18–19.

14. Ward, A. (June 1964). "A Note on the Origin of the Ku Klux Klan." *Tennessee Historical Quarterly* 23: 182.

15. Wade, W. C. (1998). *The Fiery Cross: The Ku Klux Klan in America*. New York: Oxford University Press, 34.

16. Newton, M. (2014). *White Robes and Burning Crosses: A History of the Ku Klux Klan from 1866*. Jefferson, NC: McFarland, 16.

17. Rable, G. C. (2007). *But There Was No Peace: The Role of Violence in the Politics of Reconstruction*. Athens: University of Georgia Press, 101.

18. Parsons, 21–27.

19. Aiken, C. S. (2003). *The Cotton Plantation South Since the Civil War*. Baltimore, MD: Johns Hopkins University Press, 175.

20. Hollitz, J. (2014). *Thinking Through the Past: A Critical Thinking Approach to U.S. History, Volume 1* (5th Edition). Belmont, CA: Wadsworth Publishing, 330.

21. United States Constitution (1789). Fifteenth Amendment. Section 1.

22. Martinez, J. M. (2007). *Carpetbaggers, Cavalry, and the Ku Klux Klan*. Lanham, MD: Rowman & Littlefield, 64.

23. Kaczorowski, R. J. (Fall 1995). "Federal Enforcement of Civil Rights During the First Reconstruction." *Fordham Urban Law Journal* 23: 156–160.

24. Miller, W., ed. (2012). *The Social History of Crime and Punishment in America: An Encyclopedia*. Thousand Oaks, CA: Sage Publications, 537.

25. Cox, S. (April 4, 1871). Congressional Globe. 42nd Congress. 1st Session. 451.

26. Williams, L. (2004). *The Great South Carolina Ku Klux Klan Trials, 1871–1872*. Athens: University of Georgia Press, 85.

27. Baker, B. E. (2007). *What Reconstruction Meant: Historical Memory in the American South*. Charlottesville: University of Virginia Press, 54.

28. Coulter, E. M. (1947). *The South During Reconstruction, 1865–1877: A History of the South*. Baton Rouge: Louisiana State University Press, 374.

29. Rable, 132.

30. Woodward, C. Vann (1956). *Reunion and Reaction: The Compromise of 1877 and the End of Reconstruction*. New York: Doubleday, 3–15.

Bibliography

Ableman v. Booth (1859). 62 U.S. 506.

Adams, J. (October 2, 1780). Letter to Jonathan Jackson.

Adams, J. Q. (2010). *Arguments of John Quincy Adams Before the Supreme Court of the U.S. In the Case of the U.S. vs. Cinque and Others, Africans Captured in the Schooner Amistad* (1841). Whitefish, MT: Kessinger Publishing.

Aiken, C. S. (2003). *The Cotton Plantation South Since the Civil War.* Baltimore, MD: Johns Hopkins University Press.

Airstrup, J. A. (1996). *The Southern Strategy Revisited: Republican Top-Down Advancement in the South.* Lexington: University of Kentucky Press.

Allen, W. B. (2008). *George Washington: America's First Progressive.* New York: Peter Lang.

Amar, A. R. (2005). *America's Constitution: A Biography.* New York: Random House.

Ambrose, S. (2002). *To America: Personal Reflections of an Historian.* New York: Simon & Schuster.

Atlantic (June 17, 2013). "How the Voting Rights Act Hurts Democrats and Minorities."

Bailyn, B. (1992). *The Ideological Origins of the American Revolution.* Cambridge, MA: Belknap Press.

Baker, B. E. (2007). *What Reconstruction Meant: Historical Memory in the American South.* Charlottesville: University of Virginia Press.

Baker, R. (2014). "A Better Story in Prigg v. Pennsylvania?" *Journal of Supreme Court History* 39.

Banks, T. L. (2008). "Dangerous Women: Elizabeth Key's Freedom Suit—Subjecthood and Racialized Identity in Seven-teenth Century Colonial Virginia." *Akron Law Review.*

Bartley, N. V., & Graham, H. D. (1975). *Southern Politics and the Second Reconstruction.* Baltimore, MD: Johns Hopkins University Press.

Basler, R. P. (1953). *The Collected Works of Abraham Lincoln.* New Brunswick, NJ: Rutgers University Press.

Bass, J., & DeVries, W. (1976). *The Transformation of Southern Politics: Social Change and Political Consequences Since 1945.* New York, NY: Basic Books.

Bayard, J. A. (1863). *Two Speeches of James A. Bayard of Delaware.* Baltimore, MD: W. M. Innis.

Beale, H. K., ed. (1960). *Diary of Gideon Welles,* Vol 1. New York: W. W. Norton.

Beeman, R. (2009). *Plain Honest Men: The Making of the American Constitution.* New York: Random House.

Bennett, W. J. (2002). *America: The Last Best Hope (Volume I): From the Age of Discovery to a World at War.* Nashville, TN: Thomas Nelson.

Benning, H. L. (February 18, 1861). Speech, in *Proceedings of the Virginia State Convention of 1861, Vol. 1.*

Benson, G. (1938). *Abraham Lincoln.* Garden City, NY: Garden City Publishing.

Berard, S. P. (2001). *Southern Democrats in the U.S. House of Representatives.* Norman: University of Oklahoma Press.

Bergen Democrat, May 15, 1863.

Bernstein, I. (1990). *The New York City Draft Riots: Their Significance for American Society and Politics in the Age of the Civil War.* New York: Oxford University Press.

Berwanger, E. H. (1967). *The Frontier Against Slavery: Western Anti-Negro Prejudice and the Slavery Extension Controversy.* Urbana: University of Illinois Press.

Black, E., & Black, M. (2002). *The Rise of Southern Republicans.* Cambridge, MA: Harvard University Press.

Blackmon, D. A. (2008). *Slavery by Another Name: The Re-Enslavement of Black Americans from the Civil War to World War II.* New York: Random House.

Blight, D. W. (1989). *Frederick Douglass' Civil War: Keeping Faith in Jubilee.* Baton Rouge: Louisiana State University Press.

Borchard, G. A. (2011). *Abraham Lincoln and Horace Greeley.* Carbondale: Southern Illinois University Press.

Boston Gazette, March 26, 1812.

Boston Post, November 20, 1867.

Botts, J. M. (2005, reprinted from original 1866 ed.). *The Great Rebellion: Its Secret History, Rise, Progress, and Disastrous Failure.* Carlisle, MA: Applewood Books.

Boyer, P.; Clark, C.; Kett, J.; Salisbury, N.; Sitkoff, H.; & Woloch, N. (2007). *The Enduring Vision*, 6th ed. Boston, MA: Houghton Mifflin.

Brown, C. H. (1980). *Agents of Manifest Destiny: The Lives and Times of the Filibusters.* Chapel Hill: University of North Carolina Press.

Brown, R. H. (Winter 1966). "The Missouri Crisis, Slavery, and the Politics of Jacksonianism." *South Atlantic Quarterly* 61.

Brown, T. (1985). *Politics and Statesmanship: Essays on the American Whig Party.* New York: Columbia University Press.

Buchanan, J. (1910). *The Works of James Buchanan, Comprising His Speeches, State Papers, and Private Correspondence (1860–68)*, Vol. 11. Moore, J. B., ed. Philadelphia, PA: J. B. Lippincott.

Burgan, M. (2002). *The Louisiana Purchase.* Minneapolis, MN: Compass Point Books.

Burnham, W. B. (1955). *Presidential Ballots.* Baltimore, MD: Johns Hopkins University Press.

Burr, C. (January 1863). "Abolition Preachers Versus Christ and the Apostles." *Old Guard* 1(1).

Calore, P. (2008). *Causes of the Civil War.* Jefferson, NC: McFarland.

Campos, N. F., & Fidrmuc, J., eds. (2003). *Political Economy of Transition and Development: Institutions, Politics and Policies.* Berlin: Springer.

Cannan, J. (1994). *The Antietam Campaign: August–September 1862.* Mechanicsburg, PA: Stackpole.

Canton Daily Ledger, January 29, 2011.

Card, R. (2010). "Can States 'Just Say No' to Federal Health Care Reform? The Constitutional and Political Implications of State Attempts to Nullify Federal Law." *B.Y.U. Law Review*, 1795, 1808.

Carter, D. T. (1995) *The Politics of Rage: George Wallace, the Origins of the New Conservatism, and the Transformation of American Politics.* New York: Simon & Schuster.

Cauthen, C. E. (1950). *South Carolina Goes to War, 1860–1865.* Chapel Hill: University of North Carolina Press.

Chalmers, D. M. (1987). *Hooded Americanism: The History of the Ku Klux Klan*, 3rd ed. Durham, NC: Duke University Press.

Chambers, W. N., ed. (1972). *The First Party System: Federalists and Republicans.* Hoboken, NJ: John Wiley & Sons.

Charleston Courier, February 1, 1861; February 18, 1863.

Charleston Mercury (November 8, 1860). "The News of Lincoln's Election."

Cheney, L. (2014). *James Madison: A Life Reconsidered.* New York: Viking.

Chernow, R. (2004). *Alexander Hamilton.* New York: Penguin.

Chicago Daily Tribune, March 13, 1857; February 11, 1862.

Chicago Times, November 26, 1861; September 24, 1862; July 17, 1865; November 12, 1866.

Chicago Tribune, September 24, 1862; October 21, 1862; November 16, 2014.

Cimbala, P. A., & Miller, R. M. (2002). *Union Soldiers and the Northern Home Front: Wartime Experiences, Postwar Adjustments (The North's Civil War).* New York: Fordham University Press.

Cincinnati Commercial, August 11, 1861.

Cincinnati Daily Enquirer, November 21, 1867.

Civil Rights Act of 1866.

Columbian Centinel, July 12, 1817.

Columbus Crisis, May 13, 1863; July 19, 1865.

Commager, H. S., ed. (1950). *The Blue and the Gray.* New York: Bobbs-Merrill.

Cooper, W. J., Jr. (1980). *The South and the Politics of Slavery, 1828–1856.* Baton Rouge: Louisiana State University Press.

Coulter, E. M. (1947). *The South During*

Reconstruction, 1865–1877: A History of the South. Baton Rouge: Louisiana State University Press.

Cox, J. D. (1994). *Sherman's Battle for Atlanta*. Boston, MA: De Capo Press.

Cox, S. (April 4, 1871). Congressional Globe. 42nd Congress. 1st Session. 451.

Crenshaw, O. (October 1941). "The Knights of the Golden Circle: The Career of George Bickley." *American Historical Review* 47.

Crofts, D. W. (2014). *Reluctant Confederates: Upper South Unionists in the Secession Crisis*. Chapel Hill: University of North Carolina Press.

Crouch, B. A. (July 1993). "'All the Vile Passions': The Texas Black Code of 1866." *Southwestern Historical Quarterly* 97(1).

Curry, R. (1967). "The Union as It Was: A Critique of Recent Interpretations of the Copperheads." *Civil War History* 13.

Cutler, C. C. (1984). *Greyhounds of the Sea*, 3rd ed. Annapolis, MD: Naval Institute Press.

Cutler, W. G. (1883). *History of the State of Kansas*. Davenport, IA: A. T. Andreas.

Daily Morning News, March 19, 1857.

Dallek, R. (2004). *Lyndon B. Johnson: Portrait of a President*. New York: Oxford University Press.

Davis, D. B. (2006). *Inhuman Bondage: The Rise and Fall of Slavery in the New World*. New York: Oxford University Press.

Davis, J. (D–MS) (May 7, 1860). Speech to the U. S. Senate, in Monroe, H. M. (author); Williams, K. H. (ed.); Dillard, P. L. (ed.); & Crist, L. L. (ed.) (1999). *The Papers of Jefferson Davis*, Vol. 10. Baton Rouge: Louisiana State University Press.

Davis, W. C., & Hoffman, J., eds. (1991). *The Confederate General*, Vol. 1.

Decredico, M. A. "Sectionalism and the Secession Crisis," in John B. Boles, ed. (2004). *A Companion to the American South*. Hoboken, NJ: Wiley-Blackwell.

Democratic Party platform (August 1864).

Detroit Free Press, September 28, 1862; September 1, 1864; July 1, 1865.

Detweiler, P. F. (April 1958). "Congressional Debate on Slavery and the Declaration of Independence, 1819–1821." *American Historical Review* 63.

Diggins, J. P. (1994). *Up from Communism*. New York: Columbia University Press.

Divine, R. A.; Breen, T. H.; Williams, R.

H.; Gross, A. J.; & Brands, H. W. (2007). *The American Story*, 5th ed. New York: Pearson.

Donald, D. H. (1996). *Lincoln*. New York: Simon & Schuster.

Donoghue, J. (October 2010). "Out of the Land of Bondage: The English Revolution and the Atlantic Origins of Abolition." *The American Historical Review*.

Douglass, F. (1845). *Narrative of the Life of Frederick Douglass: An American Slave, Written by Himself* (2009, reprinted ed.). New York: Cambridge University Press.

Dred Scott v. Sandford, 60 U.S. 393 (1857).

DuBois, W. E. B. (1935). *Black Reconstruction: An Essay Toward a History of the Part Which Black Folk Played in the Attempt to Reconstruct Democracy in America, 1860–1880*. New York: Russell & Russell.

Dubuque Herald, April 14, 1861.

Dugdale, A.; Fueser, J. J.; & Alves, J. (2001). *Yale, Slavery and Abolition*. New Haven, CT: Yale University Press.

Dumond, D. L. (1931). *Secession Movement*. New York: Macmillan.

Dunham, A., & Kurland, P. B., eds. (1964). *Mr. Justice*, quoting Carl Brent Swisher, "Mr. Chief Justice Taney." Chicago, IL: University of Chicago Press.

Dunning, W. A. (2010). *Essays on the Civil War and Reconstruction and Related Topics*. Whitefish, MT: Kessinger Publishing.

Dupree, A., & Fishel, L. (1960). "An Eyewitness Account of the New York Draft Riots, July, 1863." *The Mississippi Valley Historical Review* 47(3).

Easton Daily Argus, March 5, 1863.

Ehrlich, W. (1979). *They Have No Rights: Dred Scott's Struggle for Freedom*. Westport, CT: Greenwood Press.

Eicher, D. J. (2001). *The Longest Night: A Military History of the Civil War*. New York: Simon & Schuster, 2001.

Elkins, S., & McKitrick, E. (1995). *The Age of Federalism*. New York: Oxford University Press.

Elliot, J., ed. (1866). *The Debates in The Several State Conventions on the Adoption of the Federal Constitution, As Recommended by the General Convention At Philadelphia, In 1787*. Philadelphia: J. B. Lippincott & Co.

Ellis, R. E. (1987). *The Union at Risk: Jacksonian Democracy, States' Rights, and the*

Nullification Crisis. New York: Oxford University Press.

Eltis, D. (1999). *The Rise of African Slavery in the Americas.* Cambridge, UK: Cambridge University Press.

Emancipation Proclamation (preliminary), September 22, 1862; (final), January 1, 1863.

Engerman, S. L., & Sokoloff, K. L. (2005). *The Evolution of Suffrage Institutions in the New World.* Cambridge, MA: National Bureau of Economics.

Ericson, C., & Austen, B. (2000). "On the 'Front Lines' of the Civil War Home Front." *Connecticut History* 39.

Ex Parte Merryman, 17 F. Cas. 144 (C.C.D. Md. 1861).

Ferrand, M., ed. (1967). *Records of the Federal Convention of 1787.* New Haven, CT: Yale University Press.

Finkelman, P. (Winter 1986). "Slavery and the Northwest Ordinance: A Study in Ambiguity." *Journal of the Early Republic* 6(4).

Flood, C. B. (2009). *1864: Lincoln at the Gates of History.* New York: Simon & Schuster.

Foner, E. (October 1965). "Politics and Prejudice: The Free Soil Party and the Negro, 1849–1852." *The Journal of Negro History* 50(4).

_____ (September 1969). "The Wilmot Proviso Revisited." *The Journal of American History* 56(2).

_____ (2002). *Reconstruction: America's Unfinished Revolution, 1863–1877.* New York: Harper & Row.

_____ (2010). *The Fiery Trial: Abraham Lincoln and American Slavery.* New York: W. W. Norton.

Foner, P. S. (1952). *The Life and Writings of Frederick Douglass.* New York: International Publishers.

Formisano, R. P. "State Development in the Early Republic," in Shafer, B. & Badger, A., eds. (2001). *Contesting Democracy: Substance and Structure in American Political History, 1775–2000.* Lawrence: University Press of Kansas.

Forte, D. F. (1998). "Spiritual Equality, the Black Codes, and the Americanization of the Freedmen." *Loyola Law Review* 43.

Franklin, J. H. (1963). *The Emancipation Proclamation: The Dramatic Story of Abraham Lincoln's Greatest Document and Its Significance in American History.* New York: Doubleday.

Freedmen's Bureau Bill (March 3, 1865). 13 Stat. 507.

Freehling, W. W. (2007). *The Road to Disunion*, Vol. 2. New York: Oxford University Press.

Freeman, D. S. (1934). *R. E. Lee: A Biography.* New York: Charles Scribner's Sons.

Fuld, J. (2012). *The Book of World-Famous Music: Classical, Popular, and Folk*, 5th ed. Mineola, NY: Dover Publications.

Gambill, E. L. (1981). *Conservative Ordeal: Northern Democrats and Reconstruction.* Ames: Iowa State University Press.

Gara, L. (September 1964). "The Fugitive Slave Law: A Double Paradox." *Civil War History* 10(3).

Garrett, F. (1987). *Atlanta and Environs: A Chronicle of Its People and Events*, Vol. 1. Athens: University of Georgia Press.

Gates, P. W. (1954). *Fifty Million Acres: Conflicts Over Kansas Land Policy.* Ithaca, NY: Cornell University Press.

Geary, J. W. (1991). *We Need Men: The Union Draft in the Civil War.* DeKalb: Northern Illinois University Press.

Gellman, D. N., & Quigley, D. (2003). *Jim Crow New York: A Documentary History of Race and Citizenship.* New York: New York University Press.

Gibbons v. Ogden (1824). 22 U.S. (9 Wheaton) 1, pp. 33–159.

Gienapp, W. E. (1985). "Nativism and the Creation of a Republican Majority in the North Before the Civil War." *Journal of American History* 72(3).

Gray, W. (1942). *The Hidden Civil War: The Story of the Copperheads.* New York: Viking Press.

_____ (2002). *This Fiery Trial: The Speeches and Writings of Abraham Lincoln.* New York: Oxford University Press.

Gitlin, T. (1993). *The Sixties: Years of Hope, Days of Rage.* New York: Bantam.

Glaser, J. M. (1996). *Race, Campaign Politics, and the Realignment in the South.* New Haven, CT: Yale University Press.

Goad, J. (1998). *The Redneck Manifesto: How Hillbillies, Hicks, and White Trash Became America's Scapegoats.* New York: Simon & Schuster.

Going, C. B. (1924). *David Wilmot: Free-Soiler.* New York: Appleton.

Goldberg, J. (2009). *Liberal Fascism.* New York: Broadway Books.

Goodman, P., ed. (1970). *Essays on the Civil War and Reconstruction.* Austin, TX: Holt, Rinehart and Winston.

Goodwin, D. K. (2005). *Team of Rivals: The Political Genius of Abraham Lincoln.* New York: Simon & Schuster.

Goolrick, W. K. (1985). *Rebels Resurgent: Fredericksburg to Chancellorsville.* Alexandria, VA: Time-Life Books.

Graham, H. D. (1990). *The Civil Rights Era: Origins and Development of National Policy, 1960–1972.* New York: Oxford University Press.

Gray, W. (1942). *The Hidden Civil War: The Story of the Copperheads.* New York: Viking Press.

Griffith, E. (1907). *The Rise and Development of the Gerrymander.* Chicago: Scott, Foresman and Co.

Grimstead, D. (1998). *American Mobbing, 1828–1861: Toward Civil War.* New York: Oxford University Press.

Gunderson, R. G. (1961). *Old Gentlemen's Convention: The Washington Peace Conference of 1861.* Madison: University of Wisconsin Press.

Gutzman, K. R. (Winter 1995). "A Troublesome Legacy: James Madison and 'the Principles of '98.'" *Journal of the Early Republic* 15(4).

Hallock, J. L. (1983). "The Role of the Community in Civil War Desertion." *Civil War History* 29.

Hamilton, A. (May 28, 1788). *Federalist No. 78, cited in Elliot, J., ed. (1866). The Debates in The Several State Conventions On The Adoption Of The Federal Constitution, As Recommended By The General Convention At Philadelphia, In 1787.* Philadelphia: J. B. Lippincott & Co.

Harkins, A. (2004). *Hillbilly: A Cultural History of an American Icon.* New York: Oxford University Press.

Harris, L. M. (2003). *In the Shadow of Slavery: African Americans in New York City, 1626–1863.* Chicago, IL: University of Chicago Press.

Harris, W. C. (Winter 2011). "His Loyal Opposition: Lincoln's Border States' Critics." *Journal of the Abraham Lincoln Association* 32(1).

Harrison, L. H. (2000). *Lincoln of Kentucky.* Lexington: University Press of Kentucky.

Hartford Daily Times, May 6, 1865.

Headley, J. W. (1984). *Confederate Operations in Canada and New York.* New York: Time-Life Books, p. 221.

Hesseltine, W. B. (1955). *Lincoln and the War Governors.* New York: Alfred A. Knopf.

Higginbotham, A. L. (1975). *In the Matter of Color: Race and the American Legal Process: The Colonial Period.* Westport, CT: Greenwood Press.

Holcombe, J. P. (1860). Pamphlet. "The Election of a Black Republican President: An Overt Act of Aggression on the Right of Property in Slaves: The South Urged to Adopt Concerted Action for Future Safety."

Hollitz, J. (2014). *Thinking Through the Past: A Critical Thinking Approach to U.S. History,* Vol. 1, 5th ed. Belmont, CA: Wadsworth Publishing.

Holt, M. F. (1999). *The Rise and Fall of the American Whig Party.* New York: Oxford University Press.

Horne, G. (2012). *Negro Comrades of the Crown: African Americans and the British Empire Fight the U.S. Before Emancipation.* New York: New York University Press.

Hubbard, C. M. (2000). *The Burden of Confederate Diplomacy.* Knoxville: University of Tennessee Press.

Huebner, T. S. (2010). "Roger B. Taney and the Slavery Issue: Looking Beyond—and Before—Dred Scott." *Journal Of American History 97(1).*

_____ (2015). "'The Unjust Judge': Roger B. Taney, the Slave Power, and the Meaning of Emancipation." *Journal of Supreme Court History* 40(3).

Huston, J. L. (1987). *The Panic of 1857 and the Coming of the Civil War.* Baton Rouge: Louisiana State University Press.

Hutter, J. H., & Abrams, R. A. (1935). "Copperhead Newspapers and the Negro." *Journal of Negro History* 20.

Irvin, B. H. (2002). *Samuel Adams: Son of Liberty, Father of Revolution.* New York: Oxford University Press.

Jackson, Thomas "Stonewall." Last words: "Let us cross over the river, and rest under the shade of the trees."

Jaffa, H. V. (2000). *A New Birth of Freedom: Abraham Lincoln and the Coming of the Civil War.* Lanham, MD: Rowman & Littlefield.

Jefferson, T. (December 2, 1806). "Annual Message to Congress," in *The Avalon Project.* New Haven, CT: Yale Law School.

Johnson, A. (March 27, 1866; July 16, 1866). Veto Message.

Johnson, C. W., ed. (1893). *Proceedings of the First Three Republican National Conventions of 1856, 1860 and 1864.* Minneapolis: Harrison and Smith Printers.

Jones v. Van Zandt (1847). 46 U.S. 215.

Jones, H. (1997). *Mutiny on the Amistad: The Saga of a Slave Revolt and Its Impact on American Abolition, Law, and Diplomacy.* New York: Oxford University Press.

Kaczorowski, R. J. (Fall 1995). "*Federal Enforcement of Civil Rights During the First Reconstruction.*" *Fordham Urban Law Journal* 23.

Kaplan, S. (1996). *American Studies in Black and White.* Amherst: University of Massachusetts Press.

Kentucky Law Journal 97(3): 2008–2009.

Keyssar, A. (2009). *The Right to Vote: The Contested History of Democracy in the United States.* New York: Basic Books.

King-Owen, S. (2012). "To 'Write Down the Republican Administration': William Boylan and the Federalist Party in North Carolina, 1800–1805." *North Carolina Historical Review* 89(2).

Klement, F. L. (1960). *The Copperheads in the Middle West.* Chicago: University of Chicago Press.

_____ (1964). "Midwestern Opposition to Lincoln's Emancipation Proclamation." *Journal of Negro History* 49: 169–183.

_____ (1965). "Clement L. Vallandigham's Exile in the Confederacy, May 25–June 17, 1863." *Journal of Southern History* 31.

_____ (1989). *Dark Lanterns: Secret Political Societies, Conspiracies and Treason Trials in the Civil War.* Baton Rouge: Louisiana State University Press.

Konig, D. T.; Finkelman, P.; & Bracey, C. A., eds. (2010). *The "Dred Scott" Case: Historical and Contemporary Perspectives on Race and Law.* Athens: Ohio University Press.

Korsi, M. J. (2004). *A Seat of Popular Leadership: The Presidency, Political Parties, and Democratic Government.* Amherst: University of Massachusetts Press.

Krout, J. A. (December 1, 1938). "Horatio Seymour of New York (review)." *Journal of American History* 25(3).

Lampi, P. J. (2013). "The Federalist Party Resurgence, 1808–1816." *Journal of the Early Republic* 33(2).

Leonard, I. M. (1966). "The Rise and Fall of the American Republican Party in New York City, 1843–1845." *New York Historical Society Quarterly* 50.

Levine, P. (1981). "Draft Evasion in the North During the Civil War, 1863–1865." *Journal of American History* 67.

Liberator, June 24, 1859.

Lightner, D. L. (November 2004). "The Supreme Court and the Interstate Slave Trade: A Study in Evasion, Anarchy, and Extremism." *Journal of Supreme Court History* 29(3).

Lincoln, A. (March 4, 1861). First Inaugural Address.

Linden, F. van der (2007). *The Dark Intrigue: The True Story of a Civil War Conspiracy.* Golden, CO: Fulcrum Publishing.

Link, W. A. (2003). *Roots of Secession: Slavery and Politics in Antebellum Virginia.* Chapel Hill: University of North Carolina Press.

Lipset, S. M. (1960). *Political Man.* New York: Doubleday.

Loewen, J. W. (2008). *Lies My Teacher Told Me: Everything Your American History Textbook Got Wrong.* New York: New Press.

Logan, R. W. (1997). *The Betrayal of the Negro.* Boston: Da Capo Press.

Long, A. (April 8, 1864), in Stellato, J., ed. (2012). *Not in Our Name: American Antiwar Speeches, 1846 to the Present.* University Park, PA: Penn State University Press.

Long, D. E. (1994). *The Jewel of Liberty: Abraham Lincoln's Re-Election and the End of Slavery.* Mechanicsburg, PA: Stackpole.

Lublin, D. (2004). *The Republican South: Democratization and Partisan Change in the South.* Princeton, NJ: Princeton University Press.

Luthin, R. H. (1944). *The First Lincoln Campaign.* Cambridge, MA: Harvard University Press.

Madison, J. (January 25, 1788). *Federalist No. 44.*

Maier, P. (1998). *American Scripture: Making the Declaration of Independence.* New York: Vintage Press.

Malanson, J. J. (Summer 2015). "The Founding Fathers and the Election of 1864." *Journal of the Abraham Lincoln Association* 36(2).

Maloney, C. (March 23, 1999), in *Congressional Record—House.*

Maltz, E. M. (Spring 1997). "The Idea of a Proslavery Constitution." *Journal of the Early Republic* 17: 48–9.

_____ (2007). *Dred Scott and the Politics of Slavery*. Lawrence: University Press of Kansas.

Man, A. (1951). "Labor Competition and the New York Draft Riots of 1863." *The Journal of Negro History* 36(4).

Marshall, J. A. (1881). *American Bastile: A History of the Illegal Arrests and Imprisonment of American Citizens in the Northern and Border States During the Late Civil War*. Philadelphia: T. W. Hartley & Co.

Martinez, J. M. (2007). *Carpetbaggers, Cavalry, and the Ku Klux Klan*. Lanham, MD: Rowman & Littlefield.

Martis, K. C. (1989). *The Historical Atlas of Political Parties in the United States Congress, 1789–1989*. New York: Prentice Hall College Division.

Mayor of New York v. Miln (1837). 33 U.S. 120.

McCullough, D. (2004). *John Adams*. New York: Simon & Schuster.

McCulloch v. Maryland (1819). 17 U.S. 316.

McFeely, W. S. (2002). *Grant*. New York: W. W. Norton.

McKitrick, E. L., in Chambers, W. N. & Burnham, W.D., eds. (1967). *Party Politics and the Union and Confederate War Efforts*. New York: Oxford University Press.

_____ (1988). *Andrew Johnson and Reconstruction*. New York: Oxford University Press.

McPherson, E. (1882). *The Political History of the United States of America, During the Great Rebellion*. La Jolla: University of California Libraries.

McPherson, J. M. (1988). *Battle Cry of Freedom: The Civil War Era*. New York: Oxford University Press.

_____ (2001). *Ordeal by Fire: The Civil War and Reconstruction*, 3rd ed. Boston: McGraw-Hill.

McVeigh, R. (2009). *The Rise of the Ku Klux Klan: Right-Wing Movements and National Politics*. Minneapolis: University of Minnesota Press.

Malanson, J. J. (Summer 2015). "The Founding Fathers and the Election of 1864." *Journal of the Abraham Lincoln Association* 36(2).

Miller, W., ed. (2012). *The Social History of Crime and Punishment in America: An Encyclopedia*. Thousand Oaks, CA: Sage Publications.

Milwaukee News, November 14, 1866.

Moore, G. (1966). *The Missouri Compromise, 1819–1821*. Lexington: University of Kentucky Press.

Morris, T. D. (1974). *Free Men All*. Baltimore: Johns Hopkins University Press.

Morison, S. E. (1965). *The Oxford History of the American People*. New York: Oxford University Press.

Morse, Samuel (1863). "An Argument on the Ethical Position of Slavery in the Social System, and Its Relation to the Politics of the Day." Papers from the *Society for the Diffusion of Political Knowledge*. New York.

Morton, J. C. (2005). *Shapers of the Great Debate at the Constitutional Convention of 1787: A Biographical Dictionary*. Westport, CT: Greenwood Publishing Group.

Muzzey, D., & Link, A. (1968). *Our Country's History*, 21st ed. Boston: Ginn and Co.

National Archives. www.archives.gov.

National Intelligencer, January 3, 1863.

Neely, M. E., Jr. (2002). *The Union Divided: Party Conflict in the Civil War North*. Cambridge, MA: Harvard University Press.

_____ (2011). *Lincoln and the Triumph of the Nation: Constitutional Conflict in the American Civil War*. Chapel Hill: University of North Carolina Press.

Nelson, L. E. (1978). "Black Leaders and the Presidential Election of 1864." *Journal of Negro History* 63.

Nevins, A. (1947). *Ordeal of the Union: Fruits of Manifest Destiny, 1847–1852*. New York: Scribner.

_____ (1959). *The War for the Union: The Improvised War, 1861–1862*. New York: Scribner.

New Orleans Delta, November 3, 1860.

New York Express, October 20, 1862.

New York Herald, August 1, 1860; August 13, 1861; February 22, 1864; August 11, 1946; September 10, 1866.

New York Journal of Commerce, September 24, 1862.

New York Times, September 23, 1862; March 19, 1864; July 20, 1864; August 20, 1864; October 18, 1864; December 6, 1866.

New York Tribune, September 24, 1862; January 10, 1863.

New York World, June 22, 1865; October 12, 1867; March 7, 1876.

Newmyer, R. K. (1968). *The Supreme Court Under Marshall and Taney.* Storrs: University of Connecticut.

_____ (2000). "John Marshall, McCulloch v. Maryland, and the Southern States' Rights Tradition." *Faculty Articles and Papers*, p. 182.

Newton, M. (2014). *White Robes and Burning Crosses: A History of the Ku Klux Klan from 1866.* Jefferson, NC: McFarland.

Nichols, R. F. (1948). *The Disruption of American Democracy.* New York: Free Press.

Nicolay, J. G. (1917). *A Short Life of Abraham Lincoln.* New York: The Century Co.

Noonan, J. T. (1977). *The Antelope: The Ordeal of the Recaptured Africans in the Administrations of James Monroe and John Quincy Adams.* Oakland: University of California Press.

Norton, M. B.; Sheriff, C.; Katzman, D. M.; Blight, D. W.; & Chudacoff, H. (2007). *A People and a Nation: A History of the United States, Vol. 1: To 1877.* Boston: Houghton Mifflin Harcourt.

Novak, D. A. (1978). *The Wheel of Servitude: Black Forced Labor After Slavery.* Lexington: University Press of Kentucky.

O'Connor, T. H. (1997). *Civil War Boston: Home Front and Battlefield.* Boston: Northeastern University Press.

Olsen, C. J. (2002). *Political Culture and Secession in Mississippi: Masculinity, Honor, and the Antiparty Tradition.* New York: Oxford University Press.

Oswald, A. (2012). "The Reaction to the Dred Scott Decision." *Voces Novae: Chapman University Historical Review* 4(1).

Paludin, P. S. (October 1972). "The American Civil War Considered As a Crisis in Law and Order." *American Historical Review* 77.

Parsons, E. F. (2015). *Ku-Klux: The Birth of the Klan During Reconstruction.* Chapel Hill: University of North Carolina Press.

Parsons, L. (2009). *The Birth of Modern Politics: Andrew Jackson, John Quincy Adams, and the Election of 1828.* New York: Oxford University Press.

Paterson, I. (Summer 1949). "The Riddle of Chief Justice Taney in the Dred Scott Decision." *The Georgia Review* 3(2).

Patrick, R. W. (1944). *Jefferson Davis and His Cabinet.* Baton Rouge: Louisiana State University Press.

Peterson, M. D. (1960). *The Jefferson Image in the American Mind.* Charlottesville: University of Virginia Press.

Pohlmann, M., & Whisenhunt, L. (2002). *Student's Guide to Landmark Congressional Laws on Civil Rights.* Westport, CT: Greenwood Publishing Group, 2002.

Pomeroy, B. (August 23, 1864). *La Crosse Democrat* (WI).

Porter, G. H. (2010). *Ohio Politics During the Civil War Period.* Charleston, SC: Nabu Press.

Potter, D. M. (1976). *The Impending Crisis, 1848–1861.* New York: HarperCollins.

The Pilot (Boston), December 27, 1862; September 10, 1864.

_____ (1995). *Lincoln and His Party in the Secession Crisis.* New Haven, CT: Yale University Press.

Prigg v. Pennsylvania (1842). 41 U.S. 539.

Rable, G. C. (1984). *But There Was No Peace: The Role of Violence in the Politics of Reconstruction.* Athens: University of Georgia Press.

Rachel v. Walker (1834). 4, MO 350.

Rae, N. C. (1994). *Southern Democrats.* New York: Oxford University Press.

Randall, J. G., & Current, Richard (1955). *Lincoln the President: Last Full Measure.* Champaign: University of Illinois Press.

Rawley, J. A. (1969). *Race and Politics.* New York: Lippincott.

Remini, R. V. (1959). *Martin Van Buren and the Making of the Democratic Party.* New York: Columbia University Press.

Republican Party platform (June 1864).

Rhea, G. (January 25, 2011). "Why Non-Slaveholding Southerners Fought: Address to the Charleston Library Association," quoting Handy, H.

Richards, L. L. (2000). *The Slave Power: The Free North and Southern Domination, 1780–1860.* Baton Rouge: Louisiana State University Press.

Richmond Examiner, September 29, 1862; September 30, 1862; October 1, 1862; December 15, 1862.

Riggs, David F. (July 1978). "Robert Young Conrad and the Ordeal of Secession."

The Virginia Magazine of History and Biography 86(3).

Risjord, N. K. (1965). *The Old Republicans: Southern Conservatism in the Age of Jefferson.* New York: Columbia University Press.

Robertson, J. (1993). *Civil War Virginia: Battleground for a Nation.* Charlottesville: University of Virginia Press.

Rose, S. E. F. (1914). *The Ku Klux Klan: Or Invisible Empire.* New Orleans, LA: L. Graham Co.

Ross, M. A. (2003). *Justice of Shattered Dreams: Samuel Freeman Miller and the Supreme Court During the Civil War Era.* Baton Rouge: Louisiana State University Press.

Ryan, J. G. (1977). "The Memphis Riots of 1866: Terror in a Black Community During Reconstruction." *The Journal of Negro History* 62(3).

Scher, R. K. (1992). *Politics in the New South.* New York: Paragon House.

Schlesinger, A. M., Jr. (October 1949). "The Causes of the Civil War: A Note on Historical Sentimentalism." *Partisan Review* 16: 969–981.

Schlesinger, A. M., Jr.; Troy, G.; & Israel, F. L. (2011). *History of American Presidential Elections.* New York: Facts on File.

Schroeder, G. R. & Zucaek, R. (2001). *Andrew Johnson: A Biographical Companion.* Santa Barbara, CA: ABC-CLIO.

Sears, S. W. (1988). *George B. McClellan: The Young Napoleon.* New York: Ticknor & Fields.

_____ (1992). *The Civil War Papers of George B. McClellan: Selected Correspondence, 1860–1865.* Boston: De Capo Press.

Second Confiscation Act (1862). 37th Congress.

Seiple, D. W. (1998). "The Presidential Election of 1864 in Northampton County, Pennsylvania: Continued Dominance of the Democratic Party Despite Fervent Union Nationalism and Support for the Civil War." Theses and Dissertations. Paper 544.

Sewell, R. H. (1965). *John P. Hale and the Politics of Abolition.* Cambridge, MA: Harvard University Press.

Shafer, B. & Badger, A., eds. (2001). *Contesting Democracy: Substance and Structure in American Political History, 1775–2000.* Lawrence: University Press of Kansas.

Shalhope, R. E. (2009). *The Baltimore Bank Riot: Political Upheaval in Antebellum Maryland.* Champaign: University of Illinois Press.

Siegel, A. A. (2001). *Beneath the Starry Flag: New Jersey's Civil War Experience.* New Brunswick, NJ: Rutgers University Press.

Silber, S., & Sievens, M. B., eds. (1996). *Yankee Correspondence: Civil War Letters Between New England Soldiers and the Home Front.* Charlottesville: University Press of Virginia.

Simpson, B. D., & Grimsley, M., eds. (2002). *The Collapse of the Confederacy.* Lincoln: University of Nebraska Press.

Singh, M. "Traditional or Chattel Slavery." The Feminist Sexual Ethics Project. http://www.brandeis.edu/projects/fse/slavery/contemporary/essay-chattel-slavery.html.

Slave Trade Act of 1794.

Snodgrass, M. E. (2011). *The Civil War Era and Reconstruction.* New York: Routledge.

Somerset v. Stewart. (1772). 98 Eng. Rep. 499 (K.B.).

Stampp, K. M. (1944). "The Milligan Case and the Election of 1864 in Indiana." *Mississippi Valley Historical Review* 31.

_____ (1980). *The Imperial Union: Essays on the Background of the Civil War.* New York: Oxford University Press.

State of Pennsylvania (March 1, 1780). An Act for the Gradual Abolition of Slavery, amendment.

Statutes at Large of the United States of America, 1789–1873, Vol. 3. (1845).

Smith, W. H. (1903). *A Political History of Slavery.* Ann Arbor: University of Michigan Press.

Stewart, D. O. (2007). *The Summer of 1787.* New York: Simon & Schuster.

_____ (2009; 2010 reprint ed.). *Impeached: The Trial of President Andrew Johnson and the Fight for Lincoln's Legacy.* New York: Simon & Schuster.

Stidger, F. G. (1997). *Knights of the Golden Circle Treason History, Sons of Liberty, 1864.* Brandon, MS: Dogwood Press.

Stone, I. (1943). *They Also Ran.* Garden City, NY: Doubleday & Doran.

Story, J. (1873). *Commentaries on the Constitution of the United States.* New York: Little, Brown.

Strader v. Graham (1851). 51 U.S. 82, 96, 97.

Strausbaugh, J. (2006). *Black Like You: Blackface, Whiteface, Insult and Imitation in American Popular Culture.* New York: Jeremy P. Tarcher, Penguin.

Summers, M. W. (2009). *A Dangerous Stir: Fear, Paranoia, and the Making of Reconstruction.* Chapel Hill: University of North Carolina Press.

Tarnoff, B. (2011). *Moneymakers: The Wicked Lives and Surprising Adventures of Three Notorious Counterfeiters.* New York: Penguin Press.

Taylor, M. J. C. (2003). "'A More Perfect Union': Ableman v. Booth and the Culmination of Federal Sovereignty." *Journal of Supreme Court History* 28(2).

The Antelope (1825). 23 U.S. 66.

Thomas, B. P. (1952). *Abraham Lincoln: A Biography.* New York: Alfred A. Knopf.

Thorpe, F. N., ed. (April 1898). *American Historical Review* 3(3).

Throne, M., ed. (1960). "Iowa Doctor in Blue: Letters of Seneca B. Thrall, 1862–1864." *Iowa Journal of History* 58.

Tidwell, W. A. (1995). *April '65: Confederate Covert Action in the American Civil War.* Kent, OH: Kent State University Press.

Tocqueville, A. de (1835). *Democracy in America* (2000 ed.). Indianapolis: Hackett Publishing.

Trefousse, H. (1991). *Historical Dictionary of Reconstruction.* Westport, CT: Greenwood Publishing.

_____ (1997). *Andrew Johnson: A Biography.* New York: W.W. Norton.

Tregarthen, T. D., & Rittenberg, L. (1999). *Macroeconomics.* New York: Macmillan.

United States Constitution. 13th Amendment.

Trelease, A. W. *White Terror: The Ku Klux Klan Conspiracy and Southern Reconstruction.* Baton Rouge: Louisiana State University Press.

Unger, I. (1970). *Essays on the Civil War and Reconstruction.* Austin, TX: Holt, Rinehart & Winston.

United States Constitution (1776).

United States Department of Labor and Commerce Bureau of the Census (1909). *A Century of Population Growth from the First Census of the United States to the Twelfth, 1790–1900.* Washington, D.C.: Government Printing Office.

United States v. Amy (1859). 24 F Cas 792 (CCD VA).

United States v. Libellants and Claimants of the Schooner Amistad (1841). 40 U.S. 518.

Vallandigham, C. L. (1864). *Addresses and Letters of Clement L. Vallandigham.* New York: J. Walter.

Van Buren, M. (March 4, 1837). First Inaugural Address.

Vincent C. H. (1967). *Dred Scott's Case.* New York: Russell & Russell.

Virginia Slave Codes (1705).

Vorenberg, M. (2001). *Final Freedom: The Civil War, the Abolition of Slavery, and the Thirteenth Amendment.* Cambridge, MA: Cambridge University Press.

Wade, W. C. (1987). *The Fiery Cross: The Ku Klux Klan in America.* New York: Oxford University Press.

Waldstreicher, D. (2009). *Slavery's Constitution: From Revolution to Ratification.* New York: Hill & Wang.

Ward, A. (June 1964). "A Note On the Origin of the Ku Klux Klan." *Tennessee Historical Quarterly* 23.

Washington National Era, January 24, 1854.

Waugh, J. C. (1998). *Reelecting Lincoln: The Battle for the 1864 Presidency.* New York: Crown Publishing.

Weber, J. L. (2006). *Copperheads: The Rise and Fall of Lincoln's Opponents in the North.* New York: Oxford University Press.

_____ (Winter 2011). "Lincoln's Critics: The Copperheads." *Journal of the Abraham Lincoln Association* 32(1).

Weidenmier, M. (1999). "Bogus Money Natters: Sam Upham and His Confederate Counterfeiting Business." *Business and Economic History* 28(2).

Weisenberger, F. P. (1941). *The Passing of the Frontier: 1825–1850.* Columbus: Ohio State Archaeological Society.

Welles, G. (December 1872). "The History of Emancipation." *Galaxy.*

Wender, H. (1930). *Southern Commercial Conventions.* Baltimore, MD: Johns Hopkins University Press.

Wheeler, Kenneth H. (1999). "Local Autonomy and Civil War Draft Resistance: Holmes County, Ohio." *Civil War History* 45.

White, R. C., Jr. (2009). *A. Lincoln: A Biography.* New York: Random House.

_____ (2017). *American Ulysses: A Life of Ulysses S. Grant.* New York: Random House.

White, L. A. (1931). *Robert Barnwell Rhett, Father of Secession.* Washington, D.C.: American Historical Association.

Whiting, W. (1997). *War Powers Under the Constitution of the United States.* Delran, NJ: Legal Classics Library.

_____ (2002). *War Powers Under the Constitution of the United States,* 3rd ed. Union, NJ: Lawbook Exchange.

Whitman, T. S. (2012). *Antietam 1862: Gateway to Emancipation.* Santa Barbara, CA: Praeger.

Wilentz, S. (2008). *The Rise of American Democracy: Jefferson to Lincoln.* New York: Horton.

_____ (September 2010). "Book Reviews." *Journal of American History* 97(2).

Williams, E. (1994). *Capitalism and Slavery.* Chapel Hill: University of North Carolina Press.

Williams, L. (2004). *The Great South Carolina Ku Klux Klan Trials, 1871–1872.* Athens: University of Georgia Press.

Williams, T. H. (1938). "Frémont and the Politicians." *Journal of the American Military History Foundation* 2: 191.

Wills, G. (2003). *"Negro President": Jefferson and the Slave Power.* Boston: Houghton Mifflin.

Wilmot, D. (October 29, 1847). Speech. Albany, NY.

Wilson, C. R. (1936). "The Original Chase Organization Meeting and the Next Presidential Meeting." *Mississippi Valley Historical Review* 23.

Winny v. Whitesides (November 1824). Supreme Court of Missouri, St. Louis District, 1 Mo. 472.

Winters, J. D. (1963). *The Civil War in Louisiana.* Baton Rouge: Louisiana State University Press.

Wisconsin Legislative Reference Library (1962). *State of Wisconsin Blue Book.* Madison: Wisconsin Legislative Reference Bureau.

Wood, F. G. (1970). *Black Scare: The Racist Response to Emancipation and Reconstruction.* Oakland: University of California Press.

Wood, W. J. (January 1970). "The Illegal Beginning of American Negro Slavery." *American Bar Association Journal* 56.

Woodson, C. G. (1925). *Negro Orators and Their Orations.* Washington, D.C.: Associated Publishers, Inc.

Woodward, C. (1956). *Reunion and Reaction: The Compromise of 1877 and the End of Reconstruction.* New York: Doubleday.

_____ (2011). *American Nations: A History of the Eleven Rival Regional Cultures of North America.* New York: Penguin.

Woodward, C. V., & McFeely, W. S. (2001). *The Strange Career of Jim Crow.* New York: Oxford University Press.

Wubben, H. H. (1980). *Civil War Iowa and the Copperhead Movement.* Ames: Iowa State University Press.

Yearns, W. B. (2010). *The Confederate Congress.* Athens: University of Georgia Press.

Zarefsky, D. (1993). *Lincoln, Douglas, and Slavery: In the Crucible of Public Debate.* Chicago: University of Chicago Press.

Zorick, R. J. (1964). "Study of the Union and the Confederate Reactions to the Emancipation Proclamation." Master of Arts thesis, University of Montana, UMIEP36175.

Zornow, W. F. (1954). *Lincoln and the Party Divided.* Norman: University of Oklahoma Press.

Index

236 Index

corrupt bargain 56
Corwin Amendment 103
Cox, Samuel S. 140, 202–203
Crawford, William 56
Crittenden, John 102
Crittenden Compromise 98, 101–103, 104
Crowe, James 197
Cukucan 197
Curtis, Benjamin 69, 89

Daniel, Peter V. 82
Davis, Jefferson 34, 90, 101, 109, 111, 112, 113, 152, 160–163, 164
Dayton, William 61
Declaration of Independence 6–7, 8, 16–17, 19–20, 30, 63, 86, 89
Democratic Party: abandonment of Douglas 59; agricultural distinction 10; American Party (Know Nothing) 62–64; anti-slavery members of 33; anti–Union 112, 136; appointments to the Supreme Court 6, 8, 69; assassination of Lincoln 169; barnburner 51–52; battlefields 98; Bayard, James A., as member of 140; beginning 98; belongs to slavery 155–156; Benning, Henry Lewis as member of 106–107; Black Codes 178–180, 182; black suffrage 174, 175, 189, 192, 195; black vote repression 11; Bleeding Kansas as precursor 39–40; border state 168; Breckenridge, as member of 99; Brinkerhoff, as member of 33; Buchanan, as member of 43, 62, 184; casualties 15–16; Chicago platform 155; Christian Church support 59; Civil Rights Act of 1866 180–182; Compromise of 1850 8, 35, 36–37, 38, 84; concerns about civil rights 185–187; Confederacy plots to overthrow 160–161; conservative 60; conspiracy rumors 158–159; Constitutional Democrats 65; Constitutional interpretation 104; Constitutional Union Party and 59, 64, 101, 102; Copperheads 98, 112–117, 122, 135–136, 145, 155, 172–173; Cox, Samuel as member of 140, 202–203; Crittenden Compromise and 98, 101–103, 104; debates in 1860 59; declaration of principles 156; delay for 10 years 37; disarray after the Civil War 190; disaster in 1864 election 165; dissent over slavery 116, 166; dominance 6, 9, 10, 11, 37; Doughface 34, 50, 58, 91; Douglas, as member of 36, 60, 63, 106; Dred Scott decision 86; economics 44; election of 1860 65; election of 1860 65–68; election of 1868 187–189; election outcomes 59; emergence of 6; Enrollment Act 139–141; Era of Good Feelings and 54–55; favoring peace in 1864 election, 157; Federalists and 47–49; First Party System 45–47;

first well-organized national party 57; Fourteenth Amendment positions 184; Free Soil Party and 51–53; Freedman's Bureau 39, 175–178, 187, 194; Fugitive Slave Act 91; greenbacks and graybacks 153; *Habeas Corpus* suspension 118–120; Hard Shell 53; House defeat of Lincoln's amendment 167; House seats before 1854, 40; Illinois state legislature and 63; issues 24; Jackson, as member of 46, 50, 55–56; Jim Crow laws 11–14; Johnson, as a member of 165, 173, 175, 182–185, 187, 192; Knights of the Golden Circle (KGC) 42, 114, 118, 124, 159, 195–196; Know Nothing Movement and 62–64; Ku Klux Klan 13, 191–192, 200–202, 206; legislative voting 22; liberal 60; Lincoln's defeat as a goal of 164; Mason, Charles as member of 136, 174; McClennan, as member of 13, 154, 166; Military Draft Act 139–141; Militia Act votes 124–125; militia groups 160; Missouri Compromise 8, 29–31, 39, 40, 86, 91, 102–103; Morse, Samuel, as member of 136–138; National 65; National Convention of 1856 62; National Convention of 1860 65; Nationalism 55; New York draft riots 139–140, 146–147; newspaper editors 125; Northern 34, 35, 37, 53, 58–59, 104, 112–114, 123, 127, 132–133, 174; Northern support in 1864 151; Opposition Party and 64; paramilitary organizations formed by 13; Party System concerns 53–54; path toward 28, 139; peace 23, 98, 112, 114–118, 121, 144, 148, 159, 173; Pierce, as member of 40; platform against Negro supremacy 188; Platform of 1856 41, 43, 62; Platform of 1864 151, 154–158, 162; platforms and policies 114–115; political debate 172; politicians ridiculing blacks 50; Polk, as member of 81; Populist orientation 51; presidents in 6; pro-slavery 7, 9, 10, 34, 44, 67, 94, 105, 172; racialism and 52; racist sentiments 50, 133, 135–136, 155–156, 186–187; Randolph and Calhoun, as members 30; Red Shirts created by 13, 204–206; Redeemers 203–204, 207; renamed from Democratic Republicans 8–9, 45–46, 49, 53, 70; resentment by soldiers 158; rumors of overthrow 158; Rural South 9, 50; schism over the Wilmot Proviso 34; secession 63, 68, 94; secession threats 59–60, 100–102; secret societies 196, 198; Seymour, Horatio, as candidate in 1868 23, 182, 187–188, 194; Sherman, William T. 164; slave power 6, 8–9, 22–26, 34, 42–43, 51, 60, 114; slavemasters controlling 36; slaveowners 57; slavery in new territories 50; slogan 23; Soft Shell 53; Sons of Liberty 195–196;